A Cultural Approach to Emotional Disorders

In her latest contribution to the growing field of emotion studies, Deidre Pribram makes a compelling argument for why culturalist approaches to the study of emotional "disorders" continue to be eschewed, even as the socio-cultural and historical study of mental illness flourishes. The author ties this phenomenon to a tension between two fundamentally different approaches to emotion: an individualist approach, which regards emotions as the property of the individual, whether biologically or psychologically, and a culturalist approach, which regards emotions as collective, social processes with distinctive histories and meanings that work to produce particularized subjects. While she links a strong preference for the individualist construct in Western culture to the rise of the psychological and psychiatric disciplines in the late nineteenth and twentieth centuries, Pribram also engages with a diverse set of case studies tied to psychological and aesthetic discourses on emotions. These range from Van Gogh's status as emotionally disordered to the public, emotional aesthetics of nineteenth century melodrama to the diagnostic categories of the *DSMs* and the fear of "globalizing" emotional disorders in the twenty-first century. This genuinely interdisciplinary approach makes for a text with potential application in a wide range of disciplines within cultural studies, including sociocultural and historical analysis of psychiatry and psychology, gender theory, subject and identity theory, popular culture studies, and history and theory of the arts.

E. Deidre Pribram is, most recently, the author of *A Cultural Approach to Emotional Disorders: Psychological and Aesthetic Interpretations* and *Emotions, Genre, Justice in Film and Television: Detecting Feeling,* as well as co-editor of *Emotions: A Cultural Studies Reader.* She writes on cultural emotion studies, media studies, gender, and popular culture. She is a professor in the communications department of Molloy College, Long Island, New York.

T0417911

Routledge Research in Cultural and Media Studies

For a full list of titles in this series, please visit www.routledge.com.

A Cultural Approach to Emotional Disorders

Psychological and Aesthetic Interpretations

E. Deidre Pribram

Routledge
Taylor & Francis Group

NEW YORK AND LONDON

First published 2016
by Routledge
711 Third Avenue, New York, NY 10017

and by Routledge
2 Park Square, Milton Park, Abingdon, Oxon OX14 4RN

First issued in paperback 2018

*Routledge is an imprint of the Taylor & Francis Group, an informa
business*

Library of Congress Cataloging-in-Publication Data

Names: Pribram, E. Deidre.
Title: A cultural approach to emotional disorders: psychological and
aesthetic interpretations / by E. Deidre Pribram.
Description: 1 Edition. | New York: Routledge, 2016. | Series: Routledge
research in cultural and media studies; 79 | Includes bibliographical
references and index.
Identifiers: LCCN 2015027165
Subjects: LCSH: Emotions—Cross-cultural studies. | Personality disorders.
Classification: LCC BF511 .P75 2016 | DDC 152.4—dc23
LC record available at http://lccn.loc.gov/2015027165

Typeset in Sabon
by codeMantra

ISBN 13: 978-1-138-59953-6 (pbk)
ISBN 13: 978-1-138-01829-7 (hbk)

For Cliff Jernigan
Always

Contents

Introduction

The Global Epidemic

In recent years, a great deal of alarm has been expressed over the current phenomenon of a global epidemic of mental illness. Distress concerning the rampant rise in numbers worldwide focuses primarily on emotional disorders, which represent "a public health problem of vast proportions" (Horwitz 101). In the United States, projections exist that "nearly one hundred million people, 25 to 30 percent of the US population, have a mental illness during any one year, and half of the population will have a mental illness during their lifetime" (Kirk vii). Almost identical prevalence rates have been estimated for Europe: 27 percent of the population over the course of any single calendar year, and 50 percent at lifetime risk (Rose, "Disorders" 469).

Repeatedly cited statistics, extending the mental health pandemic to global proportions, originate with the World Health Organization (WHO). In a pivotal study published in 2001, and a major source for much of the current alarm, WHO maintained that over 25 percent of the world's population would suffer from a mental disorder over the course of their lives and that depression, alone, takes a toll on 340 million people across the globe at any one time (Rose, Ibid. 467).

In its classification of mental and behavioral disorders, WHO incorporates a wide range of mental dysfunctions, from the organic (dementia, as in Alzheimer's disease) and the psychotic (schizophrenia), to mood and anxiety disorders (depression, bipolar disorder, PTSD, OCD), as well as behaviors such as alcohol or drug abuse. Inclusively, mental illness is "present at any point in time in about 10% of the adult population" worldwide (WHO, *New Understanding* 20). Yet those citing WHO statistics accurately hold emotional disorders responsible for a disproportionate share of the mental health problem. In 2014, WHO provided figures of 400 million people who suffer from depression and 60 million with bipolar affective disorder globally, in comparison to 35 million with dementia and 21 million facing schizophrenia ("Fact Sheet," np).

That the unfolding mental illness epidemic has become a worldwide crisis is often blamed on the widespread dissemination of Western forms of psychological knowledge, including its psychopathologies. Such knowledge transfer occurs in a number of ways, for example, through humanitarian relief efforts in the wake of war, natural disaster, atrocity, or sociopolitical upheaval all of which, from Western perspectives, create conditions leading to psychic trauma that demand various forms of psychotherapeutic amelioration (Summerfield, "Effects of War;" Fernando; Watters). The means through which global dominance by Western forms of psy constitutes a form of psychological "imperialism" is indeed a pressing matter; however, it is not the main trajectory of this book (Summerfield, "Scientifically Valid" 992). The principal concern for this project is to explore some of the ways we conceptualize emotionality which, in turn, unveils how we configure its assumed disorders, aberrations, and pathologies. Doing so, requires scrutinizing psy explanatory systems on emotions. It also necessitates imagining emotionality, its pleasures and suffering, in alternative ways.

WHO arrives at its statistics on mental disorder by a methodology called the Global Burden of Disease (GBD). This formula calculates the burden of a specific illness by factoring in rates for mortality and morbidity, in order to arrive at what it calls disability-adjusted life years (DALYs) (WHO, *New Understanding* 25). Issues of mortality or premature death mark relatively clear criteria. WHO estimates that "persons with major depression and schizophrenia have a 40% to 60% greater chance of dying prematurely than the general population" and, for example, "15–20% of depressive patients end their lives by suicide" (WHO, *Action Plan* 7; *New Understanding* 30). In terms of morbidity, however, DALYS prove more complex and controversial. Disability-adjusted life years attempt to also factor in the costs of "disability and other non-fatal health outcomes," so that a single DALY "can be thought of as one lost year of 'healthy' life" (*New Understanding* 25). Through this method, WHO reaches its projections that, in 2000, unipolar depression was the fourth leading global cause of lost disability-adjusted life years and, in perhaps the most frequently repeated estimate, by 2020 it will become the second leading cause of sacrificed DALYs internationally and the number one disease burden in the developed world (*New Understanding* 27, 30).

WHO's predictions for the future, pointing to the startling, ongoing growth of mental illness, have sparked the most disquiet, given their delineation of prevalence rates "in the stratosphere" (Greenberg, *The Book of Woe* 171). Numerous explanations have been offered for the stratospheric figures, several of which this book explores. However, the most frequently tendered arguments indict the psychologizing and medicalizing of vast expanses of 'normal,' everyday life.

For many, both within professional psy fields and beyond, a false epidemic has been created, generated by fault lines in psy itself. As touched upon in Chapters Two, Four, and Five from varying perspectives, the extensive psychomedicalizing of phenomena currently classed as emotional disorders involves erroneously transforming what accounts depict, instead, as simple unhappiness, minor troubles, malaise, life's vicissitudes, reasonable responses to stressful conditions, troublesome problems in living, normal misery, or the suffering of ordinary people. Such accounts offer a critique of both international and domestic applications of prevailing psychiatric paradigms which, their authors believe, simply should not conceptualize so much of the everyday as psychopathology.

Since the nineteenth century, emotions have been understood as belonging primarily to the psy sciences. Historians such as Fay Alberti have begun asking and tracking, "how and when emotions became the province of science in general and the [individual] mind in particular" ("Introduction" xviii). Here, Alberti frames two historically parallel, pivotal events. The first concerns the movement of emotionality to the realm of science and medicine; the second involves the relocation of emotions within a highly personalized, internalized self. Both of these events depended upon the nineteenth and twentieth century development of psychology and psychiatry as distinct disciplines with their own bodies of theoretical knowledge, empirical study, and professional/clinical practice.

A Cultural Approach to Emotional Disorders is not a historical investigation of emotionality, work currently being undertaken by scholars like Alberti, Dixon, and others. Rather, I am concerned with exploring some of the contemporary cultural implications and repercussions of these historical transformations. This necessitates examining both how we arrived at conceptualizing emotions as we currently do, and ways we might imagine living them alternatively. On the one hand, if psy disciplines have overwhelmingly determined how we currently experience emotionality, in part resulting in the widely perceived global epidemic of emotional disorders, a nuanced cultural analysis scrutinizing how the psy sciences and social sciences have positioned emotions and their disorders becomes essential. On the other hand, I believe emotional disorders ought not to be so easily dismissed as the tribulations of the extensive but inescapable ordinary, relegating vast numbers of people to their own coping devices. Making such an argument is to suggest that emotional dysfunctions are most suitably experienced in individual silence, despite the extraordinary population involved, because those persons would render themselves, as well as society overall, better off by just getting on with their lives. Both circumstances, the powerfully influential presence of psy in the modern world and, conversely, frequent views on the negligibility of emotions because ordinary, warrant a more thorough comprehension of the cultural operations and purposes of emotionality.

Referring to the nineteenth and early twentieth centuries, Gauchet and Swain contend that if asylums failed to treat the insane, nevertheless, "they *changed* insanity" (100; italics in original). Similarly, current widespread awareness of a global epidemic hasn't managed to arrive at plausible remedies but the prevalence rates have changed mental illness, perhaps going so far, through the sheer number of people encompassed, to undermine 'mental illness' as a sustainable concept. Certainly, the global crisis has sealed the centrality of emotional disorders within the category of mental illness, an adjustment that has been underway since early in the twentieth century

(Chapters One and Two). Mental illness has been transformed by its focus on emotional disorders, in the process raising a new set of questions: What 'kinds' of mental illness do emotional disorders actually represent? Why are they so prevalent? Could they, and should they, be treated through psycho-pharmacology and/or psychotherapy, given the magnitude of the populations involved? Or should they be disregarded because they are symptomatic only of the excessive medicalization of the trials and tribulations of ordinary life?

Emotional Disorders

By 'emotional disorders,' I refer to the classes of mental illness currently encompassed by mood and anxiety disorders, collectively, as defined by the American Psychiatric Association's *Diagnostic and Statistical Manual of Mental Disorders (DSMs).*[1] I also include personality disorders (PDs) in this grouping because, as covered in Chapter Four, PDs are identified in most significant measure by their emotional characteristics.

While sometimes difficult to separate in practice, emotional disorders are non-psychotic forms of what we regard, today, as 'mental illness.' Their lack of psychosis distinguishes them, first, as *emotional* disorders and, second, as *minor* forms of mental illness (Chapter Two). When psychotic symptoms also are present, treatment tends to focus on the psychosis, returning to the more psychiatrically familiar terrain of irrationality (in contrast to emotion-ality) as represented by hallucinations and delusions. My interest focuses on the depressed, the anxious, the manic – in total, all those who populate the various contemporary classes of emotional disorders.

Collectively, the mood and anxiety disorders are referred to as affective disorders in the *DSMs* and elsewhere. However, throughout this book, I consistently employ 'emotional' rather than 'affective' for several reasons crucial to the aims of this project. Affective disorders – or moral insanity and neuroses in previous eras – reference an array of psychological, psychiat-ric, and psychoanalytical configurations of emotions, in their functions and malfunctions. Affective disorders, therefore, delineate particularly psy ren-derings of emotionality. My intent, in utilizing emotional disorders, is not to exclude psy's theoretical, scientific, or clinical formulations. As mentioned, the psy fields have been one of, if not *the,* principal locations of emotions since the nineteenth century. Certainly, *A Cultural Approach to Emotional Disorders* considers psy's importance to, and recent historical preeminence over, emotionality, devoting attention to a variety of psy conceptualizations on emotionality, albeit often critically. Indeed, in the contemporary moment, it remains impossible to talk about 'disorders' or 'mental illness' without referencing psy, the wellspring of these notions. But ulitlizing the phrase emotional disorders is intended to also acknowledge and explore other meanings and practices of emotionality beyond psy endeavors. Employing emotion rather than affect, except when affect is specifically being used by the author or work under discussion, signals my desire to investigate emotions both within and beyond their psychological manifestations. The alternative conceptualizations I turn to are principally aesthetic ones but, also, in briefer measure, nonverbal communicative and biographical configurations of emotionality (Chapter Five). The arts serve as one of few cultural arenas in which emotions are admitted and sometimes valorized. However, close examination shows that emotionality and emotional disorders often surface as sites of contention in artistic practices and theory (Chapters Two and Three).

Another motive surrounding my usage of emotional rather than affective disorders involves the current prominence of affect theories across the sciences, social sciences, and humanities. While representing a diverse range of work that cannot be characterized in a singular manner, contemporary affect theories tend to foreground the biological, the material, the embodied. In cultural theory, certain influential strands draw a sharp distinction between affect and emotion. Affect occurs as intensity, vitality, and force in ways that are "irreducibly bodily and autonomic" (Massumi 28). It manifests as "noncognitive, nonconscious, nonlinguistic, and nonrational" states that remain "relatively autonomous from the sociocultural" (Gould 25, 31). In contrast, emotions transpire as part of the sociocultural world, which "squeezes" affect "into the realm of cultural meanings and normativity" (Gould 27). In this view, emotions come into being as the product of "two planes: signification … and affect" (Grossberg, *Gotta* 82).

Although long a proponent of the need to devote theoretical attention to affect, more recently Grossberg cautions that the work of "parsing out everything that is collapsed into the general notion of affect" has not been undertaken, but such investigations remain necessary in order to understand how affect functions alongside other human and cultural modes of organization, including emotional economies ("Affect's Future" 316). I would go further, to suggest that in some branches of affect theory emotions have been quite purposefully rejected. As Greco and Stenner observe, in recent approaches as diverse as philosophy and psychoanalysis, affect tends to represent "all things sophisticated and good" while emotions have come to stand for that which is "superficial and bad" (11). Which is to say, a rather romanticized, idealized notion of affect has gained predominance. Yet, as Hemmings notes, "affects do not only draw us together," providing solely freeing, productive effects; "they also force us apart" or make certain kinds of connections more rather than less difficult (152). Like thought or emotions, affect comes into existence in a variety of ways, creating a multiplicity of outcomes. One consequence of recent affect theory has been the radical alignment of affect with body/brain, while assigning emotions to what I believe is erroneous overdetermination as cognition. If affect appears as noncognitive, nonconscious, nonlinguistic, and nonrational states of being, then emotions, as affect's socialized counterpart, are remaindered as conscious, signifying, and ideologically normative forms of meaning production. Such a view, this book argues, offers a thoroughly impoverished comprehension of the complexities of emotionality as immensely diverse ways of experiencing life.

Which brings me to the final motivation in opting for emotion over affect. In 2000, Simon Williams argued that significant expanses of what we refer to as 'mental health' should, more accurately, be relabeled 'emotional health.' Although he himself doesn't use the terms, this also suggests the redesignation of its dysfunctions to emotional illness or emotional disorders. Williams advocates using emotional health over mental health as a way of breathing "new corporeal life" into existing configurations that perpetuate sharp dichotomizations of body from mind, at a point in time that was dominated by cognitive theories (560). His position is that the notion of *mental* health locates emotions too firmly as properties of mind rather than emphasizing "the active, emotionally 'expressive' body, in sickness and in health, as the basis of self, sociality, meaning" (567). In certain respects, the theoretical landscape has changed dramatically since Williams wrote. Through the rise to preeminence of biological psychiatry, neurosciences, and affect theories, the principal threat now surrounds the continued existence of 'mind,' endangered by its displacement to 'brain.'

In other respects, however, the theoretical landscape Williams described remains much the same, particularly in dispositions towards polarization and diminishment, in this case of mind in favor of body. Another goal of *A Cultural Approach to Emotional Disorders,* then, is to assess the capacity of emotionality to be engaged as a mediating force, a role that affect, as currently construed, often has failed to serve. The connective potential of emotions was also one of Williams' objectives, in which he maintained that they are "compounds" "*irreducible* to any one domain" (566; italics in original). A variety of historical and contemporary ways of analyzing emotional disorders make evident the difficulty in attempting to render them as either body or mind, affect or cognition, conscious or nonconscious, individual or social, and other competing terrains. Emotional disorders are treated, in this book, as a means of bridging or obscuring common polarities, precisely because they have never been easily or entirely successfully reduced to one binary term *over* another. Thus, emotional disorders hold the capacity to outline the relational, connective, negotiating potentials of emotionality as a conceptual and experiential life sphere. An exploration of emotional disorders enables us to take stock of how we currently assess emotionality as ways of knowing and being in the world.

A Cultural Approach

Offering a definition of "a cultural approach" to emotional disorders is a challenging task, given the many ways the notion of culture has been activated. And I certainly rely on more than one of those activations in this book.

As a person whose home disciplinary landscape is cultural studies, I am concerned that affect theory overlooks a place for all the sociocultural work that has been done over the last decades. But I am also aware of the substantial criticisms that have been aimed at social construction approaches, for example, that they give social and political identity a determining role to the neglect of embodied and other kinds of experiences. Nor do I wish to ignore the limitations imposed by strongly linguistic and ideological theories in recent years. Yet, I also uphold the position that emotions and emotional disorders have histories, that they are experienced – felt, practiced, expressed – differently in varying social and cultural contexts, and that those profuse histories and experiences have barely begun to be accounted for. The work of chronicling such histories and experiences composes one kind of cultural approach.

Additionally, emotionality makes up a unique cultural category. Unlike thought or reason, arguing for emotionality's public and social impact necessarily has been part and parcel of its scholarly study. Cognitive processes have never been as radically personalized as emotions. Knowledge rarely is considered quite so individualized, belonging instead to public collectives. We understand, often proudly as in the cases of nationality or religion, that even as we 'think' for ourselves, our ideas, values, and beliefs are accumulated across history and received from the various social worlds we inhabit, making us part of something larger. Illustrating how emotions are more than individualized, internalized phenomena, pivotal across all life spheres, persists as another facet of the cultural endeavor.

From a cultural perspective, I also feel uneasy with the way that some strands of cultural theory, under the influence of affect, reject certain aesthetic processes, such as narrativity, in a rather wholesale manner (Massumi 26–28). Disapproval of representation, broadly understood as the product and processes of thought, has circumscribed representation in the narrower sense of artistic practices and popular culture. Aesthetics are partially but not entirely sensational experiences. They are also culturally and emotionally meaningful events, perhaps no more so than when taking shape in nonlinguistic forms, through visuals, forms of sound beyond dialogue, and performance techniques such as gesture and movement. A cultural aesthetics ought to pursue approaches that preserve both embodied sensation and emotional impact, without being forced to resort to primarily linguistic or ideological explanations.

Another aspect of pursuing a cultural approach rests in distinguishing specifically social construction perspectives from more broadly cultural contours. Certain social construction views regard emotions as fulfilling specific social functions, such as generating control, status, and adaptation to norms through scripts, rules, and roles. Culture, in this formula, provides guidelines and constraints that determine "how emotions are felt or expressed" (Turner 64). In that process, conflicts may arise between the feelings people "actually experience" versus social requirements (Ibid.). However, none of this explains how the emotions people "actually experience" come into existence, becoming possible in certain configurations at particular points in place and time, and *why* they might take shape as they do. Although the former perspective traces the ways emotions occur as part of social relations, the latter interpretation contends that the circulation of emotions actually brings social relations into being.

In these terms, biological psychiatry or the neurosciences exist as cultural entities to the same degree that, say, aesthetics, philosophy, or pop psychology self-help practices do. The sciences are not the opposite of culture; they exist at its very heart. As all cultural (rather than 'truth') entities, contestations over biological versus social origins of emotionality and emotional disorders invariably lead to an impasse. Instead of debating what emotions and emotional disorders *are*, following Sara Ahmed, the task of a cultural approach is to investigate what they *do* (*Cultural Politics* 4). To what uses are they put? What purposes and functions do they serve? What emotional and social relations do they create or render impossible? A cultural perspective accumulates versions of how we conceptualize emotional disorders, which includes how we think, feel, and live them. The goal is to investigate the modes in which various cultural enterprises realize emotionality and, thereby, configure its disorders and pathologies. This explains why, as stated earlier, the book probes psy explanatory systems of emotionality as well as pursues alternative interpretations, such as those offered by aesthetics. However, no cultural entity exists as a straightforward corrective to any other conceptualization; rather, any explanatory system can offer no more than alternative sets of narratives, each embracing its own difficulties and contradictions as well as advantages, about the phenomena we identify as emotion.

Which brings us to another vital piece of the cultural puzzle, concerning the place of and possibilities for meaningfulness. In strongly distinguishing "affect as biology" and "emotion as culture" (Ahmed, "Imaginary" 38), 'the new materialism' seeks to sever affect from all association with the generation of meaning. This is accomplished via several linked steps. First, occurs the heralded *autonomy of affect* from culture and, therefore, from meaning. Second, in order to keep affect purely autonomous, emotion becomes fully assimilated with culture and meaning. Third, meaning drastically simplifies to language, discourse, and ideology, bundled together as 'signification.' Emotion, then, exists as acculturated affect, tamed through stabilization into signification. Emotionality's purpose, in this schema, is to absorb all that might threaten the material, embodied, asignifying autonomy of affect, in order that the latter can remain isolated and *unaffected*. Through these moves, we arrive at the notion of emotionality as largely confined to cognitive, conscious, linguistic, and rational activity.

However, if we take affect theory's delineation of emotionality as our starting point, particularly its implications for the generation of meaning, social or otherwise, we move closer to emotionality's conceptual and practical potentials. Value, and vitality, attach to invoking forms of meaningfulness that are not linguistically, consciously, ideologically, or rationally derived. Pursuing such emotional avenues functions as an urgently demanded antidote against recent attempts to circumvent meaning entirely or, at best, to seriously circumscribe all that it might entail.[2] Among segments of the current theoretical backdrop, reluctance exists to engage with the thoroughly entangled domains of culture, meaning, and emotionality resulting, consequently, in too often seeking autonomy rather than connectivity.

Ultimately, a cultural approach to emotionality promises the recuperation of broader conceptualizations of meaningfulness. After all, we access emotionality – feel it and express it – through pathways other than the explicitly spoken, written, or thought. Emotions, even as 'agents of meaning,' are experienced nonverbally as well as verbally, sensationally in addition to cognitively, through images, tone, texture, and gestures as much as words. Depression, anxiety, and mania, as well as alignments of emotions designated healthy or appropriate, are lived across life spheres more extensive than the immediately affective or narrowly signifying. Indeed, one of the attractions of emotionality rests with its potential capacity to link affect and meaning, turning again to the value of its irreducibility to any single domain *over* another.

However, a cultural approach must also assess the techniques and conditions through which emotions and meaningfulness suffuse each other. Because none of what precedes is to suggest that particular meanings occur 'in' or 'with' any specific emotion. On the contrary, emotional meaningfulness relies on how any emotion becomes utilized, the contexts in which it appears, and the precise ways it comes to be activated or takes shape. How emotions are put into effect and, therefore, how they affect us, inevitably returns to the centrality of culture.

Emotions as Forms of Experience

The variability of emotionality is so great that it mitigates against establishment of a taxonomy. Emotionality's abundance and absent boundaries have operated as a source of frustration, limiting its progress as object for empirical study (Chapters Four and Five).

A feasible classification system for emotionality would have to account for a number of seemingly intractable features. First, any taxonomy must contend with the sheer multitude of existing and potential emotional states. Along with the most frequently studied, countless others exist that sometimes are considered 'minor' emotions. Those receiving the most attention often become referred to as the basic emotions – anger, fear, love, empathy, shame, guilt, jealousy, and so on – although consensus has never been reached on their exact number or which specific feeling states ought to be included and which excluded. As for those more commonly regarded as minor, they constitute that which we experience with the greatest frequency and familiarity. That is, they make up the everyday emotions that permeate our existences. Among these are:

> irritation, boredom, impatience, mild amusement, transient frustration, resignation, apprehension, nostalgia, chagrin, contentment, affection, slight feelings of envy and vague dissatisfaction.
>
> (Richards 51)

And many more. While these could be conceived of as slight, as Richards observes, collectively they compose the majority of our "quotidian emotional lives" (Ibid.).

Accompanying the issue of sheer volume, the problem of gradation also would have to be addressed in arriving at a taxonomy. In the case of emotions we identify as part of a series – for example, annoyance, irritation, anger, wrath, fury, rage – do they signal differing emotional events or can they better be understood as 'subspecies' of a more pronounced, singular state, such as anger? Making such determinations involves quite elaborate complexities. If we take the series of emotions that cluster around empathy, including pity, sympathy, and compassion, arguably the empathy sequence stands for radically different states of relationality between people, with accompanying serious political implications (Chapter Two).

A second feature of emotionality, impeding the construction of a viable classificatory system, converges on the hopelessly porous quality among emotions, in which reliable boundaries refuse to be fixed. Conceived as human conveniences rather than verifiable physical matter, any emotion moves, flows, overlaps and conjoins with others. As we will see, much contestation, and once again frustration, occurs around establishing the most appropriately accurate borders that distinguish emotional disorders from one another. However, such demarcations remain essential to defining different orders of mental illness. If we have never successfully arrived at a viable taxonomy for emotions in general, the psy fields as we know them exist only on the presumption of being able to classify – and thereby identify and treat – various kinds of emotional disorders as distinct forms of mental illness.

Finally, a third feature frustrating a defensible categorization of emotionality can be attributed to the enormous malleability of any single emotion, however defined. As experienced, emotions are not duplicable, reproduced in identical manner from one occurrence to the next. Emotions are felt in newly meaningful ways, as constantly renewable engagements, reliant upon the idiosyncrasies of moment and situation. We love in ongoingly original ways; we feel anger uniquely on each and every occasion.

All of these complications often result in emotionality being regarded as inexplicable, mysterious, ineffable (Chapter Three). The boundless plurality and variability of emotions seem to surface as insurmountable obstacles. On the contrary, this book argues, their plurality and variability marks 'the genius of the system.' Emotions are nearly infinite and, as such, infinitely productive, rendering a vast array of social relations and cultural meanings possible. They exist as ceaseless continua of change, *moving* us from one encounter to the next. Emotional relations encompass both the extraordinary and the ordinary, accumulated over a day, a year, a lifetime of engagement on a constant, moment-by-moment basis.

In speaking of all that is encompassed under the canopy of experience, Whitehead invokes the following qualities that touch upon emotionality:

… experience anxious and experience care-free, experience anticipatory and experience retrospective, experience happy and experience grieving, experience dominated by emotion and experience under self-restraint, experience in the light and experience in the dark, experience normal and experience abnormal.

(Whitehead qtd. in Brown and Stenner 10)

This book is my effort to begin with the experiences of emotions normal and abnormal, to discover where they might lead us.

Outline of Chapters

Although a cultural rather than historical account, the structure of *A Cultural Approach to Emotional Disorders* follows a roughly chronological progression. However, some chapters dwell on relatively narrow periods of time (Chapters Two, Four, and Five) while others traverse a century or more (Chapters One and Three). As a cultural account, considerable interchange occurs among eras discussed, especially when making connections to the present day. As Chapter One specifies, we continue to live in the age of mental illness, one dominated by emotional disorders. The chapters that follow track how we arrived here, why, and in what configurations emotionality has attained its central cultural position, as tracked through the ongoing individual and collective implications attached to dysfunctions of mood, anxiety, and personality.

Part of pursuing a cultural perspective entails questioning why, both contemporarily and historically, societies in the West have been so preoccupied with mental illness. One set of replies, from scholars such as Foucault or Gauchet and Swain, argues that conceptions of madness, insanity, and mental illness have been key to the development of modernity's subject or self. Chapter One, "Madness and Mental Illness," explores such assertions, focusing especially on the place of emotionality in the formulation of both madness/mental illness and the modern, Western self.

Foucault's work on madness has been especially influential. Chapter One assesses his early book, *Mental Illness and Psychology* (1954/1962), in some detail. Significant because it straddles Foucault's thinking as he moves from the notion of mental illness to the broader category of madness, the chapter explores the alterations, and their implications, as he transitions from one concept to the other. Temporally, *Mental Illness and Psychology* both precedes and parallels *History of Madness* (1961). Originally written in 1954, Foucault reissued *Mental Illness* in 1962, following the publication of *History of Madness*. The 1962 edition of *Mental Illness* retains Part I as it appeared in the first edition. However, he rewrote Part II in what has been described as a stunning summary of the *History of Madness* (Dreyfus xxvii). As a result, the two Parts invite comparison regarding Foucault's theoretical progress, although I argue that the more he turns toward madness, the less place he allocates for emotionality. In analyzing madness as an historical category that helped define reason, he largely ignores its emotional characteristics and consequences.

Foucault's well-known historical trajectory traces successive stages in the development of madness, culminating in the present era of mental illness. Chapter One, and the chapters that follow, treat the emotional aspects of mental illness in three phases. The first is the asylum era, dominated by moral insanity and moral treatment. The second phase coincides with the Freudian period, especially in its establishment of neuroses (Chapters One and Two). Finally, the contemporary moment from the 1970s through today, marks the biomedical age (Chapters Four and Five).

While agreeing with Foucault's timeline and periodization, Gauchet and Swain take exception to his characterization of the asylum era as inaugurating little other than disciplinary control. Although designating moral treatment a failure, they believe it marks the point when it became possible, within Western modernity, to regard the insane as human subjects. In part, this was achieved by recognizing that, despite their illness, the insane maintain emotional relations with others. Gauchet and Swain's work, in contrast to Foucault's, provides a departure point in accounting for emotionality's core role in the current organization of mental illness. "Madness and Mental Illness" applies these beginnings towards examining some of the conditions by which emotional disorders came to dominate the network of mental illnesses.

Two major events paved the way for today's prevalence of what we currently understand and extensively experience as emotional disorders: the asylum era's moral insanity, and the psychoanalytical turn to neuroses. While neuroses greatly expanded the parameters of mental illness, moral insanity activated changes that caused emotions, from this point on, to be judged within the framework of normality and abnormality. Ultimately, Chapter One argues that the category of 'mental illness' creates a place for emotionality, albeit a severely constrained one, in contrast to emotions' overall absence in the theoretical configuration of 'madness.'

Chapter Two engages with a particularly important version of the modern subject for emotional disorders: the psychological self, who crystallizes between approximately 1875 and 1925. The psychic subject was made possible by a number of factors, including the Enlightenment emergence of heightened individuality. Although the Enlightenment is closely associated with the elaboration of Cartesian rationality, "The Psychological Self" argues that the rise of certain emotional states, exemplified by the sensibility movement and Rousseau, likewise were fundamental to the appearance of a strongly individuated, autonomous self. A second factor enabling the psychic subject can be located in the transformation of mind to interiorized space. Mind as psyche inhabits the deepest recesses of the self, epitomizing our mysterious but most authentic essences. The two qualities, individuation and internalization, comprise the hallmarks of the psychological self, generating experience as both private (belonging to the individual) and personal (reflecting unique interiority).

Additionally, the psychological subject emerges against a social backdrop typified as a nineteenth century preoccupation with 'character' transitioning in the early twentieth century to an era dominated by 'personality.' The culture of character most often is associated with standards of social conduct aligned with morality while personality references an ethics of self-fulfillment and personal freedom. These depictions suggest movement from a climate of emotional restraint towards more open self-expression. Yet other cultural arenas offer competing accounts of the era's emotional trajectory. Drawing on the transition from theatrical melodrama to dramatic realism, which occurs in years overlapping the solidification of psychology and psychiatry, the prevailing sociality of emotions modifies towards increased concealment and privatization. Melodrama's attention to social suffering, engendered by rapid industrialization, conforms to values attributed to a culture of character, but its modes of emotionality do not. For its part, modernism's dramatic realism depends extensively on formulations of the psychological subject as deep interiority. In the theatrical context, however, changing notions of selfhood result in a transformation from melodrama's public, extroverted displays of emotionality to dramatic realism's more muted emotional experiences, in both audience behaviors and character portrayals.

Turning specifically to the implications for mental health, Chapter Two surveys the proliferation of mental illnesses *as* emotional disorders in the new epoch of psychological selfhood. The early twentieth century witnesses the expansion of neuroses, incipient forms of emotional disorders, into a separate category of mental illness contrasted to psychoses. Among their prominent impacts, neuroses vastly increase the boundaries of mental illness, enfolding emotional states previously largely disregarded. In their initial stages, the neuroses resulted in a burgeoning of psy fields. More recently, however, some of the exigencies confronting psy, especially the increased numbers of people world-wide diagnosable as emotionally disordered, have been attributed directly to the expansion enabled by the neuroses. In some quarters, the appearance of neuroses, signaling the infiltration of psy into the most minute corners of everyday life, has empowered an encroaching regulatory society. For others, the enlargement of mental disorders, initiated by neuroses, threatens the viability and continued existence of various psy fields. In either case, responses have called for the elimination of what has been depicted, in a variety of ways, as 'ordinary unhappiness' from the domain of psy. "The Psychological Self" outlines how the effort to distinguish emotional disorders from 'normal' misery and distress itself constitutes a pressing psy crisis.

Aesthetic fields represent relatively rare sociocultural arenas in which emotionality and emotional disorders have been acknowledged and, sometimes, welcomed. However, as "The Artist as Mad Genius" argues, assumptions about the receptiveness of artistic practices toward emotionality require careful investigation. Emotions and mental illness have not always been warmly embraced by aesthetics, particularly in higher status strands. Instead, aesthetics stands as different cultural terrain to psy, upon which alternative conceptualizations and difficulties about emotionality are enacted.

Chapter Three follows transitions in emotional subjectivity from nineteenth century Romanticism to twentieth century modernism. The centuries share in common an understanding of genius as exceptional inspiration, located as the inner quality of extraordinary individuals. Beyond these shared notions, however, the two aesthetic movements diverge significantly over the role of emotionality. High art modernism, in particular, has been associated with a rejection of emotions in favor of formal and intellectual principles. "The Artist as Mad Genius" focuses on modernism's organization of emotionality, in both high art and popular culture forms, as it tangles with issues of artistic genius, mental illness, and emotional suffering.

The chapter does so by undertaking an extended analysis of Vincent Van Gogh from the 1890s, the decade of his death, to the 1990s, a period coinciding with record-breaking sales of his work. My discussion does not take shape as a reflection on Van Gogh, the individual; rather, it concentrates on the critical and popular reception of his work, life story, and persona over the course of the twentieth century. Chapter Three contends that the struggle over Van Gogh's reputation corresponds to contestation between high modernism versus, in Miriam Hansen's vernacular modernism (Hansen). Throughout the twentieth century, high art was closely linked, if not often synonymous, with painting. In contrast, cinema epitomizes vernacular modernism, especially in its formative years and in movies emanating from Hollywood. Arguably, Van Gogh played a simultaneous role in both modernisms, high and vernacular, as his reputation became pulled between them. Most importantly, the struggle over Van Gogh's aesthetic reputation occurs, precisely, around the meanings and value of emotionality to his work. In critical circles, Van Gogh's standing waxed and waned over the course of the century. Aesthetics and emotionality were frequently situated in opposition to each other in high art contexts, with the result that Van Gogh's emotionality worked to preclude him from the highest echelons of the modernist pantheon. In contrast, he attained a vast and abiding popularity among a non-specialist, general public who were drawn to him exactly because he was perceived as a painter of emotion.

"The Artist as Mad Genius" also explores definitions of mental illness as they were applied to Van Gogh. In this matter, too, Van Gogh's legacy provokes contestation. The narrative of his madness, particularly as it developed in the last two decades of the twentieth century, placed great emphasis on the role of psychosis in his life, allowing issues concerning 'emotional volatility' to diminish. Part of the explanation rests with attempts to recuperate Van Gogh for high modernism in the face of his unrelenting popularity, leading to increasingly high profile exhibitions and astronomical sales prices for his paintings. By focusing on Van Gogh's psychotic/epileptic episodes, claims could be made that mental illness did not befall Van Gogh until the last year and a half of his life and, even then, only sporadically. Therefore, art commentators felt justified in asserting that madness did not affect his work. Through this maneuver, the problem of emotionality pitted against aesthetic expertise was resolved by rendering mental illness moot, in order to recover Van Gogh as an artist of the highest order, referred to as "the new Van Gogh." In the process, however, the intense emotional suffering he experienced throughout his life came to be drastically minimized, reflecting more general cultural attitudes towards emotionality.

"Personality Disorders, Biopsychiatry, and the Problem of Social Identity" bases its discussion around the category of emotional pathology known as personality disorders, as inscribed in the influential *Diagnostic and Statistical Manual of Mental Disorders.* The chapter assesses the impact on psy, in recent years, from two important but different directions: social identity theories and biomedical psychiatry. Personality disorders, as a coherent diagnostic class, were first introduced in 1980's *DSM-III,* the result of increased attention paid them during the 1960s and 1970s. Thus, personality disorders are contemporaneous with the political movements of those decades. I argue that personality disorders emerge at this time as a response to political and theoretical concerns around 'identity,' in particular, late century preoccupations with social collectivities as constitutive of individual identities. Intended as a meeting ground between 'personality,' as internalized, autonomous experience, and 'identity,' as the impact of sociocultural factors, personality disorders have resulted largely in demonstrating incompatibilities between the two concepts. Using the example of gender, in particular, I indicate some of the ways emotionality's operations, as activated through personality disorders, create struggle between the notions of psychological and social selves.

1980's *DSM-III,* the edition that codified personality disorders, itself represents a watershed moment in the history of psychopathology. As the first iteration of *DSM* to pursue the biomedical approach associated with diagnostic psychiatry, the third edition heralded the enormous changes that would be instigated by various forms of biological psychiatry. Intended to provide psychopathology with greater scientific credibility, the *DSMs'* biomedical perspective has since been blamed for much of the rampant proliferation of mental illness. By sanctioning a sharply increased number and range of official disorders, especially emotional dysfunctions, the *DSMs* from 1980 on have been widely charged with erroneously medicalizing 'normal' misery or the routine emotional problems of life.

"Personality Disorders, Biopsychiatry, and the Problem of Social Identity" concludes by looking at the manual's newest edition, 2013's *DSM-5.* Specifically, it explores *DSM-5*'s strongly contested alternative model for personality disorders. Intended to resolve problems long-associated with PDs, on the contrary, in turning to a trait-based approach, the alternative model underscores the dilemmas emotionality poses for scientific psy. Traits, regarded as the building blocks of personality, embrace an enormous variety of emotional attributes. Heated disputes surrounding a trait-based approach have focused on which emotional qualities to incorporate or omit, how degrees of emotional intensity (severity) can be quantitatively measured and, ultimately, the recurring issue of how to determine normal from abnormal emotionality.

Most recently, the neurosciences have gained primacy in psychology and psychiatry, with the result that explanations of emotions and emotional disorders increasingly occur within neuroscientific accounts. Additionally, neuroscience has generated related disciplines, such as neuroimaging, a key focus of Chapter Five. "Neuroscience and Other Narratives of Emotional Disorders" explores how scientific research on emotions incorporates aesthetics, arguing that the two often function in tacit partnership in the study of emotionality. In its most frequent usage, aesthetics refers to artistic practices and the formal techniques through which each art form takes material shape. In broader understandings, aesthetics refers to qualitative evaluations of experience or to an 'art' of living. Chapter Five takes the examples of neuroimaging, affective computing, and experimental physiology to demonstrate how the study of emotions in scientific contexts often necessitates engaging with aesthetics, in the wider sense of qualitative evaluation.

Then, turning to the more specific meaning of aesthetics, Chapter Five explores neuroimaging as a technology for visualizing the brain. Positron emission tomography (PET) scans involve complex processes for rendering large amounts of statistical data into 'simplified' colored images of the brain. In doing so, aesthetic values, such as the use of color, must be applied in arbitrary ways so that the visual images become meaningful or 'make sense.' Thus, aesthetic renderings like PET scans create explanatory narratives; in this instance, visual stories about the brain and emotions.

"Neuroscience and Other Narratives of Emotional Disorders" contends that one of the values of emotionality resides with its ability to resist dichotomization, in that it has never been definitively reduced to either mind/body, science/aesthetics, biology/social construction, individual/society. Emotionality carries the potential of moving between terms, whatever they might be. In this rendering, emotionality takes up a relational position, circulating among, integrating with, and negotiating between domains of experience. Chapter Five concludes by returning to the current global epidemic of emotional disorders. Attending to accusations that mental illness is confronting such rapid proliferation because of the extensive, erroneous psychomedicalizing of everyday life, how then might we address that which is labeled ordinary misfortune through alternate interpretations? If psy must distinguish between pathological depression and human condition suffering because it cannot accommodate the scale of current and growing distress, can we devise better narratives to account for the range of phenomena now experienced as emotional disorders? The pressing challenge is to locate interpretations of emotionality that allow for tolerable ways of living normal misery.

Notes

1. Mood disorders encompass unipolar and bipolar depressive disorders. Anxiety disorders include, amongst others, panic disorders, phobias, obsessive-compulsive disorders, and post-traumatic stress disorder (*DSM-5*).
2. For example, it is an explanatory insufficiency to say that aesthetic practices operate at the one extreme of embodied affect or at the opposite limit of cognitive signification. As in the case of narrativity, this has been used to reject certain aesthetic processes, for example forms of popular culture, because they are not primarily or adequately affective.

1 Madness and Mental Illness

Taking up a culturalist perspective on emotional disorders entails asking why as a society, from professional and theoretical quarters as well as in popular conceptions, we care so much about madness and mental illness. Why has attempting to account for 'disordered experience' troubled us historically and contemporarily, and what does it indicate about 'ordered existence'? Moyn observes that, "the history of the self is in some sense the history of the psyche" (316). This has been the case since the nineteenth century, at any rate. Over the last two centuries, the work of various Western bodies of knowledge, pivotally including the psy fields, has created the psyche and its bearer, the psychic subject. Moyn's point is that assembling a history of the self also must involve a history of the entities responsible "for theorizing it and caring for it" (322). Ultimately, endeavoring to make sense of the modern self is inseparable from the organizations and systems that have conceptualized it into existence or that maintain and nurture it.

To this end, a number of contemporary theorists, including Michel Foucault as well as Marcel Gauchet and Gladys Swain, have devoted attention to the nineteenth century institution of the asylum, which temporally coincides with the development of the psychic self, precisely because they believe the asylum to be paradigmatic of the contours of the subject within modernity (Weymans 41–42). As we shall see, however, they arrive at quite different conclusions about the qualities of modern subjectivity as constituted by the asylum, among other institutions. Yet, what they each make evident is how madness and mental illness dovetail with issues of modernity's self, subject, or individual.

Although speaking specifically about what is at stake when addressing schizophrenia, Rod Lucas takes up terms that I believe apply to mental illness more generally. Considering schizophrenia, he explains, focuses "attention on the bounds of community and the existential limits of what it is to be human" (148). A cultural exploration of mental illness operates at two simultaneous levels. First, it points to what and whom belong within society, as shared communities of humans, and what and whom lie outside or beyond those parameters. Second, it makes apparent that which, at any historical moment, it means to be a human individual. Again, who counts and who does not as a fully functional, successfully performing person. My goal is to 'get at' some of the cultural locations, purposes, and operations of emotions by means of the historically and contextually changing normal/abnormal divide of functional versus dysfunctional emotionality. Emotional disorders indicate what is acceptable within or must exist outside given communities, as well as in what configurations emotions signal whole, intact, stable persons or personalities. The emotional parameters of psy are a useful means of approaching historically and culturally specific alignments of the human being, including particular modes of subjectivity and explicit manifestations of emotional experience.

Accordingly, I am interested in exploring how emotions fit into the making of the psyche and the modern self, that is, the psychic subject. Through psychopathology, I investigate some of the ways emotions have been enveloped, or gone missing, in the history of psychology/psychiatry and, as a result, in the history of the modern self. Although this chapter, and significant portions of the book overall, address the psy-disciplines, they are far from the only fields that need to be taken into account in order to provide an adequate rendering of the place of emotions and emotional disorders in the make-up of the modern self. To this end, elsewhere I turn to other cultural arenas, most notably aesthetics, in order to offer such an alternative account. In fact, much of my exploration concerns the limitations of the psy and aesthetic fields, as currently construed, towards an appreciation of the complex significance emotions and emotional disorders hold for our contemporary lives. Emotions, I believe, are far more constitutive of personhood, social relations, and cultural existence than much current theoretical attention acknowledges.

Mental Illness

At present, the most influential historio-cultural account of madness and mental illness is Michel Foucault's *The History of Madness*, which was preceded by his *Mental Illness and Psychology*. The sequencing of these works is significant if we wish to track the development of Foucault's thinking on mental illness and, more broadly, the location of emotional disorders in the madness/mental illness edifices he constructs. *The History of Madness* was initially published in 1961; *Mental Illness and Psychology* first appeared in 1954 (under the title, *Mental Illness and Personality*). In 1962, *Mental Illness and Psychology* was republished, with a marginally altered Part I but with a substantially rewritten Part II. So while Part I, "The Psychological Dimensions of Mental Illness," reflects Foucault's thinking prior to *The History of Madness*, Part II, "Madness and Culture," is entirely shaped by the 'later' work. Indeed, Dreyfus calls Part II of *Mental Illness and Psychology* a "stunning" summary of *The History of Madness* (xxvii).[1]

Dreyfus explains the difference between Part I and Part II of the 1962, revised *Mental Illness and Psychology* in the following manner: "Foucault thus switches from an account of the *social* conditions that *cause* mental illness to the *cultural* conditions that lead us to *treat madness as* mental illness" (viii–ix; italics in original). In attempting an analysis of the cultural positioning of emotions and emotional disorders, value exists in exploring the distinctions Foucault draws between 'mental illness' (*maladie mentale*) and 'madness' (*folie*). Why does he switch from one term to the other and, in doing so, what evocations of meaning are called up or denied between one expression and the other? In particular, the more Foucault discusses madness rather than mental illness, the *less* he refers to emotions. One issue, then, concerns the degree to which Foucault constitutes reason as his foundational ground, to the exclusion of emotionality.

In Part I of *Mental Illness and Psychology*, Foucault outlines the hierarchy of mental illnesses, in ascending order from mildest to most severe, "as they are detailed in the psychoanalytic tradition" (31). First are the neuroses, which damage "only the affective complexes" of the personality. Second comes paranoia, which influences an individual's "emotional structure" but only as an exaggeration of personality; "there is as yet no damage to the lucidity, the order, or the cohesion of the mental basis." The third level he refers to as dream states in which "perceptual control and the coherence of reasoning have disappeared," resulting in illusions, hallucinations, and false recognitions. The fourth ranking falls to manic and melancholic states which exhibit both somatic symptoms and "emotional outbursts": despair for the melancholic and "euphoric agitation" for the manic. Fifth are schizophrenic states in which "thinking has disintegrated and proceeds in isolated fragments." This level is marked by hallucinations, verbal incoherency, and "sudden affective interruptions." Sixth and last is dementia in which state "there is no longer a personality, only a living being" (26–27).

Foucault's intention, of course, is to critique the psychiatric literature. His initial objection rests in what he perceives as the mistaken attempt to liken psychological illness with physiological ones. Because 'personality' cannot be divided into singular or discrete functions in a manner similar to the organic body, the two cannot be considered conceptually or pragmatically equivalent. Psychiatry having done so, as in the six levels he outlines of increasing severity of mental illness from neuroses to dementia, resulted only in "a qualitative appreciation that opened the way to every kind of confusion" (12). Categories of mental illness are qualitative conveniences that enable us to speak about varying pathological phenomena, but do not reference clear-cut, separable biological entities. Such categorization represents simply "the concrete forms that psychology has managed to attribute to" mental illness (13). In other words, the taxonomy he outlines belongs to historical, not organic, fact. However, as long as we understand the descriptions he provides as historical rather than physiologically natural traits, at this stage in his thinking Foucault does not take exception to the specific, dominant symptomatic features of mental illness in the West. My interest in the hierarchy of mental illness he outlines is the degree to which Foucault recognizes "psychological personality" as a formation of emotional elements, as well as cognitive and somatic characteristics (12).

Foucault's principle objection to Janet's and Freud's schemas (the psychoanalytic tradition) does not reside in symptomology but, rather, with their attributions of origin or cause. He describes their explanations as "psychological evolution" because they position the purported causes of mental illness in regression to either archaic social states or to infancy, which he describes as "serial determinism" (30, 45). The notion that mental illness is a retreat to more 'primitive' stages of human social interactions or a relapse to earlier childhood states, he calls "myth" (24). In place of evolutionary theories of human social or libidinal development and regression, in sequentially increasing stages of severity, he offers up his version of "psychological history" (30). In Part I of *Mental Illness*, in the mid-1950s and under the influence of phenomenological psychiatry (Lanzoni; Dreyfus), Foucault speaks in terms of the specificity of the individual morbid personality wherein a patient experiences internal affective contradictions as a direct response to encountered, irresolvable social conflicts in the world within which he or she exists. The ill person is responding to a "present situation" in which pathological behavior occurs as "a compromise between two contradictory tendencies" that the surrounding social world produces (36, 38). These are the social causes of mental illness that Dreyfus refers to versus the cultural approach of Part II that, in contrast, works to explain why we treat madness as mental illness.

In Part I, mental illness occurs as a reaction to externalized situations that the neurotic or psychotic responds to in two ways. First, he or she internalizes the social conflict as personal experience; second, the affected person moves to derealize some portion of the 'normal' world because the conflict cannot be resolved or solved (39, 35). Normal conflict is understood as ambiguity embedded in a given social situation, while pathological conflict becomes accepted as contradiction within one's very existence, the latter of which Foucault refers to as 'experience.' "The patient's psychological history is constituted as a set of significative acts that erect defense mechanisms against the ambivalence of affective contradictions" (42). For Foucault, at this stage in his thinking, important aspects of mental illness as experience take place in terms of affective life, in particular, as affective conflict.

Affective contradictions are felt, by those who suffer them, as insurmountable anxiety. In an effort to combat or diminish such intense anxiety, mentally ill persons create a morbid world for themselves that they experience alongside the 'normal' world, but which embody a private community of meanings. This morbid world is the erected defense mechanism that Foucault refers to in the quote above. While these morbid defenses appear as pathological to others, they embody logical meaning to the person who is mentally ill (40–41, 19). It is because the morbid behaviors have meanings for the patient that Foucault can call symptoms of mental illness simultaneously pathological and significative (42, 55, 19). However, attempted remediation of socially-derived conflicts through the establishment of pathological behaviors, lodged in a personalized morbid existence, inevitably fails because it is based on a misapprehension of the problem (as individual not social) and, as such, ends only in ongoing or even increased anxiety that leads, in turn, to further pathology.

Although Foucault attributes the cause of mental illness to affective contradictions, within the framework of phenomenological psychology, he depicts the morbid world constructed by the mentally ill in terms of rational, cognitive faculties. In analyzing what distinguishes the morbid world "from the world constituted by the normal man," Foucault pinpoints four qualities (55). First, potential exists for "a major disturbance in temporality," in which the past, present, and future take on alternative configurations (51). Second, space may lose its cohesion so that objects and relations appear either more distant or more oppressively immediate. Third, relations with the social and cultural 'normal' world are distorted to the effect that the person may feel isolated or persecuted. Finally, the mentally ill may come to experience their own bodies in distorted ways that diverge from common perception. In all these ways, morbid existence abandons the normal world "by losing the significations of the world ... being unable to possess its meanings," to be replaced for the mentally ill by a world of their own making that is, simultaneously, pathological yet logical to those experiencing it (56).

On the one hand, then, in the earlier phase of Foucault's thoughts as exemplified in Part I, he follows psychiatric tradition that views mental illness as manifested in somatic, affective, and cognitive symptoms. Mania, for example, "involves motor agitation, a euphoric or choleric mood, a psychic exaltation characterized by verbigeration, rapidity of the associations, and the flight of ideas" (4). For its part, depression "takes the form of motor inertia against the background of a mood of sadness, accompanied by a psychic slowing down" (5). Schizophrenia involves "a disorder in the normal coherence of the associations" as well as "a breakdown of affective contact with the environment" (6). On the other hand, although Foucault considers somatic and affective symptoms as well as cognitive characteristics in his earlier writing, the terms 'psychic' or 'psychological' refer most specifically to issues of cognition or reason. Thus, as noted above, a difficulty in concentration or focused thought associated with depression becomes "a psychic slowing down." Similarly, paranoia is accompanied by "psychological hyperactivity" or delusions, while dementia is "the total disorganization of psychological life," in which the personality sinks into "incoherence" (5). In Part I then, the notion of psychic or psychological is already most equivalent to rational thought while physiological and emotional symptoms are of a different order. Indeed, in describing dementia as the state "in which there is no longer a personality, only a living being," he equates rationality or lucidity with personhood itself. Although dementia entails disintegration in cognitive faculties, the person continues to exist as a physical and feeling being. But for Foucault, even at this early stage in his writings, physical and emotional existence without cognitive abilities is to live without subjectivity.

An affective life does not in and of itself qualify as personhood; therefore, loss of emotional equilibrium without cognitive deficiency does not impair constituted personhood. That is to say, affect is a less crucial component of personhood than an accompanying symptom of its demise. Psyche or mind, then, is most closely associated with rational thought that, in turn, is indispensable for subjectivity.

In the sense of possessing greater gravity, cognitive symptoms are of a higher order than affective and somatic ones. This is evident in Foucault's definition of psychoses versus neuroses.[2] Psychoses affect the personality "as a whole," including disordered thinking and "a disturbance in conscious control" along with an "alteration of the affective life and mood" (8). Neuroses, in contrast, affect "only a part of the personality" because "the flow of thought remains structurally intact" as does the patient's "critical lucidity" (8). In his description of psychoses and neuroses, we see a similar hierarchy to Foucault's borrowed taxonomy of ascending genres of mental illness in which the mildest forms of neuroses and paranoia concern only "the affective complexes" or "emotional structure." However, levels three, five, and six (dream states, schizophrenia, and dementia, respectively) interfere with "the coherence of reasoning." The flow in this ascending pattern of severity of illness is disrupted solely by mania and depression (level four), which are classified by predominantly affective symptoms, yet are positioned at a stage of greater severity than the initial phase (three) of loss of rational coherence. We can see that, in a number of ways, emotional disorders represent a 'problem' or 'disruption' in psychiatry's taxonomy, leading "to every kind of confusion" (12).

In describing the more severe forms of pathology as "a loss of consciousness," resulting in a style of "total incoherence," Foucault prioritizes rational deficiency over emotional suffering as the most devastating attribute associated with mental illness (17). In doing so, he is far from alone. A longstanding, still currently applied tradition refers to psychoses as 'serious,' 'severe,' 'major,' or 'acute' mental illness, while neuroses or the contemporary mood and anxiety disorders are regarded as 'minor,' 'milder,' 'less severe' forms of mental distress (MacDonald 10; Dallaire et al. 147; Palmer 117; Bentall 7, 94; Horwitz 50–51, 208). Yet it remains difficult to imagine more serious or severe repercussions than the suicide, self-injury, or intense pain that often accompany emotional disorders.

For Foucault at this stage, if the reality of the mentally ill person is not necessarily logical or coherent, it is, at any rate, meaningful in that the behaviors and ideas taken up are filled with significance for the person experiencing them. Therefore, he notes that the difference between the doctor and the patient is not the distinction between knowledge (understanding of illness) and ignorance (incomprehension of illness) (46). The patient is aware that something separates him or her "from the world and the consciousness of others" (47). Instead, the distance between doctor and patient is that of medical expertise versus experience, in which experience is consciousness "from within the illness," manifested in terms of how the patient feels and expresses the illness (47).

Out of Madness

In "Madness and Culture," Part II of *Mental Illness and Psychology,* Foucault relies on the term 'madness' to a far greater degree, while mental illness refers to a specific development in the history of madness, beginning in the nineteenth century. At the same time, references to emotional and physiological phenomena are notably reduced. Foucault partly acknowledges this, stating that he has "purposely not referred to the physiological and anatomicopathological problems concerning mental illness" (86). And of course, he would go on in future work to devote much attention to the body, particularly as the locus of disciplinary power and, therefore, pivotal to the establishment of certain modern forms of subjectivity. Emotions in Part II, however, are referenced only in passing and without explanation for their disappearance.

Part II comprises more familiar Foucaultian arguments on mental illness, a result of the influence of *History of Madness.*[3] In this section, the shift Dreyfus describes as moving from "the *social* conditions that *cause* mental illness to the *cultural* conditions that lead us to *treat madness* as mental illness" becomes actualized. Now madness is located at the margins of a culture as that which the culture refuses to integrate or recognize (Foucault, *Mental Illness* 62). But through a consideration of what a culture marginalizes, we can also locate that which it constitutes as central and valuable. Certain cultures regard the symptoms that we identify as indicative of madness in quite dissimilar ways: as magical or mystical, as spiritual, religious or demonic, or as simply ordinary (63, 76). However, Western culture in the modern era renders these same symptoms as deviancy, requiring social exclusion (63). For Foucault, this reveals more about the culture that excludes than about the mad individuals who are ostracized and silenced (68, 80, 87). Although "the doctor thinks he is diagnosing madness as a phenomenon of nature," that is, as organic or biological reality, in fact he or she is identifying the margins of what is and isn't permissible in that particular culture (78).

The historical trajectory Foucault traces, in his work on madness and mental illness, begins in the pre-modern era in the West, encompassing Medieval and Renaissance times. In broad outline, in the pre-modern world the mad lived within the bounds of society. While the general population regarded the mad with fear and fascination, they did not view them as essentially different or removed from themselves. In the Early Modern period, from the mid-seventeenth to the end of the eighteenth centuries – the classical age – the circumstances of the mad altered drastically. Along with "the poor and disabled, the elderly poor, beggars, the work-shy, those with venereal diseases, libertines of all kinds," and other exemplars of social deviancy, the mad were secreted away from general society, in the period referred to as 'the great confinement' (67). Following the French Revolution and until the end of the nineteenth century, the mad were further singled out, serving now as the principal representatives of 'unreason.' In this new guise, they were housed separately in asylums where they were attended to under the auspices of moral treatment. With the failure of the asylum movement, beginning in the late nineteenth and early twentieth centuries, the mad increasingly became the concern of the psy-function, "the psychiatric, psychopathological, psycho-sociological, psycho-criminological, and psychoanalytic function" (Foucault, *Psychiatric Power* 85).

Foucault's historical trajectory, then, tracks the movement in what, "through successive divisions, becomes *madness, illness,* and *mental illness*" (*Mental Illness* 80). In the pre-modern era, when the general population lived with the insane, madness was not conceived of as pathological. With the classical era, and the advent of scientific forms of knowledge, madness begins to be medicalized, coming into view as illness. In the nineteenth century, madness in not simply an illness but becomes, more specifically, a disorder of the psyche and, at this stage, transitions to mental illness (Major-Poetzl 112). In Foucault's historical trajectory, madness is relocated repeatedly, and systemically reordered in those movements. Major-Poetzl describes these historical developments as madness successively "divorced from the world, from nature, and from society, until it was located exclusively in the personality of the madman" (118–119). While a part of the world in the pre-modern era, madness in the classical age becomes "a deterioration of nature" (Foucault, *Mental Illness* 64). Thus the advent of modernity separates madness from the world, to constitute it as an aberration of rationally operative, scientifically determinable, immutable physical principles. For Foucault, illness is the particular form that madness took from approximately 1650 "with the arrival of the calm, objective, scientific gaze of modern medicine" (Ibid.). It is the "medical consciousness of madness" that enables its recognition as illness (79). More generally, the Enlightenment facilitated the perception of a structured natural order, in which both the world and human beings could be measured in terms of how they ought to function, resulting in the establishment of norms and, simultaneously, their opposite, the abnormal. It is at this historical juncture that reason becomes a property of human nature. At the same time, madness becomes "a nature of nature, that is to say, a process alienating nature" (87). Henceforth, madness as illness is perceived as a malfunction in the properly ordered nature of human existence. Similarly, society came to be viewed in terms of how it ought to function, as a replication of nature in the form of a rational and orderly organism. Those who represented "derangement" or disruption to this organization, including the mad among others, were marginalized and silenced because they were "no longer fit to belong to society" (67, 68).

In comparison, in the asylum era, madness increasingly is regarded "as alienation from society and the self" (Major-Poetzl 119). Over the course of the nineteenth and twentieth centuries, madness becomes a function of the individual and, in particular, of his or her discrete, interiorized psyche.

Thus, the nineteenth and twentieth centuries are characterized by "a vast technology of the psyche" (Foucault qtd. in Caputo 245). 'Mental illness' occurs with the further-heightened medicalization of the nineteenth century, by which time madness has become the principal face of unreason (Foucault, *Mental Illness* 70, 71). In particular, the nineteenth century invents 'mind' as "interiority," an inner, private world both constituted and studied by psychology (72, 83). The formation of mental illness, therefore, depends on a notion of mind as distinct from body, although Foucault argues that no historical or cultural necessity mandates such a division, given that for other cultures and in other eras "each pathological form involves man in his totality" (79). The development of interiority of mind becomes a means to more closely discipline madness, through psychology, in every social corner in which it might exist or appear.

Mental illness, then, is the series of phenomena created by psychology. Psychology, in turn, is the body of knowledge founded on the concept of psychopathological experiences (73). As such, it inevitably discovers only abnormal mental activities, from which 'normal' psychic functioning may be extrapolated. For its part, madness is a larger, more general configuration of what we now perceive as mental illness, as it existed prior to the Enlightenment. In this sense, psychology did not discover madness; rather, in the opposite movement, madness made psychology possible (73). Efforts to define and confine madness enabled psychology to come into being. Madness, and the exertions to marginalize and silence it, provided the conceptual and ideological foundation for all forms of psychology, including psychiatry and psychoanalysis (87). Not madness in and of itself, but madness as a marginalized and silenced set of phenomena was required in order to precipitate the invention of psychology. Psychology, therefore, is the discipline that secures and ensures that which has already been achieved (Ibid.).

Caputo, adapting an often-quoted statement of Foucault's, describes the era of mental illness as constituting "the monologue of reason with itself we call psychology and psychiatry" (239).[4] More specifically, psychology and psychiatry function as monologues of reason about madness, in its historical manifestation as mental illness, not as madness may have existed in earlier configurations. If we follow Foucault's historical trajectory into and through the era of mental illness, we can say that three phases have occurred to date. The first phase of mental illness covers the nineteenth century asylum period with its focus on moral treatment. It is marked by the invention of mind as interiority (see Chapter Two). The second phase, coming into its own around the beginning of the twentieth century, revolves around Freudian psychoanalysis and other forms of dynamic psychiatry. This is the period in which the neuroses take form alongside the psychoses. The third phase, from about the 1970s to the present,[5] designates a stage in which psychology and psychiatry have been dominated by biomedical explanations, especially the rapid emergence and influence of the neurosciences (see Chapters Four and Five). The movement from the second to third phase can be regarded as a major cultural transformation from the unconscious mind to the biological brain.

The formulation of neuroses, marks a crucial moment for the development of emotional disorders, rendering possible the creation of affective maladies as a distinct order of mental illness. Horwitz, for example, is quite definite that asylums only "managed a small number of very serious mental conditions," "reserved for people whose behavior was extremely strange, incomprehensible, and disruptive" (1). These very serious mental illnesses were synonymous with psychoses (Ibid. 39). Indeed, Horwitz describes psychoses as "the classical entities of psychiatry," expanded in the early twentieth century to include "sexual perversions, hysteria, obsessions, compulsions, phobias, and anxiety," as a direct result of the emergence of psychoanalysis (67, 42). Today, nonpsychotic forms of mental illness have broadened even further to encompass depression, anxiety, phobias, obsessions and compulsions, panic disorders, substance abuse disorders, eating disorders, and so on (Ibid. 109, 218).[6] However, the development of the category of neuroses was not simply an augmentation to the existing concept of mental illness. For significant portions of the psy fields, their introduction represented a deviation *from* psychoses *to* neuroses. In this regard, Freud's claim that psychoanalysis is best suited for addressing neuroses but that he doubted its efficacy in connection with psychoses has been regularly referenced over the years (for example, Gauchet, "Redefining" 6).

It is clear that, for Foucault, in the turn to the era of mental illness something of madness' energy, joy, and audibility has been lost, creating a deficit in our contemporary world. The historical trajectory from madness to illness to mental illness marks a diminishment, an insurmountable circumspection in which each successive move 'forward' (temporally) has proven to be a further narrowing of the capacities and creativities of human life or, conversely, a greater abandonment of productive forms of strangeness, abnormality, and unreason. Foucault describes the treatment of madness in the modern age as "its confiscation," reminding us not to forget its "original exuberance" (*Mental Illness* 65). In his use of the term 'confiscation,' we understand that he perceives modernity as having taken something from humanity, robbing it of that which once held great value. But it is also arguable that the historical trajectory from madness to mental illness, as Foucault has theorized it, omits certain aspects of human capacity and creativity, in particular, those vastly important and minutely executed cultural phenomena we recognize as emotions. In following the reverse trajectory in his own work, *from* mental illness *to* madness, Foucault can be said to have lost that with which he earlier engaged, the "affective complexes" or "emotional structure" of human existence (26).

The Freudian revolution can be credited with establishing the complexity and 'messiness' of emotions more prominently in the equation of mental illness. Although psychoanalysis is closely associated with libido and the unconscious, in this sense it also can be ascribed with positioning emotions

on the visible horizon, rendering them more accessible in their specific, contemporary, but often muddled modes of existence: Foucault's qualitative
system that leads to every confusion. Freud, his contemporaries, and followers offered an increased recognition of emotions, but at the same time,
in creating the neuroses, rendered them distinctly morbid, as emotional disorders. The historical move to mental illness, therefore, can be regarded
as changing emotions by making them both more visible and pathological. As 'mental illness' developed over time, its emotional phenomena have
grown to cause many of its subsequent conceptual and pragmatic difficulties, including the current global epidemic (see Introduction). Some believe
this to be the inevitable outcome of abandoning the 'simplicity' and 'clarity'
of the psychoses as irrationality, because of the greater ease by which reliable diagnosis can occur on the basis of delusional thinking, in contrast to
the murkier and much more debated criteria for determining the presence
of emotional disorders (Chapter Four).[7] Gauchet, for example, points out
that psychoses, historically, have been a largely stable category while, in
contrast, the makeup and definitions of neuroses have shifted considerably
("Redefining" 14). This is to say, the emotional phenomena of psychological
subjectivity, rendered as 'personality,' are more susceptible to revision in our
understanding and, therefore, in their manifestations. Changes in emotional
subjectivity necessarily are accompanied by variable configurations in personality's pathologies.

Indeed, Gauchet and Swain refer to the psychoanalytic revolution as 'the
Freudian reversal,' in part because it diverted the psychiatry of the previous asylum era to a focus on neuroses rather than psychoses. And like the
asylum project before it, the Freudian reversal also failed, the talking cure
proving to be as "hopelessly utopian" as the moral treatment ideal of returning the mentally alienated to society and to themselves (Gauchet and Swain
145). They contend that one of the reasons for the failure of the Freudian
reversal has been, precisely, its inability to contend with psychoses, leaving
dynamic psychiatry to tend solely to the neuroses, rendering it an incomplete, diminished response to the problems of madness/mental illness. However, I am arguing that the psychoanalytic turn eventually led to the present
circumstances in which mental illness has become dominated by emotional
disorders although, as this book goes on to argue, by incorporating emotions in chiefly constricted, unsatisfactory ways.

Major-Poetzl points out that madness continues to exist in the contemporary moment as 'mental illness' (112). This is the case; we continue to
live in the era of mental illness. But what is now encompassed when we
refer to 'mental illness' has both expanded and altered over time. It is an
historically changing, dynamically evolving classificatory means of making
sense of important aspects of human existence. My preoccupation, here,
is the centrality of emotions to the historical and cultural transformations
that resulted in the movement from relatively select manifestations of
madness to the widespread appearance of mental illness and how, in these

revolutions or reversals, emotions and their disorders have come to be conceptualized.

One may agree with Foucault, as I do, that the psy-functions are equipped primarily to understand human relations – including emotions – in pathological terms. If so, the question he leaves us with is how might we consider them otherwise? The task here is to track, via psychopathology, what has happened to emotions in the history of psychology and psychiatry and, thus, in the history of the self.

Reason and Unreason

Madness is the manifested behavior Foucault associates most distinctly with 'unreason,' although unreason is rendered largely equivalent to madness only at the end of the eighteenth century, in the period following the French Revolution (*Mental Illness* 70). From this historical moment, madness comes to exist as unreason's most visible marker. Prior to this time, in the classical age that inaugurates the great confinement, madness is not distinguished from other forms of unreason, such as the diseased, criminals, and the poor. In other words, in the earlier era unreason encompassed the entirety of those who were physically removed from the general public, by being placed into institutions, because they were unfit, in some manner, to belong within society's parameters, "all those who, in relation to the order of reason, morality, and society, showed signs of 'derangement'" (67). Thus, their persons marked the borderline between society and social deviance.

From the end of the eighteenth century, madness as the loss of rationality grows into society's greatest fear in the Age of Reason. For those existing within society's embrace, the mad come to stand for a lived experience in which "the comforting reassurances of scientific and philosophical knowledge have collapsed" (Caputo 238). The mad threaten to unveil the deception of reason's totality precisely because they exist outside its comforting reassurances. Through their very presence, the mad risk unraveling and destroying "the world that reason builds around itself" (Ibid. 241). Foucault's effort to recapture unreason as a positive experience is an attempt to counteract the deadening restrictions of reason, as he believes it has been construed in the West from the mid-seventeenth century.[8]

A number of scholars have argued that Foucault's intention, in harshly criticizing reason, is to abandon it altogether. For instance, Barham speaks of Foucault's "animus against the achievements of modernity" (49). Ingram argues that Habermas' opposition to Foucault's work rests on the latter's "disenchantment" with and "wholesale criticism" of the Enlightenment project, the notion of human progress, and the very possibility of a rational, knowing subject (215, 230). Other scholars, however, contend that the chief concern throughout Foucault's studies is, precisely, reason and that, in his later work, he returns to it in a more accepting manner. Ingram, contra Habermas on this point, states that Foucault's later efforts "to situate his life's work in the Enlightenment tradition presumably laid to rest any lingering doubts about the rational basis of his work" and that "by 1983 he had come to see his own work as a continuation of the Enlightenment ethos he had formerly repudiated" (215, 237). I would take Ingram's point a step further. Foucault returns to reason but not simply in a mode of acceptance; rather, his purpose is to activate unreason, principally in its appearance as madness, in order to resuscitate and revitalize reason. His is an operation intended to rescue reason, largely from its own limitations, in which unreason serves as an antidote to the constrictions of rationality. Thus, through madness, he can enact the great confrontation "that is the relation between Reason and Unreason" (*Mental Illness* 74). In seeking an alternative that counters the rigidity and tediousness of reason as guiding cultural principle, he attempts to capture for it a state of joy, creativity, and strangeness, an "original exuberance" that he believes existed in the fifteenth and sixteenth centuries but that, with modernity, was laid open to "confiscation."

In establishing these relations, however, Foucault sets in motion a universe of reason and unreason as the sum of all possibilities or, at any rate, as the totality of the states that matter. Just as he contends that the category of 'mental illness' is exclusionary in narrowing the field of madness solely to its medicalized form, so his conceptualization of madness constrains unreason to irrationality, defined narrowly as the absence of rationality. The question here concerns what occurs to emotionality in this process. In his vision of reason and unreason, the status of emotions remains unclear. Everything that doesn't belong to reason might well be unreason, including emotions. Conversely, reason/unreason may well have been the dynamic that fascinated Foucault, to the exclusion of other experiences or aspects of life, like emotionality.

Certainly there exists a long-standing Western tradition that understands emotion as reason's opposite. In Foucault's analysis of unreason, however, this does not appear to be the case; instead, emotions largely disappear beyond the horizon of visibility, in favor of rational, economic, embodied, and sexual factors, as symbolized by the psychotic, the poor, beggars, the disabled, libertines, and so on. Positioning unreason as reason's opposite does not necessarily open the way for emotion as an acknowledged, significant field of experience. Unreason as the desirable counter-force to reason may still be limited to the realm of the cognitive, as it appears to be for Foucault: a closed system in which rationality and sanity are largely synonymous. We can clarify this issue by turning to Gauchet and Swain's disagreement with Foucault, which turns on the issue of non-subjectivity as the loss of rationality.

Gauchet and Swain adhere to Foucault's historical timeline in which, during the Medieval and Renaissance periods, the mad lived at large in society (Weymans 35). In early modernity, from approximately 1650, the mad, along with others, increasingly come to be excluded from society through institutionalization, in the process of the great confinement (Ibid.).

Subsequently, the asylum era comes to the fore, with its concepts of moral treatment (Ibid.). It is inaugurated symbolically in the mid-1790s, when Pinel is said to free the mad from their chains. For Gauchet and Swain, the last is a pivotal metaphorical moment in the history of mental alienation because what Pinel recognizes, marking his original contribution, is that the mad retain some portion of their capacity as self-aware and feeling subjects.

> Their isolation no longer means they are totally locked up in themselves. Instead, they remain accessible from within because they maintain a basic level of subjectivity like other human beings.
>
> (Weymans 40)

Pinel's 'discovery' rests in the realization that the mad continue to possess some level of rational or conscious awareness, as well as ongoing emotional connections to others, even during "the most extreme forms of derangement" (Gauchet and Swain 141).

With Pinel's insight, Gauchet and Swain argue, the mad are rendered subjects from this historical moment forward because they come to be perceived as not entirely different from the non-mad. If the mad enter their illness at a certain point in their lives, and if they emerge from it, even if only partially or temporarily, then those departures from the state of madness require explanation. "People *become* psychotic just as they also *cease* to be it. … it is still necessary to account for the existence of the subjective formation before its eclipse in the psychotic episode and *a fortiori* for its possible reappearance" (Swain qtd. in Moyn 337). According to Gauchet and Swain, the mad may well be perceived as failed or disordered subjects but, with modernity, they exist as subjects nonetheless (78). Indeed, society could not establish a pathological *in comparison to* a normal until 'others,' like the mad, came to be considered human subjects, albeit aberrant ones (13). Pinel's, and subsequently Esquirol's, reconceptualization undermines the distinction of the mad as completely foreign, alienated beings.

This marks one of the points on which Gauchet and Swain believe Foucault is incorrect. Whereas Foucault understands pre-modern eras as a time of freedom for the mad, in that they existed with and were accepted by surrounding society, Gauchet and Swain contend that the mad living among the general public was made possible, precisely, because they were not yet perceived as human subjects (Weymans 37). The physically shared social space was enabled by the conception that the mad belonged to a distinct order of being and, as such, they posed no threat to the larger, 'ordinary' populace.

For Gauchet and Swain, a pivotal outcome of the recognition of the insane as human subjects, in a process through which they came to at least resemble the majority population, was that the connection of the mad to society-at-large was also reconstituted. First, the insane now belonged in society in a new way, given that a mad person's reason was recoverable. Second, as human subjects they were deserving of attempts at amelioration. Thus, "the discovery of the curability of the insane" led to the asylum's organizing mission: to retrieve the mad from their internal isolation and reintegrate them into society (Gauchet and Swain 46). As a result, the asylum's ambition to treat and cure the insane signals the beginning of modern therapeutic society. Of course, the asylum "failed to cure the insane in the sense in which its inventors intended," demonstrating "its own uselessness" (Ibid. 48). But in that process, perhaps inadvertently, asylums "*changed* insanity" (100; italics in original). They did so just as a century later, the Freudian reversal and its introduction of the neuroses, would drastically alter mental illness.

Gauchet's and Swain's belief that the asylum era in particular, and modernity in general, bestowed subjectivity on the mad demarcates their greatest difference from Foucault's position. For Foucault, "modernity means the exclusion of everything strange and uncontrollable in the name of a reason and science which impose its norms on those who do not fit in" (Weymans 36). In contrast, for Gauchet and Swain modernity "attributes to the mad a human ability to experience" (Ibid. 40). For his part, Foucault understands Pinel's apocryphal release of the mad from their chains as marking the origins of a new order of internalized discipline, enabled by medical science and moral treatment. Gauchet and Swain consider the same moment as the beginning of a new era of subjectivity for the mad, in which the *idea* of the insane joining human society becomes possible.

To understand the significance of these varying positions on the conceptualization of emotional disorders, we can return to Foucault's characterization of the most severe forms of mental illness, in which by the sixth level of dementia, "there is no longer a personality, only a living being" (27). For him, rationality is the human capacity most closely associated with personhood. I have argued that in Foucault's ambitious depiction of madness, rationality and subjectivity are equated to the degree that reason and sanity largely become synonymous, in opposition to unreason/insanity. Further, it is the loss of cognitive reasoning that signals the demise of subjectivity, that is, psychosis not neurosis. Again, Foucault is not alone in this. Moyn cites Lacan's position as "psychotic disturbance (as opposed to neurotic illness) meant ... the inability of subjectivity itself to take hold. Briefly, those without reason were those without selves" (Moyn 324). Similarly, Gauchet and Swain are most concerned with what they believe was the nineteenth century realization of glimmers of reason in the minds of the psychotic insane. However, in that process, Gauchet and Swain clear a path for locating emotions in both madness and in subjectivity.

Due to their stake in psychoanalysis, especially Lacanian, Gauchet and Swain emphasize the importance of "early relations" in terms of interpersonal dynamics (141). They do so in order to argue that the discoveries of the asylum era led, in the early 1900s, to "a new awareness that there is no such thing as solitary and self-sufficient subjectivity, that the self comes into being and structures itself only in relation to the other" (Ibid.). The new experience of the self that Gauchet and Swain describe is constituted through emotional ties and interactions with a world of other subjects, as well as by cognitive comprehension. Subjective experience as relational exists in contrast to the isolated individuality of *both* the insane *and* the self-determining, self-sustaining rational being. As a result, the final contact with a surrounding world to be surrendered by the mad during their withdrawal into isolation is "the affective circle" (Ibid.). The last tie to a world of others, to a world outside one's madness, is emotional, suggesting that subjectivity, and I would add emotionality, is irreducibly social. Gauchet and Swain point the way to a fuller understanding of emotions as core markers of human subjectivity through their analysis of the changes to insanity from Pinel to Freud and, in doing so, indicate a route along which, by the twenty-first century, emotional disorders move to the forefront of mental illness.

In contrast, for Foucault in Part II of *Mental Illness*, little space exists for accounts of emotionality. Yet in Part I, although the determinants of mental illness within the framework of phenomenological psychology largely are cognitive and even embodied (time, space, sociocultural relations, experience of one's body), emotionality remains a factor in comprehending the morbid world created by the mentally ill. For example, a distorted relation with space may result in feeling isolated or persecuted. While emotionality is restricted in Part I, it is not entirely excised. In this sense, Part I comes closer to Gauchet's and Swain's position. Thus, for Foucault in Part I, "mental illness always implies a consciousness of illness; the morbid world is never an absolute in which all reference to the normal is suppressed" (50). In this conceptualization, the mentally ill simultaneously occupy two worlds: the morbid one created by their illness and the 'normal' world that, in some ways or to some degree, they remain in touch with and continue to recognize. Indeed, Foucault takes as his example of the simultaneous existence of both morbid and normal worlds, the account of a schizophrenic who remembers and describes her experiences of disconnection from reality in retrospect, once she is no longer symptomatic (49–50), recalling Swain's position that a turning point for subjectivity occurs in the recognition of the ongoing, fluid state of mental illness, involving movements of immersion into and departure from insanity. Here Foucault comes closest to Gauchet's and Swain's arguments regarding the historical importance of acknowledging ongoing subjectivity within the insane because they retain or return to some form of conscious awareness and *affective connection* with the world that surrounds them.

In these terms, the effort in Part I to understand the morbid world of the mad, because it maintains meanings for them even if it manifests as nonsensical to others, attempts to grasp mental pathology "from within the illness" to a greater degree than Part II (47). It does so through the recognition of the relevance of ongoing felt experience for the mentally ill. This is why, in Foucault's earlier conceptualization, he can speak of both an understanding based on expertise, on the part of the doctor, and the knowledge of experience, from the perspective of the ill person. In Part I, knowledge as experience versus knowledge as expertise holds considerable credibility for Foucault, in which his notion of experience can accommodate emotionality.

Moral Treatment

If Foucault's focus on reason circumscribes a place for emotions in Part II of *Mental Illness,* so too does his interpretation of 'moral,' as used in 'moral insanity' or 'moral treatment.' Foucault locates the source of moral treatment in the interning practices of the classical age when economic deviants, sexual deviants, and the mad as rational deviants were excluded from society and all confined. General confinement usually included forced labor; this compulsion for work took on "the role of a sanction, of moral control" (68). All those interned shared in common the omission of a productive economic contribution to society. Thus, the moral control of the period served as rebuke for nonparticipation in a burgeoning, mercantile, bourgeois economic and cultural system. The "space of exclusion" created an association among the mad, "sufferers from venereal disease, libertines, and innumerable major or petty criminals," all of whom entered into "a relationship with moral and social guilt" from which the mad, according to Foucault, have yet to be detached (69). Here, Foucault indicates that the moral sanctions of the great confinement were not limited merely to economic failure but encompassed transgressions of sexuality and the law as well.

Following the French Revolution, houses of internment came to solely confine the mad. At this point, asylums "assumed a medical character," but only in a superficial sense (70). For example, Tuke's asylum in England subjected its internees to "uninterrupted social and moral supervision" (71). For his part, Pinel may have released the mad from their "material bonds," but "he reconstituted around them a whole network of moral chains that transformed the asylum into a sort of perpetual court of law" (Ibid.). Thus asylums existed principally as institutions for moral intervention under the guise of medical, therapeutic aims.

Two aspects of Foucault's explanation of moral treatment are worth exploring further. First, the development of the psy disciplines was made possible not only by the increased medicalization of the nineteenth century; the moralizing context of the asylums was an equally important determinant in the emergence of psychology and psychiatry. The "punishing morality" in which asylums were grounded, necessitated "the dimension of interiority" in order for moral guilt to be internalized as the problem and responsibility of the mad person as deviant (72). Psychological interiority was the means by which a punishing morality became institutionalized within both social structures and individual selves. Moral treatment demanded two facets: "the external dimension of exclusion and punishment," that is, internment and bodily deprivation, *and* "the internal dimension of moral assignation and guilt," or the bestowing of moral blame and its acceptance as guiltiness on the part of those to whom it was directed (73). The psychologization of the subject, then, was both a product of the nineteenth century asylum's "*moralizing sadism*," and the means by which moral control was accomplished (73; italics in original).

The issue of guilt leads us to the second aspect of Foucault's arguments about moral treatment that merits further exploration: the place of emotionality in the historical process he outlines. Foucault clearly, albeit only in passing, invokes emotionality as part of the asylum's moralizing processes, so that Tuke's institution instilled in internees:

> feelings of dependence, humility, guilt, and gratitude that are the moral backbone of family life. To achieve this end, such means as threats, punishment, deprivation of food, and humiliation were used; in short, whatever might both *infantilize* the madman and *make him feel guilty*. (73; italics in original)

Instilling feelings of guilt, via practices that included other emotions such as humiliation, holds a pivotal place in the techniques of moralization. Foucault outlines a complex operation entailing somatic punishments to achieve emotional feelings for ideological purposes positioned as moral (ethical) values.

For example, he describes some of the physical 'treatments' or punishments (cold showers, food deprivation, rotating devices that induced fainting) designed to inculcate feelings of humiliation and guilt in order to regulate the behavior of the mad. However, he does not develop the uses of emotions further, despite invoking them as a route to the asylum's "*moralizing sadism*" and noting that "cruelty" underlies all psychology (73). Yet, in suggesting that asylum professionals sought to instill feelings of dependence, humility, guilt, and gratitude in order to regulate the behavior of the mad, Foucault intimates that emotionality could well be instrumental in the formation and circulation of power relations. His account alludes to the centrality of emotions in the achievement of moral control, in terms of internalizing a sense of morality within a psychological being upon whom one can assign guilt and who, in turn, can be *made to feel guilty*.

Here, in *Mental Illness,* Foucault links the set of moralizing emotions comprising dependence, humility, guilt, and gratitude to the structure of family life. Some years later, in *Psychiatric Power,* he describes himself as having been wrong about this. Instead, these emotions are part of the microphysics of power specific to the discourses, institutions, and practices of psychiatry (*Psychiatric Power* 15–16). In the later work, Foucault signals a shift in his thinking from institutions, such as the family, as the source of subjectivity to power relations as the dynamic that constitutes those social institutions as well as individual subjects and bodies of knowledge.[9] My point in bringing to attention Foucault's relocation of this set of emotions from one social body of knowledge and practice to another, from family to psychiatry, concerns the flexibility and adaptability of the emotions he cites. Dependence, humility, guilt, and gratitude do not belong singularly to certain social structures, either the family *or* psychiatry. Rather, they are useful to the institutions and practices of innumerable social entities. Guilt, for example, has extensive portability and flexibility. It can be taken up in a variety of social settings, shaped into an array of experiential practices, toward a host of meanings and purposes.

Yet in *Mental Illness,* Foucault predominantly discusses moral treatment as the process through which "madness was associated with guilt and wrong-doing" (73), using the notion of guilt more narrowly in its ethical and legal senses and, therefore, overlooking the pivotal, potential roles of guilt as emotionality. We see this definitional narrowing of guilt in his description of early moral control as sanctions against lack of economic productivity or as punishment for criminal activity and sexual transgression. It becomes evident in his account of Pinel's "moral chains" that made of the asylum "a perpetual court of law," and in his characterization of the asylum doctor's role as "ethical supervision" (71). Guilt as ethical or legal wrongdoing is a matter of right and wrong, rather than a determinant of how one does or ought to *feel*. Thus, the guilt induced in the mad largely is tied to that of wrongdoing rather than in emotional terms of wrong or bad feeling. Although he harshly critiques the practices associated with this punishing morality, he doesn't seem to question that they are primarily ethical or juridical matters, in keeping with our contemporary understanding of morality. However, the nineteenth century sense of 'moral,' as it was used in 'moral insanity' or 'moral treatment' is far broader. Thomas Dixon observes that moral, in addition to its association with issues of right and wrong, could be used *in opposition to* intellectual or cognitive faculties, so that "the passions and emotions of the mind could thus be distinguished from its rational operations" (Dixon, "Patients" 39). The establishment of the emotional components of moral treatment or moral insanity set the stage for the subsequent historical development of emotional disorders.

With regard to moral insanity in particular, passions and emotions were among its principle causes (Ibid. 40). James Cowles Prichard established the nomenclature, moral insanity, in 1835 to enable the identification of "disordered emotions combined with an apparently sound intellect," which subsequently was relabeled 'emotional insanity' (Ibid.). Dixon contends that the concept of moral insanity was important in the historical partition of emotions from intellect (in which moral insanity was associated with the former), so that each could "separately be judged healthy or diseased" (41). Moral insanity, therefore, marked a turning point in which emotions, too, could be evaluated in terms of normal and abnormal manifestations. Similarly, moral treatment, in addition to its other connotations, "involved engaging the sympathies and affections of the insane individual as a stimulus to the restoration of their reason rather than relying purely upon physical restraint and the administering of medicines" (Dixon, Ibid. 43). Appealing to the sympathies and affections of the mentally ill as part of moral treatment recalls Gauchet's and Swain's contention that the final connection to the world surrendered by the insane is the affective circle. According to them, the recognition of this in nineteenth century psychiatric practice, as part of the realization of ongoing conscious awareness in the mad and, therefore, of their subjectivity, marked the asylum era's most important contribution. In all the above ways, the concept of 'moral' was linked directly to emotionality, along with notions of ethical or legal wrongdoing. If emotions in Foucault's conceptualization of madness are overshadowed to a great degree by rationality, they are further displaced by morality as ethical or juridical claims.

Emotional Distress

As outlined earlier, emotional disorders have been regarded as minor illnesses in comparison to psychoses, traditional psychiatry's major preoccupation. A prominent tendency in the history of Western views on mental illness prioritizes illnesses of reason while minimizing emotional disorders as less harmful or socially disruptive and, therefore, less necessary of attention or cause for concern. For example, Scull discusses the career of John Monro, physician at Bethlem Hospital from the mid-eighteenth century. Monro also had a thriving private practice, attending to patients who represented a range of social classes, from merchants and professionals to shopkeepers and the poor. Scull describes Monro's private practice as including cases of melancholy, fear, and distress, in which many patients "suffered rather dramatic reversals in their fortunes, either precipitated by or precipitating their mental troubles" (61). Yet he also characterizes Monro's existence when treating these same patients in the following manner: "his daily experience was more extensively preoccupied with the less florid and more harmless manifestations of mental disorder" (58). The question, of course, is less harmful to whom?

   The hierarchy of mental illnesses that views emotional disorders as less harmful does so primarily on the basis of the judgments of medical professionals and lay society and to a far more negligible degree on the experiential descriptions of the mentally ill. The weighting of severity toward illnesses that affect rationality (which is madness or psychosis as defined) reflects the extent of disturbance that mental illness poses to others, to the socially 'normal.' For example, MacDonald describes the discrepancy in perspectives between those who are mad versus those social actors who interact with the mad as "the most solitary of afflictions to the people who experience it; but the most social of maladies to those who observe its effects" (1). Here, MacDonald points to the state of madness as a personal problem for those undergoing it while existing as a social difficulty for those observing it. Traditionally, determinations have been made on the degree of social disruption, not necessarily on the level of suffering experienced. For example, in delineating the 'personal' versus 'public' aspects of mental illness, Kirk, Gomory, and Cohen contend that "personal distress" becomes "public concern" only in instances leading to actions that "physically or emotionally damage other people" (31).

Yet, the commonality amongst all forms of mental illness is the presence of emotional distress. Both psychoses and neuroses involve emotional suffering, while neuroses/emotional disorders need not encompass cognitive dysfunction, only emotional pain. Interacting with non-lucid or disorderly thinking may well be more disturbing and threatening than confronting those who suffer emotional illnesses, often privately. Madness as a breakdown in the operations of external behaviors, understood to be regulated by rationality, can be regarded as having a greater impact on the surrounding social world – whether medical, legal, professional, or interpersonal – than emotional disorders which are more possible to isolate or quarantine in the internalized feelings and experiences of those who suffer them. That is, emotional disorders can more easily be *privatized* than disorders of reason.

This adds further motivation to the long-standing Western maintenance of emotions as an inner, personal series of experiences or a state of existence relegated to familial and domestic spheres, rather than regarded as a function of public culture. Yet culture surely defines emotions and permissible emotional practices as much as it constitutes and regulates rationality and other forms of knowledge. In the specific cases of mental illness and madness, in which the confrontation between reason and irrationality is one of the ways the normative subject is constituted and recognized, normative emotions contrasted with emotional disorders also serve as a means by which individuals are made subjects either within or beyond the parameters of the permissible social world. The totality of known and recognized feelings, and their accompanying practices, in a given culture at a certain period in time, constructs the range of possibilities for emotions as experience. And emotional pain is entirely bound up in the experience of mental illness. Nineteenth century alienist, Henry Maudsley, described moral insanity as involving "no real derangement of the mind: there is only a profound pain of mind paralyzing its functions. Nevertheless, they are attended with worse suffering that actual madness is" (Maudsley qtd. in Solomon 322). It remains open to debate whether emotional disorders cause as much suffering as psychoses. Certainly, quoting Maudsley is not an attempt to pit respective forms or degrees of mental suffering against one another. As already noted, some range of emotional distress or misery is the shared factor in all the circumstances we describe as mental illness. But it is to say that we cannot create a satisfactory cultural account of psychopathology without a sounder, more robust consideration of the workings of emotions, beginning with the ways they have been positioned within psy. This is especially the case given that, in the contemporary moment, emotional disorders pose a serious dilemma for psy, as exemplified by the current and growing global epidemic (Introduction). Emotions stand as decisive factors in the possibility of the ongoing existence of psy, including the configurations it can and will take in the near future and beyond.

As noted earlier, we continue to exist in the era of mental illness. I agree with a number of the criticisms Foucault and others have expressed: that mental illness has been transformed into a suitable object for specific bodies of knowledge, particularly the sciences and social sciences; that the concept of 'mental illness' positions human beings predominantly in terms of psychic subjectivity, formulated in an image conducive to the psy disciplines and other sociopolitical interests. Yet mental illness as a scientific and psychological category has kept emotions visible on the horizon, unlike other conceptualizations of madness based on reason and unreason which have tended to sideline emotions, leaving it unclear where they lie and in what modes they exist. At the same time, in the past two centuries the conceptual category of mental illness has struggled to incorporate emotions into its paradigm, largely pathologizing them. Scientific and social scientific attempts to keep emotions in play largely have proven unsatisfactory, theorizing them in limited ways (as largely biological or individual) that, nonetheless, have led to their proliferation and to the current crisis in confidence both about and within the psy professions. We see this crisis in the ongoing view of psychoses as 'real' or severe mental illness, while the grouping formerly known as neuroses are understood to be less harmful, even as they spread exponentially. And as we will see in the next chapter, the crisis in confidence is evident in the growing opinion of many in the psy fields that emotional disorders have been inaccurately medicalized rather than recognized correctly as, and more properly relegated to, the problems of 'ordinary unhappiness.' This chapter and the next consider where emotions and their disorders are located, how they are understood, and some of the ways they could be envisioned otherwise. Equally importantly, I examine how they have been circumscribed, neglected, or entirely overlooked in order to shape mental illness into a suitable object of knowledge.

Returning specifically to Foucault, Sawicki contends that his "self-conscious preoccupations with the identity and role of the intellectual" leads to a sense of detachment in his work that includes a "noticeable absence of attention to the logics of desire and feeling" (308, 307). She contrasts him to Nietzsche whom, she believes, shows a greater awareness of, for instance, "the role of pain and anger in projects of identity formation" (307). Given that Foucault's work focuses on the intersections of knowledge and power, it is understandable that he devotes most of his attention to aspects of intellect and the sociocultural functions of rationality. However, the question remains to what degree Foucault's interest in reason as fundamental to the establishment of modern bodies of knowledge overshadows considerations of emotionality. For his part, Caputo criticizes Foucault's romanticization of both madness and art when he depicts aesthetics as the antidote to the silencing of madness.

> There are, after all, only a few Nietzsches, Hölderlins, and Van Goghs among the mad. ... But for the majority madness does not mean genius but pain, and they cry out for help, not for the immortality of the work of art. (259)

'Genius,' following Caputo, functions largely for the benefit of and in order to provide comfort to those who witness madness in its manifestations as social disruption, members of specific cultures who observe it but who do not live with it as feeling participants. For those who experience it directly, madness largely signifies pain, not the comfort or reward of artistic genius.[10] Although he continues to strongly disavow the validity of scientific and medical expertise, Foucault offers up, instead, the antidotal experience of aesthetic mastery. Gutting is even more blunt, charging that due to Foucault's "romanticization of madness as a source of truth" in *History of Madness*, he overlooks the ways "the mad are often cripplingly afflicted by the distortions and terrors of madness itself. Here he has forgotten the perceptive analyses of his earlier book," *Mental Illness and Psychology* (109). For Gutting, Foucault forgets the suffering associated with mental illness in his transition to madness. In contrast, *Mental Illness* keeps the afflictions and terrors of mental illness visible, at least in Part I, to a greater degree than his subsequent work. Missing in his later accounts of madness are the experiential manifestations of emotions, replaced by concerns with irrationality. Lest he or we forget, what Foucault attempted to locate were not solely lost forms of strangeness, abnormality, and unreason. Equally, he sought to release from confiscation creative modes of joy and exuberance in the history and present content of experience. He pursued moments of joy and exuberance because they provided potential countermeasures to the cruelty he believed serves as psychology's foundation.

One of the difficulties in attempting an analysis of cultural structures of feeling, in Raymond Williams' phrase, lies in the predicament that while the historical demarcation between rationality and irrationality has been clearer, as in diagnoses of psychosis, the boundaries between 'normal,' healthy, or acceptable emotions versus emotional disorders is far more ambiguous, context-dependent, and open to contention, as this book goes on to explore. Just as Foucault, in the early portion of *Mental Illness*, argues that mental illnesses do not function like physiological illnesses and, therefore, cannot be measured by the same criteria or analyzed analogically, the same assertion can be put forth concerning the relationship between emotions and cognition or rationality. The distinctions between the normal and abnormal workings of emotions are obscured to a far greater extent than in the demarcation between reason and irrationality, although categories labeled emotional disorders are an attempt to coerce emotions into recognizably distinct criteria of normal and abnormal. For example, anger is situated in a spiraling system of interactive cultural contexts like nationality and ethnicity. It is affected by social relations from gender, race, and age to the most specific localized circumstances such as the person with whom one is angry or the site (home, work) where the anger event takes place. Whether anger is normal or abnormal in any particular instance is a function of this web of contextual circumstances. To determine if anger in a specific context is justified, effective, unwarranted, or 'irrational' is an even more complex question.[11] To return to Foucault's examples from the asylum era of punishing morality and feelings of dependence, humility, guilt, and gratitude *each one* generates intricate, versatile structures or networks, and does so in different ways in the asylums of the nineteenth century than it does at other spatial and temporal points. Emotional relations are infinitely renewable and ceaselessly ongoing. A direct link exists between the complexity of emotions and the complexity of human social relations. By which I mean, social relations are capable of such diversity in significant part because emotional meanings and relations themselves are creatively flexible, variable, and abundant in forms and purposes. Another way to say this is that the microphysics of emotions, which works to create sociocultural relations, is ordinary, prolific, and always in process.

Obviously, this is not to say that, due to their complexity, cultural deployments of emotions should not be theorized and historicized. Quite the contrary, emotionality should not be accepted in a taken-for-granted manner, as if the operations, meanings, and uses of specific emotions such as anger, guilt, or gratitude were self-evident. It is only to suggest that such analyses cannot be accomplished satisfactorily via the binary criteria of normal and abnormal, healthy or ill, sane or irrational. Gauchet describes the contradictions of mood or emotion inherent in human existence as "polarities" (Redefining 8). However, nothing requires that emotions be viewed as contradictions or polarities. Rather, they exist as the ongoing distinctions, variations, and changes that contribute to the very experience of selfhood. A notion of polarities forces us into considerations of 'positive' or 'negative' emotions, a simplification of how they operate in practice and which, too often, becomes an attempt to model emotions on the purportedly more discernible boundaries between properly functioning reason and its malfunctions as unreason. Due to the sheer number of potential emotions, the multiplicity of prospective configurations for each one, and their endless structures when combined, as well as the degree to which they work by degrees – continuously coalescing, forming, dissolving, and reforming in varying alignments – a cultural analysis of emotions demands its own unique criteria.

Next, Chapter Two examines further the development of modernity's psychological self and the ways in which the emerging psy disciplines positioned emotionality, contrasting these to other contemporaneous formulations of emotions, particularly those found in theatrical melodrama.

Notes

1. Dates given are for original publications in France. An edition of *Mental Illness and Psychology*, with the same translation by Alan Sheridan, was reissued in English in 2011 but under the revised title of *Madness: The Invention of an Idea*.
2. In Part I of *Mental Illness*, although Foucault disagrees that the various illnesses established by psychiatric tradition represent discrete states, that is, comparable to physiology, he continues to use those categories, referring to the hysteric, the obsessional neurotic, the paranoic, and the schizophrenic, for example.

3. Although I use *History of Madness* in this and other instances for the sake of consistency, it should be noted that most commentators are referring to *Madness and Civilization* (1988), the only translation available in English until 2006.

4. Foucault's original wording, as given in the 2006 translation of *History of Madness* reads: "The language of psychiatry, which is a monologue by reason *about* madness, could only have come into existence in such a silence," by which he means the silencing of madness (xxviii; italics in original).

5. The third phase is often dated as coinciding with the appearance of the 1980 version of the *Diagnostic and Statistical Manual of Mental Disorders*, published by the American Psychiatric Association. *DSM III* represented a major departure for the manual, in which it moved to a dominantly medical model based on categorization of mental illness by symptomology (see Chapter Four).

6. Use of the term 'neuroses' as a disease category was eliminated with *DSM III* in 1980 because it was deemed an etiological concept, referring to the causes of mental illness and, as such, a contradiction to the new biomedical approach based on symptomology, taken up from *DSM III* on (Horwitz 73, 231; Wilson 407). For an explanation of the origins and definitions of neuroses, see Foucault, *Psychiatric Power* 326–327.

7. This is not to suggest that psychoses do not encompass emotional attributes; they most certainly do. It s only to say that their 'clarity,' for purposes of psychiatric diagnosis and in order to demarcate the very existence of mental illness, have been based on cognitive traits.

8. Here I use 'positive' in Foucault's sense of something that has affirmative attributes, providing a presence, not solely an absence or lack, although the alternative meaning of desirability resonates in this instance as well (*Mental Illness* 17).

9. For an explanation of how I interpret Foucault's notion of power specifically in terms of emotional relations, see Pribram, "Feeling Bad: Emotions and Narrativity in *Breaking Bad*."

10. It is worth noting that aesthetics is a cultural realm that has kept emotions in sight, which this book turns to in order to identify alternative formulations of emotions to those of psy. However, stating that aesthetics as a cultural practice engages with emotionality is not the same as suggesting aesthetic activity as compensation or consolation for madness.

11. For an account of some of the ways anger might be deployed in social relations, and to what effects, see Pribram, *Emotions, Genre, Justice in Film and Television*, Chapter Two.

2 The Psychological Self

This chapter engages with a particularly important version of the modern subject: the psychological self. More specifically, Chapter Two tracks the centrality of the psychological self to our contemporary understanding of emotionality and emotional disorders. As "The Psychological Self" demonstrates, psychic subjectivity was made possible by the Enlightenment emergence of heightened individuality. A second factor enabling psychological selfhood occurs through the recasting of mind as interiority.

Scholars like Miller and Rose have argued that the increasing diffusion of regulatory society into all aspects of the everyday has been achieved, in no small measure, through the operations of psychological interiority. Through this process, "a whole range of social ills come to be seen as flowing not so much from major mental pathologies as from remediable failures of individual subjectivities to function at their optimally adjusted levels" (Miller and Rose 5). In the course of the evolving development of the psychic self, emotionality increasingly becomes enclosed within the notion of the psychological. Emotionality, then, is further demarcated into neuroses versus psychoses, and eventually reconfigured into stand-alone subcategories of mental illnesses, such as mood, anxiety, and personality disorders. Following Miller and Rose's argument, the conceptualization of a category of 'minor' mental illnesses, first in the form of neuroses and subsequently as emotional disorders, rather than the psychoses they describe as "major mental pathologies" in the preceding quote, come into existence in conjunction with a vastly intensified, public scrutiny of the everyday. Emotions and, more specifically emotional disorders as "failures of individual subjectivities," serve as the means of expansion into ordinary life. In this view, the twentieth century has been, and continuing into the twenty-first remains, the age of emotions as a terrain upon which Western societies have staged their regulatory expansion.

The challenge in making sense of the class of difficulties considered emotional disorders, then, is part of a larger dilemma concerning the conceptualization, location, and purposes of emotionality in general. "The Psychological Self" pays attention to the limitations of a disciplinary approach. It argues that emotions are too far-reaching as modes of experience, and too complex, to exist solely as regulatory instruments. More broadly, the chapter acts to distinguish between forms of emotionality embraced by psy disciplines and modes of emotionality beyond. It does so chiefly through the example of theatrical melodrama giving way to dramatic realism in the late nineteenth and early twentieth centuries. While emotions, since the nineteenth century, have been claimed as primarily the purview of psy (Alberti, Dixon), their ubiquity and intricacy exceeds any singular epistemological body or social landscape.

Ultimately, the goal of "The Psychological Self" is to explain how we have arrived at the present problems emotional disorders pose for psy. Difficulties have lead to directing emotionality into one of two principal avenues. The first opts for physiological, biological, and neuroscientific explanations to circumvent the immateriality and supposed ineffability of emotional experience, topics discussed further in Chapters Four and Five. The alternative avenue, focused on in this chapter, converges on efforts to exclude from the category of mental pathology various degrees of 'ordinary unhappiness,' in order to return to more valid descriptions of mental illnesses as they purportedly once existed. "The Psychological Self" contends that efforts to distinguish emotional disorders from 'normal' misery and distress, as the failures of individual subjectivities, also hold responsibility for psy's current crises.

Emergence

A number of scholars concur that the psychological subject – the conceptualization of mind as interiority – relies upon the processes of individuation that began with the Enlightenment (R. Porter 3–4; Smith 56; C. Williams 97). Smith argues that the modern concept of internalized human consciousness developed alongside the rational subject of science: "the understanding of what is outward in mathematical and mechanical terms, the shift for which Descartes is emblematic, seems also to have involved a shift towards understanding what is internal in terms of a private world of qualitative truth and feeling" (56). The centralized knowing subject who could come to comprehend the intimate workings of the universe that surrounded him or her was accompanied by the corresponding desire to grasp the composition of this knowing, masterful self.

While the importance of reason to the Enlightenment has been thoroughly deliberated, lack of consensus exists concerning the role of emotions in the journey to humanist individuated consciousness. The specific part played by emotions in the emergence of modern subjectivity remains open to debate. Jean Jacques Rousseau serves as a key figure in this dilemma. For Gutman, Rousseau's importance rests with the French author's sympathy for the eighteenth century sensibility movement, which led him to "rebel against the overvaluation of reason by asserting the claims of the emotions" (107). Likewise, Cardinal describes nineteenth century Romantics who wrote about their travels as prioritizing "the agitation of personal perception" over "sober, objective observation," and "creative vision over good sense" (136). In these instances, emotions are perceived as the antitheses of reason, pursued by Rousseau and his Romantic followers as a means of counterbalancing the limitations of rationality as guiding life principal.

Yet Gutman also takes pains to argue that Rousseau's emphasis on emotions is essential to the very process of Enlightenment individuation. Thus, Rousseau celebrates "the emotive life" because it provides a basis for the "atomistic, autonomous self" (100). The valorization of emotions and the development of individuality "exist in a reciprocally defining relation" (101). In these last examples, emotions are not positioned in opposition to the goals of the Enlightenment. Rather, emotionality is viewed as vital to Enlightenment activities that enable the emergence of the modern individual. For these reasons, Gutman insists on Rousseau as a figure who very much belongs to his time: "Despite the stress on his emotive life in the *Confessions*, he still highly values the clarity of thought so prized in the Age of Reason" (119). However, Gutman's use of "despite" at the beginning of this quote underlines the dilemma in his position. On the one hand, emotions often have been perceived as reason's opposite, calling for the 'despite' to acknowledge their distinction. On the other hand, if emotions and rationality both are pivotal to the formation of modern individuality, then emotion is corollary, not antithetical, to reason in the Enlightenment project.

Elsewhere, I have argued that the sensibility movement in the late sixteenth and seventeenth centuries was central to the Enlightenment's formulation of the modern individual and, therefore, to the development of a certain kind of emotional as well as rational being (Pribram, "Individual of Feeling"). Intense focus on an autonomous self led to corresponding increased attention towards emotions which, like reason, came to be perceived as properties of the individual. Emotions associated with sensibility, such as sympathy, pity, compassion, and attention to the suffering of others, helped formulate the humanist subject. Ultimately, the onset of modernity required a specific type of feeling, as well as knowing, being. In these terms, Rousseau stands as a figure of his time who, in his 1781 *Confessions,* persuasively argues for the centrality of emotions in creating unique, autonomous individuality. The altered historical circumstances symbolized, respectively, by Descartes and Rousseau share a common goal, bringing emotionality along with reason to the heart of the Enlightenment. In these circumstances, reason and emotion are implemented toward similar ends, not in rivalry, rendering them partners in both the accomplishments and limitations of the modernity project. Further, it is emotionality that, to a significant measure, guarantees the authenticity of the individual. Emotions ensure our specificity, distinguishing us from others, rendering us unique. While our thoughts, ideas, and beliefs are received from and shared with the larger social worlds we occupy, modernity conjectures emotional experience as idiosyncratic and private.

Just as the emergence of the psychological self relied upon the formulation of modern, individuated subjectivity, it also demanded the reconfiguration of mind as interiority. If individuality privatizes the self, interiority personalizes it.

The Psychic Subject

In *Mental Illness and Psychology*, Foucault contends, first, that the totality of human functioning has been sharply delineated between mind and body – a process that begins with the establishment of Cartesian duality – and, second, that 'mind' is reconfigured as "interiority" in the nineteenth century (79, 72). Both of these moves were necessary to the development and successful implementation of psychology and psychiatry. According to Hutton, Foucault understands the nineteenth century development of mind as the invention of "the psyche as an abstraction conjured up by public authority" to meet the demands of modern disciplinary societies (126). However, if this altered conceptualization of mind is an "abstraction," it is a very real phenomenon in terms of its effects on the modern self.

Rose argues that the psy-disciplines, which emerged and solidified between 1875 and 1925, "have profoundly shaped the kinds of persons" we are capable of becoming, in both the sense of productively modeling as well as constraining our development as subjects ("Assembling" 226, 225). He states that the "'psy-interior'" – the notion of the psyche as inhabiting an internal space within each individual – "has been hollowed out within us as our truth" (Ibid. 226; "Disorders" 480; "Psychology as Social Science" 447). This deep inner truth, in turn, is a world that only psychology and psychiatry can unearth and explain to us. Thus, the psy-disciplines justify their existence through their ability to reveal the "laws and processes" of this new modern self, a self they initially conceptualized and continue to maintain ("Assembling" 226).

Rose's point is that despite the notion of a deep and true inner self, we can only become the subjects "that our culture makes available to us" (Ibid. 237). Institutions and practices concerning the self determine particular formulations of that self. In other words, human existence becomes intelligible and able to be practiced through different but specific understandings of personhood or subjectivity. In the modern era and emanating from the West, the prevailing possibility for self takes the shape of psychological interiority. This psychological being is a complex personality partially hidden and partially overt, an individual with an unconscious, with internal conflicts that have to be unearthed, a person both mysterious and endlessly fascinating to him or herself – in short, a subject of deep, internal truths.

Rose's difficulty with the psychological self lies in his belief that beneath the veneer of self-realization and self-fulfillment, positioned as personal 'empowerment,' psychological individuals are, in fact, closely monitored social subjects whose purpose is to self-regulate the minutia of their daily lives, including "their bodies, their emotions, their beliefs and their forms of conduct" ("Assembling" 244, 245). Thus, the conceptualization of an inner psychological domain, or mind as interiority, does not lead to a politics of freedom, personal or otherwise, but instead serves as the means for further surveillance and discipline, now diffused throughout both the external social and internal mental landscape of all aspects of human existence. Miller describes this intensification as "the modernized psychiatry of everyday life that has replaced the carceral psychiatry of the nineteenth century" ("Psycho-therapy" 144). Although nineteenth-century asylum psychiatry involved the extreme of incarceration for those judged insane, it also confronted limits on the kinds of conduct considered to fall under its jurisdiction, that is, a circumscribed range of usually severe, socially disruptive behaviors that could be judged pathological and, as such, in need of psychiatric intervention. Thus, for Miller, nineteenth century practices placed boundaries on the aspects of a person's life that fell within psychiatric purview, a constriction that has been lost in the twentieth century expansion of psychiatry to include the "everyday" (Ibid.). The psychiatry of the everyday involves all facets of human existence, down to the most minute, mundane, and previously inaccessible moments of daily life, an expansion made possible by the psychological interiorization of the modern subject.

At the same time, the psychological self came into being within a specific social context that both facilitated and was brought about by psychological interiority. Typified by a preoccupation with 'character' for much of the nineteenth century, by the early twentieth century altering social perceptions created a dominant focus on 'personality' instead. Susman, for example, characterizes this shift as a move from a culture of self-sacrifice to one of self-realization (276). Using the phrase, "modal types of persons" to refer to forms of subjectivity or self, he describes the culture of character as follows:

> By 1800 the concept of character had come to define that particular modal type felt to be essential for the maintenance of social order. ... But it also provided a method of presenting the self to society, offering a standard of conduct that assured the interrelationship between the 'social' and the 'moral.' (273)

In this reading, the main functions of character were to maintain social order, to instruct people how to exist appropriately as social beings, and to link the social world closely with morality.

Although Susman does not specify the point, like character, personality also works to ensure social order and provide instruction in proper social behaviors. However, over the course of time different techniques became necessary in order to maintain similar goals of social stability. That is to say, different modal types of subject are required for changing eras. Susman is clear that one of the major factors that enabled the turn to 'personality,' beginning in the first decade of the twentieth century, was "the development of psychological and psychiatric studies" (274). The culture of personality, then, was indebted to the age of psychic subjectivity as described by Rose and others.

Analyzing advice manuals and similar literature from the respective epochs, Susman finds the words most frequently connected to the culture of character included, "citizenship, duty, democracy, work ... honor, reputation, morals, manners, integrity" (273–274). In contrast, the vocabulary of the early twentieth century phases of the age of personality emphasized attributes such as, "fascinating, stunning, attractive, magnetic, glowing, masterful, creative, dominant, forceful" (277). Susman, then, tracks the transformation from the morality of a "higher law" to a personal ethics of a "higher self" (280). Yet, Susman perceives a deep contradiction within the culture of personality in which, on the one hand, "one must be oneself," stressing values of "being different, special, unusual, of standing out in a crowd" (277). On the other hand, people of personality are urged to present themselves "in such a way as to make oneself 'well liked,'" which involves doing away with "the little personal whims, habits, traits that make people dislike you" (280, 277). While Susman understands this as a paradox in the subject type associated with personality, in actuality it is consonant with the analysis provided by Rose on the social functions of the psychological self. Personality, like character, focuses to a significant extent on how others view and judge an individual. Despite its nomenclature, 'self-realization' stresses social acceptance and popularity, tasking the individual with fitting in and getting along with others.

In his analysis of character, as noted above, Susman outlines several functions central to its rationale for existing. It provided a method of presenting the self to society that, in turn, offered standards of conduct ensuring integration between the 'social' and the 'moral.' And, in adopting those standards of conduct, "the maintenance of social order" was ensured. Arguments have been made that the culture of personality also exists to fulfill these functions, if in altered forms. The relationship between self and society is now maintained by the imperative to be well-liked and accepted instead of enacted through the restraint of living a morally correct existence. The individual remains secured to the social body but the new relation occurs between the 'social' and the 'psyche' in place of the dynamic of 'social' and 'moral.' Under the guise of personal freedom, people remain socially obliged. In Rose's anslysis, this enables not less but more social monitoring of the self through the expanded access to the individual initiated by the development of interiorized space or personhood.

Although Susman does not invoke a specifically Foucaultian argument, his data and discussion are amenable to the proposition that self-realization through personality leads to further encroachments in management of the self. Simultaneously, through the more intimate and minute forms of discipline and control established via a culture of personality, Susman's second function – the maintenance of social order – is also assured. In this matrix, the development of a "higher self" becomes a time-consuming, exacting activity in which individuals focus on self-manipulation motivated by the desire to attain "self-fulfillment, self-expression, self-gratification" (280). Self-regulation occurs on the basis of an individual's intimate knowledge of and meticulous attention to one's own finely-tuned, psychological operations.

From this perspective, the contradiction Susman identifies as belonging to the culture of personality – being unique but conforming – is not paradoxical at all. On the contrary, the consistency in these 'competing' messages is clear if we understand personality to involve management of the self, concealed beneath the promise of personal freedom and self-fulfillment. In this view, the development of the psychological subject as a unique, internalized identity ostensibly valorizes individual differences but, in that process, actively works to eradicate, control, or moderate such differences.

Rose makes an additional key argument for purposes here, contending, like Foucault (Chapter One), that although psychology is widely presumed to be the study of "the normal mental functioning of human beings," in fact, psychology and psychiatry developed around groups of people who were deemed abnormal in one form or another (*Psychological Complex* 2, 5; "Psychology as Social Science" 448). The scientific credibility and social productivity of the psy-disciplines came to prominence, precisely, on the basis of their claim to be able to manage populations considered socially dysfunctional (*Psychological Complex* 5, 187, 226). Therefore, psychology always has been primarily the study of pathologies. Two significant factors emerge from Rose's contention. First, his argument bolsters the viewpoint that the psy-disciplines have been focused, above all, on social constraint and social order in their designated roles of treating, curing, or managing various kinds of pathology. Second, 'normal' psychological functioning was established only in distinction to the expressions and manifestations of conduct considered abnormal. Rose provides an 1890 quote from French philosopher, Ernest Renan, who observes that "the madness of mankind, the dreams and hallucinations" provide a far more favorable source of data than "the normal state" in determining the true nature of human psychology (Renan qtd. in Rose, *Psychological Complex* 1). Thus, our understanding of normal mental operations is based, not on direct inquiry into perceived optimal or healthy activity but, rather, on extrapolation from thoughts, feelings, or behaviors deemed abnormal, as determined by social expectations and values.

Rose believes that "psychological normality was conceived as merely a lack of socially disturbing symptoms, as absence of social inefficiency: *that which does not need to be regulated*" (Ibid. 6; italics in original). His statement, like Miller's earlier, suggests that when the psychological and social sciences developed in the nineteenth century, there remained aspects of human behavior that did not fall under regulation. However, with the social changes that occurred early in the twentieth century, evolving into the era of personality, the 'normal,' too, came to demand constant supervision, explaining the intensification of the psy-disciplines across every aspect of contemporary human existence. This explains Miller's characterization of modern psychiatry as that which oversees all aspects of the most mundane forms of "everyday life," in place of the more constrained carceral psychiatry of the nineteenth century ("Psychotherapy" 144).

Descriptions of a shift from a culture of moral character to one emphasizing personality suggests that the transition in the emotional tenor of the psychological self is from nineteenth century emotional restraint to twentieth century emotional expression. However, such an implication would be, at best, a simplification. I explore some of the emotional implications of the change from character to personality through the example of the transition from the dominance of melodrama to the emergence of dramatic realism in theatre, which occurs in the same period as the development of psychology and psychiatry (1875 to 1925 per Rose). Other cultural arenas, beyond psy, offer competing versions of emotionality. In the instance of stage performance, an existing sociality of emotions moves towards increased concealment and privatization.

Melodrama and Dramatic Realism

Late in the nineteenth century, melodrama begins to decline as it gives way to the emerging prominence of dramatic realism, a historical transition that pinpoints a change in the conceptualization of emotional subjectivity. An ethos of self-restraint and moderation has long been associated with the Victorian era and with the growth of the middle classes. For instance, Peter Gay speaks of the "nineteenth-century ideal of self-control for the sake of exquisite, if postponed, psychological rewards" (23, 88). This altered subjectivity has been conceived, in physical terms, as a withdrawal to hearth and home, accompanied by an affective relocation in which emotions are felt and enacted in private, if at all.

The case of theatrical melodrama is interesting because it is a form of aesthetics closely linked to strong and highly visible emotion, indeed, it is often associated with an embarrassing excess of feeling, in an era in which emotion is said to be facing increasing confinement. Further, theatrical melodrama occurs in a public venue where displays of emotion are, in general, more social than with other aesthetic modes, such as the novel. The theater's visibility, in terms of both performance and audience, helps provide a gauge of accepted or expected social forms of emotional behaviors.

Like all artistic modes, melodrama as an aesthetic practice provides an organizational framework for interpreting or constructing the world. Gledhill notes that melodrama served as a central cultural paradigm in the nineteenth century ("Introduction" 19). Its qualities of sentimentalism and spectacle and its moral dilemmas based on binary antagonisms of good and evil seemed able to articulate the values and conflicts of a swiftly industrializing society and the concurrent solidification of the bourgeoisie as dominant social group. Yet this mode of representation that seemed to so adequately explain the world from which it sprang met its demise relatively soon after the end of the century. Booth, for instance, dates melodrama's decline from 1905 (174). By the turn into the twentieth century, theatrical melodrama was becoming, in middle class and elite circles, a disparaged dramatic form, an attitude that largely has persisted to the present day. Even a proponent such as Booth justifies melodrama by branding it escapist, offering up to its audiences the antithesis of reality (187). Descriptions of melodrama's shortcomings can easily be found (Brooks 11–12; Gerould 7–9; Hauptman 281; L. James 5; Postelwait 42, 56; R. Williams, "Social Environment" 214). Yet the question remains, how do we account for melodrama's validation and widespread popularity in the nineteenth century, turning so abruptly to derision early in the twentieth? Is it possible to understand how it can make sense of the world at one moment while failing miserably so soon in the next? For the disparagement of melodrama, I am arguing, is also the disparagement of emotion.

Theatrical melodrama was closely linked to emotion, from the intensity of feelings felt and displayed by audiences, to the "extravagant gesture, high flown sentiments, declamatory speech" of acting techniques (Gledhill, "Signs" 212). Most significantly here, melodrama's emotional functions were viewed as closely aligned with its moral purposes, especially notions of virtue, in which the key to the dispersal of desired values was the audience's strong emotional reaction to the narrative and its characters. Emotions associated with moral virtue focused on the ability to feel for the suffering of others, especially pity, sympathy, and compassion for the poor, the weak, and the otherwise victimized. Melodrama's aesthetic aspects and narrative structure used emotional means to arrive at 'moral legibility.' Further, whether any moral improvement was actually effected, or whether audiences attended for reasons of virtue or not, the emotional power of melodrama, as critics of the day recognized, was central to the genre's widespread appeal across the full spectrum of social classes. By the 1840s in England, Buckley notes, critical and public discussion made it clear that melodrama's emotional aspects primarily accounted for its popularity and had become the genre's most "enduring" feature (181).

In contemporaneous critical understandings of melodrama, the ability to recognize correct moral behavior and so, presumably, to enact moral reforms upon one's self and others, is based upon the capacity to feel, that is, grounded in one's own emotional responses to, in this instance, drama. The spectator's virtue is revealed in his/her emotional reactions to the event. In this respect, emotions were central to the nineteenth century culture of character. As a result, it was socially permissible, indeed necessary, to openly and publicly display certain emotional effects, including tears, in response to a play. Doing so said something publicly about the kind of person one was. More than simply pleasurable releases, the experience and expression of emotions were signs of a person's capacity for deep feeling and, therefore, of their virtue (Gledhill, "Introduction" 34; Hyslop 74). The depiction of a melodramatic world based on binary antagonisms of good and evil, portrayed in such a way that each side was easily recognized by spectators, helped develop a 'feeling audience' that was emotionally responsive in socially and ideologically useful ways.

Signposted in London by the 1889 debut of Ibsen, dramatic realism emphasizes, in Singer's words, "the depiction of ordinary quotidian reality, with an attempt to portray fully developed, psychologically multidimensional characters" (49). Our contemporary conceptualization of "fully developed" characters more often than not is linked to psychological understandings of experience and selfhood. With the advent of Ibsen and other modernist playwrights, theatrical experience becomes divided, in critical perception, into two groupings towards the end of the nineteenth century and into the early twentieth: melodrama, associated with the emotional, the simplistic, and the frivolous; and realism, an intellectual, complex, and serious form of drama (Hauptman 281–282; Booth 132, 167; Postlewait 39, 42–43). High culture – realism and tragedy – becomes associated with up-market, metropolitan, middle- and upper-class consumers, while popular entertainment, including melodrama, revises into pleasure for the urban, laboring and provincial, agricultural classes. As early as 1875, Henry James bemoans the state of affairs in which audiences go to melodrama "to look and listen, to laugh and cry – not to think" (James qtd. in Postlewait 56). Here James not only devalues the relevance of emotion – laughing and crying – in favor of thinking, he also makes the questionable assumption that people engaging with melodrama don't think and that tragedy's audiences don't feel.

High art practices are classified, in part, by their rejection of emotionalism in favor of other – intellectual, aesthetic – qualities. In the case of realism, emotion becomes its antithesis. And in response, in aesthetic practices in which emotions are regularly acknowledged, like melodrama, such attributes come to be widely considered in terms of their exaggerations and excesses. Realism, based on new conceptualizations of the psychological being, render melodrama's narrative and performative techniques outmoded. A new set of techniques develops that encourage audiences to focus more intently on "the inner life and private personality of the characters" (Gledhill, "Signs" 219). A move occurs from sentiment – emotion aligned with morality – to psychology, in characterization and narrativity. Restrained performances and dialogue became more valued than melodrama's physically and emotionally extroverted, gestural qualities. The unconscious replaces the expressive.

Tied to the perception of realism's truth-telling function, psychologically based characterization became accepted as more fully revealing, that is, apparently able to journey into the interior of the individual heart and mind, in contrast to melodrama's lack of psychological underpinning, character development, or depth. Brooks, a proponent of melodrama, is explicit on this point: "There is no 'psychology' in melodrama in this sense; the characters have no interior depth, there is no psychological conflict" (35). In contrast, Gerould poses the question, "Why should we always assume that the psychological level is the deepest?" (20). In the twentieth century, following acceptance of the psychic self, the psychological becomes the truest depths to plum, not the social, the moral, the spiritual, or the political. The shift from sentimental morality to psychological interiority thus signals a moment of historical change in emotional subjectivity. In the case of drama, the moment of change to a more completely privatized individual of feeling does not occur in the nineteenth century, in the era of melodrama, as is usually supposed. It can more properly be said to arrive with the twentieth century, the age of the unconscious, and the emergence of realism, leaving behind melodrama's focus on the social ills of a rapidly industrializing world. The development of a wholly 'private' emotional self as contemporarily understood, that is to say, a fully interiorized subject, can more accurately be dated to the *demise* of melodrama.

Postlewait argues that in prevalent critical opinion, the historical narrative on genre conflict reads as follows:

> nineteenth century entertainment – popular, romantic, sentimental, and quintessentially melodramatic – gives way to twentieth century drama in the modernist mode, predominantly realistic. (39)

From this perspective, between the 1880s and 1920s "American drama comes of age when modern realistic drama supplants melodrama as the definitive dramatic form" (Ibid.). And along with it, intellect is victorious over emotion, and elite or high art defeats popular entertainment. Indeed, the twentieth century prevailing notion of high art *becomes* the victory over melodrama and emotionality.

Melodrama and its viewership come to be disparaged, often for the very same qualities, particularly emotionality aligned with virtue, that previously had rendered the genre so valuable. By the latter part of the nineteenth century strong emotional responses to forms of representation begin to be regarded as signs of ignorance on the part of lower, working-class audiences – in the perception of members of the middle and upper classes. Displays of pity and compassion are considered indications of virtue less frequently than they had been throughout much of the nineteenth century.

The advent of psychologically motivated characters helped push emotions further 'inward' and caused the diminishment of a previously dominant public demonstration of emotions, in character construction, performance styles, and audience conduct. With melodrama, emotions and the public sphere are closely intertwined in both audience behaviors and in the social nature of subject matter, such as feelings of empathy for various forms of victimization. Subsequently, however, there is a concealment of emotions as they shift from public manifestation to a more privately appreciated, introspective mode. In this new organization, the psychological overtakes an earlier understanding of emotionality. Emotions shift from belonging in the realm of sentimental social morality to relocation in the region of the psyche. And as a result, certain kinds of publicly displayed, performed, or expressed emotions decline along with melodrama. Emblematic of this is the Victorian practice of viewing theatrical performances with full house lights on, the goal of which was for audience members to be seen as much as it was to focus on the stage (Booth 62; McCormick 38; Mayer 100). Only late in the nineteenth century did theaters begin extinguishing house lights during performances, resulting in a more isolated, less communal viewing experience, in which the darkened playhouse can be said to represent the retreat into a private psyche. Similarly, an earlier "raucous interactivity between audience and stage," in which viewers routinely cheered, booed, shouted responses to actors' dialogue, and otherwise made their presence felt "as a ritual part of the melodramatic experience," gives way to "the repressed quietude of realism" (Singer 179, 50).[1] Emotionality as repressed quietude becomes taken up as a new, middle-class ideal of appropriate, public behavior and, at the same time, serves as the antithesis of melodramatic unruly excess. A cultural reconceptualization of emotions creates altered circumstances in which externalized displays of emotion increasingly become considered overwrought and ill-mannered.

Contemporary forms of melodrama live on of course, for instance, in twentieth and twenty-first century film and television. The emotional impulses of nineteenth century theatrical melodrama represent similar structures of feeling to those underpinning much of contemporary American popular culture, in its paradigmatic emphasis on righting wrongs, on seeking justice for the innocent or victimized, however ideologically naïve such representations may be (Linda Williams; Pribram, "Melodrama"). Emotions serve as melodrama's foundation, activating audiences' desires to see social imbalances redressed. Further, melodrama's 'failures' are in critical and high culture terms. Many of those who practice popular cultural forms understand their terrain and rationale to very much include emotional representation and expression. Indeed, unlike high art formulations, popular culture practices claim emotionality as central to their endeavors. In contrast, high art categories, such as dramatic realism, have tended to reject or minimize the presence of emotional expression as part of their aesthetic. Instead, realist practices often have sought to abandon the representation and expression of emotion in favor of intellectually and psychologically oriented explanations.

In cultural terms, if we attempt to account for the journey from nineteenth century sentimental morality to twentieth century psychological realism, it becomes possible to trace that trajectory, not from emotional restraint to emotional expression, but precisely the opposite. So while emotions are accounted for in dramatic realism – in character interiority and narrative development – they are simultaneously constrained, becoming closely guarded. Melodrama's attention to social suffering conforms to values attributed to a culture of character, but its modes of overt emotionality do not. For its part, modernism's dramatic realism depends extensively on formulations of the psychological subject as privatized, personalized interiority.

Neuroses: The Advent of Emotional Disorders

Now I turn to considering implications arising from the era of psychological selfhood for emotional dysfunctions, specifically. The development of the neuroses signals a transformation in emotional subjectivity comparable in magnitude to the move from melodrama to dramatic realism, although not identical in nature. As discussed in Chapter One, the formation of the neuroses marks a crucial moment in the advent of emotional disorders, establishing affective maladies as a distinct order of mental illness. Their derivation changed much of the focus of psy from psychoses to neuroses and, eventually, made possible the current circumstances in which emotional disorders dominate mental illness. However, while rendering them more visible, the concept of neuroses largely pathologized emotional experience.

The emergence of neuroses resulted in a tiered system, in which disorders perceived as minor, mild, or less harmful took shape next to other mental illnesses regarded as major, acute, or severe by comparison. While both historical movements – from melodrama to realism, and the distinguishing of neuroses from other forms of mental illness – appear to give augmented credibility to emotions, the effect, in practice, amounts to their devaluation. That is, the separation of emotions from other forms of mental illness becomes a means to their diminishment in psy as minor, even as they then proliferate in numbers. Just as dramatic realism in the age of personality appears to give a more prominent position to emotional life through notions such as self-fulfillment, its focus on "inner life and private personality" works to constrain emotions by internalizing them. They are reconfigured as the effects of personal hearts and minds, creating a privatized individual of feeling, and thereby isolating emotional experience, now no longer considered of public or social significance in the ways it once was.

Especially in their earlier phases, neuroses varied considerably from how, contemporarily, we understand emotional disorders. Initially, they were attributed to physiological causes, as malfunctions of the nerves, explaining their nomenclature. However, various neuroses manifested in markedly emotional, as well as embodied, symptomology. Recognized under the category of partial insanity, over the course of the nineteenth century neuroses surfaced, most notably, in disorders such as monomania, hysteria, and neurasthenia. Goldstein notes that by 1850 a number of "loosely defined nervous conditions … had come to the fore in the medical community" and, from mid-century in France, were widely referred to as neuroses (*névroses*) (332, 334). Most psy professionals did not consider these cases comparable to complete madness, but as "intermediary nervous pathologies" or partial insanity, identified as "an individual who could pass for an ordinary citizen, who certainly did not disturb the public peace" (Ibid. 333, 338). Neurotics weren't 'ordinary,' but they appeared so. And although they did not pose a high level of threat to social order, they were abnormal in certain ways that fell to psy professionals to recognize and tame. With the emergence of the broad category of neuroses, mental health specialists were newly tasked with rendering determinations over illnesses that non-experts could not identify. Psy experts became designated as social arbiters, uncovering "the hidden signs of disorder behind the appearances of reasonable behavior" (Castel 154).

Castel contends that the new class of mental disorders "destroyed any objectivist perception of insanity," because they materialized in ways that resisted detection by scientific means, like empirical measurement, based on already established distinctions between normal and pathological (Ibid.). However, I would argue that the arrival of the neuroses set in motion a *more* intense search for just those measures. The specific nature and attributes of emotionality provoked an intensified mission for "hidden signs of disorder," presumed concealed but still extant, so as not to undermine an identifiable division between function and dysfunction, normal and aberrant. Consequently, the effort to discover a boundary between normality and pathology applicable to emotional disorders became a holy grail for the psy disciplines. The elusive objectivist criteria of emotional disorders continue to be both sought and eluded, a topic returned to later in this chapter (and in Chapters Four and Five).

According to Rose, by the early twentieth century neuroses had grown to be a vital focus of attention. They became a grouping of mental disturbances "which did not themselves amount to insanity, but were nonetheless severe enough to disrupt normal functioning" (*Psychological Complex* 180). Rose outlines factors that he believes enabled neuroses to become matters of social concern at this particular historical juncture. An expansion occurs from mental illnesses considered most disabling – those requiring asylum care – to others that previously had been left to family responsibility and individual coping. Formerly privatized illnesses now demand attention because of the recognition that they, too, prevent individuals from functioning 'normally,' that is at maximum capacity in their proscribed social roles. In this argument, neuroses came to the fore as a psychological category when the physical, cognitive, and emotional attributes they designate become recognized as impediments to economic efficiency and social productivity. With this realization, previously inconsequential 'personal' issues became matters of public concern, the encroachment into the ordinary and everyday identified by Miller. Neuroses emerge at the historical moment when certain 'lesser' emotional behaviors can be identified as socially, rather than solely individually, detrimental, that is, when they become a matter of public and not just personal distress.

As discussed earlier, in Rose's view neuroses came into existence, through the operations of the psy disciplines, at the same time and as a mechanism for the increased social regulation of individuals. As the regulatory sweep of a disciplinary society grew both more minute and more widespread, the neuroses facilitated a new permeation into what once were unregulated or less regulated aspects of individual, private existence. Therefore, the discovery of the neuroses – the historical moment when they became a matter of social and professional concern – signals the transition from nineteenth century carceral psychiatry, focused on those cases deemed to require social segregation through asylums, to the twentieth century psychiatry of everyday life, which accesses a far greater percentage of the population, indeed, everyone.

However, the difficulty for Rose, as a result of his belief that the development of the neuroses represents psy encroachments into previously personal or unregulated aspects of daily existence, serving to negate individual freedoms in favor of the augmentation of ever-widening social control, means that he, first, comes to accept the major/minor distinction of psychological ills and, second, tends to participate in the diminishment or dismissal of those conditions described as minor. As a consequence, the "burgeoning empire of psy" in the early twentieth century includes "nerve doctors whose principal remit was the minor troubles of emotion and conduct of the wealthier classes and predominantly their women" ("Assembling" 232). Rose appears to suggest that "minor troubles" of emotion and conduct do not constitute legitimate pathologies ("Disorders" 476). Yet, at other points, he acknowledges that the life disturbances encompassed by neuroses or emotional disorders include the debilitating. For example, Rose describes the function of community therapy and out-patient services in the 1950s as aimed at "the young neurotics and personality disordered, the persistently self-damaging, the repetitively suicidal, the ostentatiously anti-social, those who continually act-out and those who are continually manipulated by others" ("Psychiatry" 77). These itemized dysfunctions are clearly serious and far from minor. They represent often extreme degrees of suffering and, indeed, it is difficult to conceive of an outcome more acute than suicide.

Rose's goal of critiquing the psychological and psychiatric colonization of everyday life leads him to diminish the emotional experiences that have been incorporated as part of the psy empire, instead of attempting to account for their current prevalence. Might there be reasons beyond disciplinary control that prompted neuroses to emerge at this historical juncture? Do they express an aspect of human existence, social and individual, that pleads for attention? Understanding neuroses principally as a category engineered to ensure social productivity risks regarding emotional disorders as only worthy of attention when they cause identifiable public harm, threaten social productivity, or drain social resources, reinforcing the long-standing notion of attending to mental illnesses only when they signal social disruption rather than personal despair.

Castel remarks that, during the nineteenth century, the non-institutionalized insane outnumbered those confined to asylums. In France in 1872, even at the height of the asylum era, "the number of 'insane living at home' ... exceeded the number in asylums" (194). Further, the asylum population was dominated by compulsory rather than voluntary patients (Castel cites 80 percent of the former in Paris in 1853), meaning they were confined primarily by administrative authority instead of individual or familial request

(197). As a result, asylums largely housed "spectacular cases in the name of a conception of public order," because compulsory placement was preoccupied with those regarded as the most egregiously dangerous or disruptive to the social order (195–196). Castel points to serious socioemotional consequences due to the dominance of compulsory placement and the specific population on which its attentions focused. It led to "the almost exclusive linking of mental illness to the degree of danger" the disordered appeared to pose for members of the public, a disturbing association between mental illness and harm to others that continues to this day (198).

The correlation between mental illness and disruption or danger reinforces psychopathology as threatening to the safety of others and, therefore, to the larger social order, rather than attending to the distress of the ill, regarded as a personal matter. In Castel's example, the more numerous 'insane living at home' were composed of a less threatening category: the "harmless" mentally ill (Castel 197; R. Porter 131). Those perceived as less of a threat tended to be hidden in domestic spaces, 'privatized' away from public visibility. In such cases, severity of mental illness is adjudicated by perceived threat to others, not on the degree of an individual's suffering.

My concern is that to see emotions primarily in terms of their disciplinary functions renders it more challenging to regard as legitimate the experiential miseries in people's lives. As a consequence, Rose finds himself in the difficult position of asserting that the psy disciplines "promise succor to anyone who experiences a discrepancy between the reality of their lives and their desires," a false hope because such a discrepancy results from the "intractable features of desire and frustration" that inevitably accompany life ("Psychiatry" 81). Yet, isn't the space between our desires and the realities of people's lived circumstances precisely the appropriate location for political and other forms of social action? For Rose, the solution appears to rest with the acceptance of a full range of emotional difficulties as non-remediable, as simply "intractable features" intrinsic to the inevitable distance between life's desires and its frustrations. To reach this conclusion is to reinforce emotions as personal, private problems, properly left to the coping devices of individuals.

Ordinary Unhappiness

Miller asks: "How, where and through what processes do madness, depression and simple unhappiness become constituted as problems amenable to psychiatric treatment?" ("Critiques" 39). He expresses concern that some portion of these states lies appropriately within the purview of psychiatric treatment while the balance does not, although it remains unclear where the line of demarcation falls. While madness appears to rest securely within, "simple unhappiness" exists beyond that which is suitable for psychiatric treatment. To accept that simple unhappiness falls within the jurisdiction of psy would accede to the penetration of social regulation into the most minute aspects of daily existence. Meanwhile, the appropriate status for depression remains unclear.

The position Miller and Rose take up, in response to their apprehensions about disciplinary control, enacted through the cultural expansion of psy constraining and managing too much of contemporary life, bears consequences for our understanding of emotions (unhappiness) and emotional disorders (depression). While delimiting psy encroachment by setting emotions aside as matters of routine life helps place them out of the bounds of psy knowledges, it also tends to bolster them as private, individual events.

Additionally, regarding unhappiness as a normal or acceptable part of life's vicissitudes, part of the inescapable ordinary, returns us to the difficulties of applying criteria of normal and abnormal to emotional states. Unhappiness is not 'normal' in that the desired condition most people strive for is happiness or, at any rate, lack of unhappiness. But neither can we call unhappiness 'abnormal,' in the sense that it is experienced at certain moments in every individual's life. However, the means by which Miller and Rose distinguish madness, and perhaps depression, from unhappiness occurs by recognizing the former as abnormal states but withholding a similar status for the latter. Thus unhappiness is left taking up the position of normalcy, as the non-pathological form of madness or depression. Unhappiness is situated as an intractable feature of the vicissitudes of life, enabling it to serve as a condition of normality against which legitimate mental disorder may be measured. Yet it would seem curious to suggest that people strive for unhappiness as a stable, healthy set of circumstances. In the many variations in which it takes shape, unhappiness cannot attain a clear or permanent status of either normality or dysfunction; rather it fails, as do most emotions, at either state because emotions are frustratingly fluid, variable, and contextually dependent forms of experience.[2]

Rose and Miller were forward thinking when they began their critiques on psy encroachment. Since Miller posed his dilemma in the 1980s, questioning the rationale for including madness, depression, and simple unhappiness all within the purview of psychiatric treatment, this query has pervaded psy fields, chiefly in response to the worldwide, exponential growth of emotional disorders in the same time frame.[3] In the intervening years, Rose and Miller's concerns have grown into major preoccupations for significant portions of the psy worlds.

I take, as specific example, Horwitz's *Creating Mental Illness* because it offers up a specific schema as redress to the problem posed by Miller. For many writing as professional members of various psy fields, their primary concern is not the excessive growth of a regulatory society but, instead, the potential demise – some would argue either imminent or already underway – of the psy disciplines as socially, epistemologically, and professionally valid enterprises *due to* the rapid and far-reaching expansion of mental illness. Where psy was viewed, historically, as seeking to broaden its scope to encompass more and more aspects of human existence, current fears focus on it being under threat as a result of having encompassed too much. Thus we find spokespersons for psy arguing to return to more delimited specialization. "Treatments for mental illnesses are no longer directed at a small number of seriously ill persons. Instead, they are aimed at the many millions of people who presumably have some mental disorder" (Horwitz, *Creating* 4). Horwitz is clear that emotional disorders have been central to the movement from select madness to widespread mental illness, beginning with the Freudian period of dynamic psychiatry, and its focus on neuroses, through the contemporary era, beginning in the 1970s, that follows the biomedical approach associated with diagnostic psychiatry (Chapters Four and Five).

The problem is one of numbers, so that we consider "much ordinary social behavior as pathological and [are] overestimating the prevalence of mental disorder," leading to the current global epidemic (Ibid. 15). The task, then, is to reduce the numbers, for if everyone is mentally ill then, effectively, no one is mentally ill. A 'normal' would no longer exist against which to delimit the pathological. Mental illness must return to affecting a select minority, as madness did, instead of remaining so "common, pervasive, and ubiquitous" (214). Historically, the relative rarity of mental illnesses was one of their advantages, certainly from the perspective of maintaining the psy fields as definable bodies of knowledge and practices. In describing mental illnesses as having become ordinary and omnipresent, Horwitz aligns them with emotions, which have played such a pivotal role in the changes to the psy fields, from the advent of neuroses to the current array of recognized emotional dysfunctions. The increased integration of emotionality has altered psy's organization so this it comes, inevitably, to more closely resemble those emotional phenomena it has grown to incorporate.

Yet Horwitz maintains that the current fault line lies with both dynamic and diagnostic psychiatry for "breaking down the boundaries between the normal and the pathological" (105). Rather than considering efforts to maintain that distinction as itself the problem, which has become less and less sustainable given how psy has developed, he suggests, and is far from alone in doing so, that the solution rests in re-solidifying the distinctions between the mentally ill and the 'normal' population, as he believes once existed between psychoses and soundness of mind. In this pursuit we will discover that what appears to be "a public health problem of vast proportions" is only erroneously perceived as such (101). Thus, he calls for a rejection of incorrect categories of illness and a return to classification based on genuine mental disorders. The seemingly impossible task, of course, rests in determining which are or ought to be authentic illnesses, circling back to the elusive holy grail of psy, located precisely in finding a verifiable empirical borderline between the normal and the pathological.[4]

What Horwitz and others are responding to is the rampant spread of mental illness, as a result of the rise of emotional disorders, that now threatens the disciplinary foundations of psy, first, in terms of the validity of certain mental illnesses and, second, in the professions' abilities to cope with the vast public health problem emotional disorders apparently have become.[5] Mental illness as a viable concept, and, therefore, psychology and psychiatry as the fields that describe it and attempt to ameliorate it, finds itself in crisis. In this scenario, the survival of psy is dependent upon a return to mental illness as affecting "a small number of seriously ill persons." To this end, Horwitz argues that only psychoses are both mental diseases and mental disorders (diseases because they have some biological or organic component) (215–216). States that qualify as mental disorders, but not diseases, include "persistent depressions, crippling compulsions, inexplicable anxiety, or self-starvation" (13). To be constituted a legitimate mental disorder, two criteria must be met: internal dysfunction and cultural evaluation. Dysfunction necessitates an internal "psychological system that is incapable of performing within normal limits" (11). Cultural evaluation is required because adjudicating disorders involves assessments "such as 'inappropriate,' 'unreasonable,' 'excessive,' and 'normal'"(Ibid.). Altogether, then, properly constituted and recognized mental disorders exist only if they are composed of "internal dysfunctions that a particular culture defines as inappropriate" (12).

In addition to mental diseases and mental disorders, Horwitz outlines a third overarching category of emotional issues which he labels, variously, as "problems of living," "personal problems," "personal troubles and disruptive behaviors," "generic human problems," and "the suffering of ordinary people" (20, 51, 211, 220). None of these constitute genuine mental disorder because they do not reflect internal dysfunction. Rather, in these instances, individuals are responding normally and appropriately to stressful environments and circumstances (14, 27). By these criteria, mental disorders *cannot* include "expectable reactions to stressful conditions, culturally patterned forms of deviant behavior, and general human unhappiness or dissatisfaction" (15). The vast category of those who would be excluded from states of mental disorder comprise, among others, children who act out in abusive environments, jilted lovers, laid off workers who drink too much, and people with "persistent feelings of hopelessness and helplessness" due to living in conditions of "chronic deprivation" (30). Further excluded are those who display "immoral or idiosyncratic behavior, bad character traits, personal inadequacies, bad judgment and poor choices," because these point to social deviance, not internal dysfunction (35).

In attempting to establish a boundary between 'normal' versus disordered emotional functionality, Horwitz leads us into difficult, if not impossible, distinctions, discussed in greater detail in Chapter Five. As example here, however, if persons who experience feelings of hopelessness and helplessness because they exist in circumstances of chronic deprivation are excluded from diagnoses of mental illness, given that they are responding reasonably and understandably to their life situations, then those who survive in the most stressful or deprived contexts are the least likely to be considered emotionally disordered and, thereby, most liable to be denied medical and other forms of attention. Horwitz acknowledges some of these difficulties, for instance, conceding that distinguishing between behaviors caused by dysfunctional internal mechanisms versus those that arise as a consequence of weak character traits, immorality, personal inadequacies, or poor choices (individuals who "won't" conform in contrast to those who "can't") remains "far more a value judgment than a judgment based on psychiatric knowledge" (35).

Yet Horwitz's motivation in delineating among mental disease, mental disorder, and ordinary suffering reproduces Miller's concern about having reached the point of treating madness, depression, and simple unhappiness as all belonging equally to psychiatric purview. Horwitz's tripartite system of disease, disorder, and ordinary suffering presents an attempt to address this complex dilemma. The result, however, is that on the one hand depression, which in Western cultures encompasses "emotions, personal mood, and subjective experiences of hopelessness, withdrawal, anxiety, and grief," represents "the most widespread mental disorder and is the cause of an immense amount of human suffering" (127, 97). On the other hand, due to the currently too-inclusive psychiatric diagnostic system, the ranks of the depressed are filled with false positives, people erroneously diagnosed as having a mental disorder, Horwitz and others contend, when in fact they do not. Thus psy fields currently struggle with attempting to distinguish between normal versus abnormal unhappiness or between appropriate rather than pathological hopelessness, grief, or anxiety.

Horwitz locates psy's error with the emergence of dynamic psychiatry and neuroses, continuing into the contemporary era of diagnostic psychiatry, in which the fields have moved to a focus on "normality" rather than "insanity" (52). In this scenario, psy's increased openness to neuroses and emotional disorders, the turn to "normality," has led the discipline astray from its original focus on exceptional cases of insanity. Horwitz's call for a return to insanity – mental diseases and disorders as he has defined them – effectively addresses psy's numbers problem by drastically reducing those who qualify as mentally ill. But it does so by setting adrift extensive, complex configurations of 'simple unhappiness,' which are rarely that simple. It fails to solve the problem of appropriate social and epistemological criteria for conditions of valid but ordinary suffering. In other words, psy is resuscitated by largely abandoning the complexities of emotionality.

Despite accusations that the exponential growth of psy's cultural purview is due to flaws (excessive diagnosis) or machinations (the pharmaceutical industry) within aspects of psy itself, the presence of expanded notions of emotional disorders, from dynamic psychiatry on, has taken hold among sizeable, still growing segments of the general population. Such a response suggests the desire to express complex feelings and points to legitimate needs. Neuroses and emotional dysfunctions represent, for many, experiences that cause real hardship. To dismiss the costs associated with "difficulties in interpersonal relationships, uncertain futures, bad jobs, and limited resources" (Horwitz 14), risks dismissing the validity of those emotional experiences. Further, the expansion of emotional disorders has brought into visibility the affects of dire circumstances like childhood abuse, rape, war, injustice, poverty, and oppression. The attendant pain and life costs of many such events persist as legitimate struggles and deprivations for which people, understandably, seek relief. These experiences, and their corollary material and emotional effects, warrant accommodation, even if, or especially if, they cannot be adequately encompassed within the bounds of psy.

The Socioemotional Self

I conclude this chapter by returning to Castel and his observations on insanity in the period following the French Revolution. I do so because he brings emotions to bear on his arguments. Primarily interested in the implications of insanity for a newly established juridical society, based on legal codification and penal sanctions, Castel positions emotions in primarily disciplinary or regulatory ways. However, he also begins to outline how thoroughly enmeshed emotionality proves to be in any form of social order.

For Castel, insanity grew to be such an important issue in the nineteenth century because "it revealed in concrete form a gap in the contractual order" (43). He argues that insanity threatened the juridical system by making evident its inability to control all that it claimed within its purview. The insane then function as markers for the limitations of a legally administered society, precisely because they exist as a quite real 'beyond.' The mad person, "who is both frightening and guiltless [in the legal sense] escapes the juridical classifications" (36). As a result, alternative management is demanded, creating a parallel but differently ordered system of mental health medicine, beginning with the asylum, to oversee those who cannot be made to fit within the claims of rule by law.

As we saw earlier, because asylums largely housed "spectacular cases in the name of a conception of public order," insanity became closely linked with the danger, threat, and disruption that "spectacular cases" appeared to pose for members of the general public, rather than associated with the far more numerous 'harmless' mentally ill (195–196). Thus, fear becomes instilled as common social response to insanity, and the mentally ill become, as Castel notes above, "frightening." However, in addition to fear, for Castel the mentally ill also invoke what initially appear to be diametrically opposed emotions. "Just as he is dangerous, the insane person is also an object of pity" (36). For Castel, pity and compassion do not contradict the fear instilled by the insane. Quite the contrary, both emotions function as replacements for the inadequacies of a juridical society, which fails to capture insanity within its bounds.

"Compassion for the 'unfortunate'" comes to compensate for "the deficiencies of the law" by supplanting the juridical through alternative means, such as the asylum or other techniques of mental health medicine, that work equally well to restrain and manage, but by means other than jurid-ical administration (37). In place of legal order, the mad are recuperated as the objects of "philanthropic attitude" so that, ultimately, "there is no contradiction between compassion and science, or between benevolence and authority," because they all function toward the same ends (Ibid.).

However, it is important to note that Castel's account describes only a single manifestation of pity and compassion, just as Foucault's deployment of guilt, discussed in Chapter One, limits other possibilities for that moral *and* emotional concept. Castel's interpretation does not exhaust or dismantle other cultural conceptualizations of pity or compassion. While pity, follow-ing his arguments, serves as a means of closing the gap created by a society newly constituted through legal principles, we have seen that the purposes and productivity of emotions such as pity, sympathy, and compassion func-tioned quite differently in the eighteenth century sensibility movement or in the instance of nineteenth century theatrical melodrama.

In the case of the sensibility movement, sympathy and compassion were integral to the formation of a certain kind of feeling, as well as rationally thinking, being, required towards the creation of the unique, individuated modern self. The concept of sensibility was not a means of excluding those who did not 'fit' into the contemporaneous social order, as Castel argues about pity, compassion, and benevolence in the circumstances of the insane. Quite the contrary, sympathy and compassion, as rendered through the notion of sensibility, served to provide *entry* to social acceptance by proving one's suitability for the upper echelons of a transforming, humanist social landscape. In the instance of theatrical melodrama, social status through morality was signaled by one's capacity for sensitivity to the suffering of others. Deeply, exquisitely felt emotions of pity, sympathy, and compassion were the marks of virtue and, therefore, gentility. The series of emotions associated with sentimental morality could call attention to the often bru-tal, social injustices incurred as a result of a rapidly industrializing soci-ety. Simultaneously, those who ascended to social, political, and economic dominance, as the direct beneficiaries of the transformations accompanying industrialization, could be distanced from its worst injustices through their moral virtue in attending to the suffering of others.[6]

The formulation of any emotion or series of emotions, in this instance of pity, sympathy, and compassion, are contextually and culturally specific. They each had significant but different public ramifications, in shaping the kinds of socioemotional selves that became possible, desirable, or undesirable at their particular historical juncture and in those specific configurations. Evaluations of normality or abnormality are aftereffects of emotions, applicable only once they already have been put to explicit uses or have acquired outcomes. Assess-ments of emotional functionality can only follow from their contextualized occurrences. Considerations of health or illness, normality or aberration, ben-efit or harm, make little sense unless applied to the effects accumulated once specific emotional configurations have been activated in precise ways.

The next chapter considers aesthetics as an alternative cultural canvas to the psy fields, through which emotions are recognized and expressed but, as "The Artist as Mad Genius" explores, in far from unproblematic ways.

Notes

1. With the phrase, "the repressed quietude of realism," Singer is quoting from a 1902 theatrical review.
2. Some of the complexities surrounding the concept of happiness, and its corollary unhappiness, can be found in Ahmed, *The Promise of Happiness*.
3. Such concern is evident in book titles like *Making Us Crazy: DSM: The Psychiatric Bible and the Creation of Mental Disorders* (Kutchins and Kirk), *The Loss of Sadness: How Psychiatry Transformed Normal Sorrow into Depressive Disorder* (Horwitz and Wakefield), and *Manufacturing Depression: The Secret History of a Modern Disease* (Greenberg).
4. The search for an indisputable, scientifically-derived dividing line continues. Darrel Regier, co-chair of the American Psychiatric Association's Task Force responsible for overseeing the development of iteration 5 (2013) of the *Diagnostic and Statistic Manual of Mental Disorders*, argues that once psychiatry is able to "establish better syndrome boundaries" in diagnosing between disorders, the field would be better prepared to determine "the statistically valid cutpoints between normal and pathological" (Regier qtd. in Greenberg, *The Book of Woe* 128).
5. Greenberg notes that "the current mental health treatment system," as of 2013, comprises about "45,000 psychiatrists and half a million psychologists, social workers, and counselors" (*The Book of Woe* 176). If the current prevalence rates prove to be accurate, the situation would be dire because "then we would truly be awash in mental illness, our treatment resources swamped" (Ibid.).
6. For an additional, alternative analsysis of compassion, see Pribram, *Emotions, Genre, Justice*, Chapter Five.

3   The Artist as Mad Genius

Social psychologists Brown and Stenner contend that the psy fields, driven by the mandate to stay within the empirical parameters of the biological, brain, and cognitive sciences, have lost sight of psychology's original ambition – to determine, in an encompassing manner, what it means to be a person in both our individual and collective states (4, 21). As a consequence, "psychology typically falls far short of providing a convincing account of the rich diversity of human experience" (4). If psychology too often "kills its subject matter" in trying to grab hold of it, Brown and Stenner believe that the arts are much better prepared to "bring it back to life" (2). Among their examples, they invoke novelist Herman Melville who, in *Moby Dick*, compellingly and creatively elaborates on "the nature of obsession and vengeance" (3).

Obsession, vengeance, and a great number of other emotional states constitute significant elements in the rich diversity of human experiences, which the psychological disciplines, as Brown and Stenner observe, often grapple with in only limited ways. Further, they caution that the psychological aspects of human experience do not belong solely to the psy fields. Instead, 'the psychological' appears across the vast landscape of human individual and sociocultural activities including, in the aesthetic realm, the visual arts, literature, music, and theater (4). Brown and Stenner's principal concern resides in attempting to revitalize psychology as a set of disciplines, while I'm primarily interested in the respective place and purposes of emotionality in both psy and aesthetics. On the one hand, I agree with many of the limitations they ascribe to psy regarding its ability to successfully capture and elucidate the plurality of experiences that comprise emotionality, a central contention of this book. On the other hand, I question their faith in the power of aesthetics to come closest, "of all human endeavors," to the rich diversity of experiential, including emotional, life (200).

But theirs is not an uncommon view of the arts, as we saw in Chapter One with Foucault, who has been both lauded and criticized for finding any remaining traces of madness in the work of 'mad' artists, such as Artaud, Hölderlin, and Van Gogh. Certainly, the aesthetic fields, the primary focus of this chapter, represent a relatively rare sociocultural arena in which emotions, and emotional disorders, have been viewed as productive, as Brown and Stenner point out with regard to Melville's treatment of obsession and vengeance. For various artistic practices, emotions and their accompanying dysfunctions, are acknowledged and, sometimes, demanded.

However, assumptions about the receptiveness of aesthetic practices to emotionality and its disorders require careful investigation. Emotionality and mental illness have not always been warmly welcomed into aesthetic fields, particularly in higher status branches of artistic activity compared to popular aesthetic endeavors (see Chapter Two's discussion of theatrical melodrama and dramatic realism). To believe in an unquestioning openness toward emotionality in the arts, to trust that aesthetic practices, overall, come closest to elucidating the rich diversity of emotional experiences, is to paint with the broadest brushstrokes available. Aesthetics, *tout court*, hardly exists as a straightforward, simple antidote to psy's limitations in encompassing significant swathes of human experience. Rather, aesthetic practices stand as a different cultural terrain upon which alternate conceptualizations of *and* difficulties over emotions are played out.

"The Artist as Mad Genius" investigates how specific forms of emotionality have been engaged with or expunged in order to shape varying networks of aesthetics. In particular, I explore modernity/modernism's renditions of high art in contrast to popular culture's practices and preferences, which together have dominated twentieth century artistic activity in the West. Central to the exploration of emotionality, as both sources for and generated by modern art, stands the crucial role of madness and moods: specifically, the interconnections among artistic genius, mental illness, and emotional suffering.

In order to accomplish this investigation, I take up the arts of painting and cinema, in particular, as they come to be configured in the late nineteenth and well into the twentieth centuries. I do so through extended use of the example of Vincent Van Gogh, focusing on his reputation from the 1890s, the decade of his death, to the 1990s, a period of record-breaking sales of his work. However, as is the case throughout this book, although I turn to an individual painter, a singular mad genius, this analysis pursues a cultural approach. I utilize a specific case in order to arrive at an assessment of much broader conceptualizations of emotionality as applied to aesthetic activity, rather than an individual perspective or biographical history. In other words, this chapter does not seek to analyze what may or may not have been going on in Van Gogh, the person's, life, mind, or heart. Instead, a range of others' narratives about Van Gogh serve as means of 'getting at' some of the ways emotional experiences and expressions have shaped the nature of the art world, the value of artistic creation, and the pleasures or displeasures of its cultural reception.

Linking Genius, Madness, and Moods

Battersby explains that by 1800 Europeans believed human beings to be superior to the animal world because they possessed "feelings, imagination, sensibility, and 'genius'" (2). In 1800, genius largely remained a quality that could apply to all people, linked to attributes such as talent, skill, judgment, and knowledge. However, by 1900 "'genius' had acquired Romantic grandeur," referring to "a superior type of *being* who walked a 'sublime' path between 'sanity' and 'madness,' between the 'monstrous' and the 'superhuman'" (103).

Signaled first by Rousseau's 1781 *Confessions*, the Romantic definition of genius entailed two aspects. First, it relied upon qualities such as emotions, imagination, creativity, sensitivity, and inspiration "that welled up from beyond the limits of rational consciousness" (Battersby 103). Second, while reason and talent were properties within the potential grasp of most people, genius could only be summoned by an extraordinary handful of individuals. "The genius's instinct, emotion, sensibility, intuition, imagination – even his madness – were different from those of ordinary mortals" (Ibid. 3).

In prior epochs, the artist's task was to replicate nature as it had been divinely created. Thus, medieval art was "essentially mimetic," in which an artist reproduced "divine truth and Christian teaching as faithfully as possible" (Ibid. 25). During the Renaissance, the notion of "divine inspiration" came into existence but only to the extent that it enabled the inspired artist to replicate "the most perfect and most universal natural forms," not his or her *own* vision (26). Therefore, prior to the Enlightenment personal or authorial subjectivity was an impediment, not an asset, to artistic endeavors.

However, with Romanticism the work of art became directly linked to its specific creator. "Consequently, the uniqueness and individuality of the artist's own character also became aesthetically significant" (13). Great works of art grew to be perceived as a reflection of the unique depths of its creator's feelings, a view now naturalized. Thus, an artist's individual existence and subjective experiences began to matter because they functioned as the source for inspired art.

Battersby is concerned primarily with the relationship of gender to notions of artistic genius; however, her work provides insight into perceptions of emotionality due to the frequency with which the latter has been linked to the feminine (and genius to the masculine). She traces the cultural outcome of emotions once they are claimed as part of genius, while simultaneously retaining their association with women and femininity. The reclamation of "emotionality, sensitivity, and imaginative self-expression" results in the characterization of the great Romantic artist as androgynous: male in body but with a feminine soul (23, 7). In this formula, women remained unable to access the heights of genius but exceptional men could encompass the feminine in their character and dispositions. Such a belief is summarized by Goncourt's aphorism: "there are no women of genius; the women of genius are men" (Goncourt qtd. in Battersby 4).

Although connections were made between artistic activity and melancholy during the Renaissance, Battersby finds that it is only with the nineteenth century "that the modern concept of genius became fully associated with madness" (88). Women could certainly go mad in the nineteenth century, as exemplified by the figure of the madwoman in the attic. But while doing so, they could not reach a comparable level of creative genius to men. In Battersby's argument, male geniuses became 'mad,' while women, artistic and otherwise, were viewed as hysterical, failing to rise to a sufficient level of either genius or madness. Schnog outlines the efforts of a number of American women writers who, under the influence of Romanticism, tried to reclaim 'moods' as their own during the last three decades of the nineteenth century. In Schnog's analysis, female-authored sentimental literature of the pre-Civil War era "constituted moodiness as a major problem and flaw in female temperament" (193). Readers followed central female characters whose journeys involved learning to become 'the cheerful woman' by suppressing perceived negative emotions, including anxiousness, sadness, nervousness, irritability, self-absorption, sulkiness, standoffishness, and coldness (Ibid.).

In contrast, a number of women authors in the latter part of the century, for instance Louisa May Alcott in *Moods* (1864) and Elizabeth Stuart Phelps Ward in *The Story of Avis* (1877), sought to explicitly endow their female protagonists with moodiness as a means of accessing notions of the romantic individual and inspired artist (193). Schnog contends that "masculine romantic philosophy ... had equated moods with individualism, creativity, and emotional depth," traits which women were viewed as largely incapable of possessing (Ibid.). Like Battersby, Schnog argues that the inner life of the romantic genius normally was depicted as "tempestuous, unstable, and, in some cases, mad" (202). Writers like Alcott and Ward used emotions, especially certain moods or moodiness, as a way of establishing a "'deep' inner life" and, therefore, the potential for artistic genius in their female characters (206). Thus particular emotions, which already existed as a literary key to individuality, creativity, imagination, intensity, and excess in male Romantic figures, were appropriated by these authors in order to argue similar capacities for women.

Battersby notes that nineteenth century Romanticism largely merged into modernism (38). While this may be true with regard to notions concerning artistic genius, it is not so neatly the case with emotionality. The circumstances affecting emotions grew more complex in that, at the end of the eighteenth century, two broad accounts of the origins of artistic genius were developed, over which contestation would continue. In his 1781 *Confessions*, Rousseau identified emotions as the fire driving aesthetic genius. However, as Battersby observes, Kant, in *The Critique of Judgement* (1790), objects to such emphasis on the passions; it is "still reason, understanding and memory – as well as the imagination – that makes Kant's genius sublime" (76, 77). Rousseau and Kant represent two distinct avenues that conceptualizations of aesthetic activity and artistic genius will follow: one that extensively incorporates emotions and the other that works to curtail their impact. If Rousseau's view dominates in the age of Romanticism, Kant's understanding prevails in twentieth century modernist notions of high art.

Modernity's Modernisms

In his sociological analysis of art, Bourdieu's stated intention is to address "the old questions of Kant's critique of judgement" which calls for a "pure pleasure, pleasure purified of pleasure" (*Distinction* 1, 6). This pure aesthetic drained of traditional pleasure, which Bourdieu refers to as the pure gaze, eschews the senses and emotions in favor of disinterestedness, distance, and detachment, descriptors Bourdieu returns to repeatedly (Ibid. 4, 7, 32, 34). In his view, those who take up aesthetic issues surrounding modernist high art do so in the terms established by Kant's *Critique of Judgement*, whether overtly or tacitly (*Distinction* 564–565; *Rules* 285).

The pure aesthetic of modernism arrives with and continues onward from Manet and the Impressionists; its original contribution to the history of aesthetics consists in the primacy given to form over function (*Distinction* 3, 30; "Historical" 208; *Rules* 132). Form references the mode or style of representation while function points to the object or content that is depicted. As we saw in Battersby's account, in previous epochs the artist's primary mission was to portray the essential aspects of nature as they are found to exist. With modernism, the equation is inverted so that *how* the content is displayed becomes of greater importance than the 'what' of the depiction. Bourdieu cites Flaubert who argues "there is no such thing as subject – style in itself being an absolute manner of seeing things" (Flaubert qtd. in Bourdieu, *Rules* 160). Thus, the aesthetic qualities of the representation displace the aspects of the world that earlier artists sought to render. Bourdieu references Flaubert's injunction to "[w]rite the mediocre well," because the novelist's phrase encapsulates the principle that even the most "base or vulgar" or ordinary objects can be turned into aesthetic gems through the artist's innovative brilliance (*Rules* 94, 132). Indeed, by choosing mundane, trivial, or even unpleasant subject matter, the pure artist is able to better display the creative invention of his/her aesthetic abilities than if the chosen content, in and of itself, embodied some aesthetic quality, such as beauty. In this formula, the function or subject matter is arbitrary to the creation of the work of art. Instead, it is the content's *treatment* in the hands of the artist and in the eye of the connoisseur that proves its exceptionality.

Further, shifting the focus of attention from function to form results in the invention of both modern art and modern artist. In that creation now resides with the artist, rather than in the world he or she depicts, the significance of what is portrayed recedes while the figure of the creator moves to the fore. Foregrounding form instead of function necessarily promotes the artist-figure because, "with the emergence of the artist in the modern sense of the term," aesthetic *intention* creates the aesthetic object (*Rules* 291). The content depicted no longer exists naturally in the world for the artist to discover, prior to its representation in or as a work of art. Now, art is a work of imagination that only the artist can envision. In this sense, all modern art becomes a portrait of the artist rather than a portrayal of objects. Art historian, Griselda Pollock, calls the production of the modern artist the very purpose of the discipline of art history. "Art and the artist become reflexive, mystically bound into an unbreakable circuit which produces the artist as the subject of the art work and the art work as the means of contemplative access to the subject's 'transcendent' and creative subjectivity" ("Artists" 59). The art work exists to reveal the artist as its ultimate content, regardless of what is depicted. Art's purpose exists as the material means of access to the transcendent creator, not to an exteriorized world.

However, foregrounding the artist as transcendent creator necessarily advances other people as well. The pure aesthetic also relies on all those who play a role in determining the value of a work of art. Aesthetic production includes the "entire set of agents engaged" in the art field, from those who establish the merits of a particular artist or work to those who verify the value of art in general (Bourdieu, *Distinction* 205). For Bourdieu, then, a work of art is produced

> hundreds of times, thousands of times, by all those who have an inter-est in it, who find a material or symbolic profit in reading it, classifying it, decoding it, commenting on it, reproducing it, criticizing it, combat-ing it, knowing it, possessing it.
>
> (*Rules* 171)

The entire panoply of dealers, curators, art historians, critics, patrons, col-lectors, and other agents in the field are not attendant to but, rather, take their places at the very heart of the creation of the modern work of art.

Additionally, the "charismatic ideology of 'creation'" is dependent upon another group of people: pure art's spectators (*Rules* 167). Bourdieu con-siders those who view, and appreciate, modern art among its ranks of pro-ducers. For, in order to apprehend a modernist work, the consumer must possess the cultural competence that a modernist aesthetic presupposes. Lacking such knowledge and training, the viewer feels lost or judges the work by incorrect measures, for instance, through sense impressions or "the emotional resonances" the piece arouses (*Distinction* 2). The *interpreta-tion* of a work of art is fundamental to the creation of "its meaning and value" (*Rules* 170). Therefore, the reception or consumption of a work, by a specialized viewership of cognoscenti, must be central to the process of production, now understood not simply as the manufacture of an aesthetic object but also as the formation of its significance, in cultural and economic terms. Thus, not only artists and those employed in the art field become endowed with cultural distinction. Viewers who are capable of apprehend-ing the special qualities of the work, *as they are intended to be appreciated*, themselves become special, inspired persons, recognized as such by their role in this chain of aesthetic production (*Distinction* 31).

The link to genius, by all those who participate in the creation of the pure gaze, is guaranteed by art's supposed universal and transcendental qualities (*Distinction* 3–4; "Historical" 202; *Rules* 130). However, Bourdieu con-tends such a notion is wholly inaccurate because all art is actually situated in history and "dated," for example, from the specific context of France in the 1890s (*Rules* 286). The belief in the transcendental and universal character of modern art (and, retrospectively, of masterpieces from earlier epochs) can only be sustained by "the active forgetting of the history which has produced it" (Ibid. 288, 289). In turn, the transcendental nature of the pure aesthetic is ensured by the vagueness and indeterminacy of the language used to describe it, rendering art largely unavailable to explanation ("Historical" 205–206). Bourdieu criticizes the widespread practice (in philosophy as well as art history) that takes the work of art to be "ineffable, that it escapes by definition all rational understanding," and therefore is destined to remain mysteriously unfathomable (*Rules* xvi).

At this juncture, however, Bourdieu finds himself in something of a predicament. Toward his goal of historicizing artistic practices and values in social, economic, political, and ideological terms, he vigorously questions the inexpressible and transcendental aspects of modern aesthetic experience. Yet, he also acknowledges that a sociological analysis, such as his, remains open to the charge that it "might succeed in killing pleasure, and that, capable of delivering understanding, it might be unable to convey feeling" (*Rules* xviii). On the one hand, he could claim that, through historical analysis, aesthetic experience is capable of full availability to rational understanding. On the other hand, if rational understanding is not entirely sufficient for such a task, then something is left that must be accounted for, beyond intellectual discernment, which he points to in the notion that art conveys feelings.

Defending against anticipated accusations that his attempt to analyze aesthetic practices in a reasoned manner undermines their emotional aspects ("killing pleasure") or, at any rate, that rational historical analysis fails to deplete aesthetic experience of all its meaning and value, Bourdieu returns here to emotionality as a significant feature of experience. Indeed, in linking the pleasure provided by emotions to art's ineffability, emotions arguably become a core aspect of aesthetic experience. Ultimately, Bourdieu concludes that surrendering the mysterious eternal of pure art for a grounded historical understanding of various literary and artistic fields is worth the sacrifice because it leads to an alternate, perhaps richer because "more true," comprehension of aesthetic practice (*Rules* xx).

Yet, there is something of value in Bourdieu's hesitancy to surrender entirely the notion that there are ways of 'knowing' or forms of experience beyond rational comprehension. Without requiring the acceptance of modernism's tenets of exceptionality – the irreducible genius of those who create through inspired insight or of those, because they recognize such genius, also embody the spirit of inspiration – the longing to express other modes of existence beyond the rational stands as one of the purposes served by aesthetic activities. For example, speaking of the popular art of theatrical melodrama, Gledhill points out that it was formulated on the basis of "an aesthetics of the visible" in which its elements of spectacle, gesture, and tableaux enabled it to express that which escapes other forms of language ("Introduction" 22, 30). While dramatic realism assumes "the world is capable of both adequate explanation and representation," in contrast, melodrama "attests to the forces, desires, fears which … appear to operate in human life independently of rational explanation" (Ibid. 31).[1]

For, as Bourdieu also acknowledges, the pure aesthetic of formal experimentation over functional content has not been the only mode of aesthetic activity in the twentieth century. Bourdieu also discusses the popular or everyday aesthetics against which modernism's pure gaze was formulated, largely as popular culture's corrective. Among the traits found wanting in the popular aesthetics of the day was its emphasis on "the passions, emotions, and feelings which 'ordinary' people invest in their 'ordinary' lives" (*Distinction* 4). In the modernist view, based on the pure gaze, investing too much passion is "naïve and vulgar," a submission to "easy seduction and collective enthusiasm" (Ibid. 34–35).

Pure aesthetics, then, becomes established as the antithesis of the popular aesthetics of the era. In place of 'ordinary' emotional investment, the pure gaze valorizes "detachment and disinterestedness," "indifference and distance" (*Distinction* 4, 32). High art dismisses the accessibility of the everyday in favor of "erudition," requiring a learned, intellectual cultural competence (Ibid. 30). Delight in emotional identification with plot and characters – as an example of which Bourdieu specifically cites theatrical melodrama – are all forsaken (Ibid. 34). The everyday of popular entertainment is jettisoned for the exceptional; the ordinary gives way to the inspired; the delayed gratification of the ineffable replaces the immediate impact of the expressive.

High modernism, in its rejection of sentimentalism and emotion-based content in favor of disinterested formal experimentation, represents a transformation from Romanticism. However, high modernism and Romanticism remain in concert through their mutual validation of the pure artist, following notions of aesthetic genius and its links to madness or moodiness, as outlined earlier. Although the nature and purpose of the work has changed between the two movements, he (almost always) remains a struggling, misunderstood figure, a martyr to the cause of art and, often, "a saturnine person destined to bad luck and melancholy" (Bourdieu, *Distinction* 134, 133). Thus, while the modes of representation differ markedly in the transition from Romanticism to high modernism, the concept of the artist-figure as an isolated, troubled, but inspired genius persists.

I now would like to turn to the specific case of Vincent Van Gogh for several reasons. Certainly, he stands as one of the most influential and popular modernist painters of the twentieth century. His dominance prevails in terms of Bourdieu's criteria of both cultural and economic impact. Further, his persona endures as the epitome of the mad genius. In his exemplification of simultaneous insanity and inspired brilliance, mental illness plays a key role in his cultural legacy. Additionally, his vast popularity has triggered considerable scholarly research, particularly for purposes here on the development of his reputation and cultural standing in the century following his death. Finally, I argue that the struggle over Van Gogh's image and reputation corresponds to twentieth century contestation between high modernist and popular aesthetics over the place of emotionality for each.

The Van Gogh Legacy

Ownership and control over Van Gogh's "meaning and value" are fought over the distinction between an intellectual versus an emotional aesthetics. In this regard, the history of the Van Gogh legacy certainly confuses and, at moments, contradicts some of Bourdieu's contentions about the dominance of high art aesthetics in the twentieth century, especially as it concerns the thorny problem of the role of emotions. For in Van Gogh's case, it is a general public, largely composed of popular audiences, who inscribe Van Gogh's work with its most familiar meanings and value, and who sustain its prominence over the course of the century. In response, the artistic field of the pure aesthetic works to reappropriate Van Gogh on its own terms. This contestation, among differing forms of modernism, takes place over the terrain of an emotion-based aesthetics of the everyday versus a pure aesthetics of the exceptional. For the general public, the authority to fight this struggle is based on emotionality, which denotes a less specialized form of knowledge, in principle, felt by and accessible to all and thus not the prerogative of experts. When Bourdieu refers to agents in the art field, the prominent dealers or publishers who function as the "inspired discoverers" of great art and its creative geniuses, he describes them as motivated by both "disinterestedness and irrational passion" (*Rules* 168). Disinterested because their assessments are objectively and rationally derived through meticulous expertise; passionate because they believe intensely in their cause and because art is meant to stir and rouse. I am arguing that the curiously contradictory states of disinterestedness and irrational passion are compelled to co-exist, precisely because of a lack of cultural accord over the meanings, values, and functions of emotionality. Indeed, it is this contradiction between disinterest and passion that haunts the figure of the modern artist and modernist aesthetics as a whole.

In an article in *Newsweek* titled "Tortured Souls," with the subheading, "Do Artists Really Have to Suffer Greatly to Make Art?," critic Plagens reviews major exhibits of the work of Vincent Van Gogh and Jackson Pollock that both took place in the autumn of 1998.[2] Plagen writes, "the shows also raise the question of whether great artists are always tortured, self-destructive souls" (78). Although Plagens, citing the work of Warhol, ultimately concludes that not all artists need be tortured souls, the article makes clear an intimate link between artists' psychic disorders, their artwork, and their capacity to feel intensely. In the case of Van Gogh, Plagens describes his only "natural qualification" as an artist to be "the lack of a psychological shield to protect him from the pain of feeling everything – *everything* – right down to the quick" (Ibid., italics in original).[3]

In this view, it is precisely their intense capacity to feel that makes great artists, first, great and, second, mentally ill. Additionally, their ability to translate their powerful emotional sensibilities onto the canvas both explicates and authenticates their popular reception. A front page article in *USA Today*, similarly using "Tortured Artist" as part of its subtitle, reviews the same 1998 Van Gogh exhibit.[4] Describing him as "the exemplar of the crazy, starving, tragic artist," the author turns to the opinions of two of the show's curators as well as Van Gogh's great grand-niece (Puente 2A). All three sources attribute the artist's enormous popularity to his emotionality and, specifically, to the way museum-goers are able to recognize and respond to the work's affective intensity (Puente 1A–2A). The paintings, crafted by and saturated with emotion, cause their viewers, in turn, to feel – a positive, desired outcome. Yet it remains a sought-after effect with clear limitations, as exemplified by the artist-figure with his/her perilously excessive emotionality. A boundary exists in which enhanced emotional capacity is safe and highly valued as long as it falls short of the dangerously acute emotional sensibilities, leading to mental illness, embodied by such artists.

Additionally, both articles indicate that the emotional quality of the works makes them popular because they are rendered *accessible*, a word repeated frequently in connection with Van Gogh's paintings (Plagens 79; Puente 2A). His art is accessible, and hence popular, because of its emotional qualities, which every viewer has the capacity to recognize. The condition of recognition, grounded in the work's emotionality, constitutes that to which all viewers relate, not solely a select few. Emotionality is the basis of the work's, and our, common "humanity" (Puente 2A). Thus, the capacity to feel, and to chronicle those feelings in one's artwork, draws viewers to certain artists. Simultaneously, this same quality sets the artist apart, marking him or her as exceptional in a troubling way. Exceptional emotionality, although it may be universally recognized, necessarily distances the true artist from ordinary folk. Intense emotionality remains the preserve of a select few because of the dangers it represents, for example, ending in some form of madness or mental illness. Thus, two different varieties of artistic distinction develop. The first is an intellectual and aesthetic understanding associated with the connoisseur, the knowing expert. The second is a capacity for feeling belonging to those artists who possess the emotional equivalent of connoisseurship but for which we lack analogous language.

At the same time that the artist of emotional distinction is lauded, particularly by popular audiences, many of the most highly valued attributes of modernist artistic practice, on the part of those actively engaged in the art field, exemplify the pure aesthetic as delineated by Bourdieu. Modernist high art largely eschews inner turmoil and emotionality in favor of formal properties and the ideational aspects of the work. As we have seen, following Kant's principles, as modernist high art travels up the echelons of aestheticism, a mounting distance from emotionality accompanies it. Both high formalism and high emotionality exist as features of various modern artistic practices; however, they usually have been structured as contradictory, competing impulses.

Van Gogh is a significant figure in this conflict due to his vast popularity, because of his standing as one of the twentieth century's most influential painters, and as a result of the conceptual struggles that have taken place over his paintings and his person. He is a figure who brings the contestations surrounding emotionality and art into high relief. And arguably, he serves as an instance in which emotions 'win out,' emerging as the attribute of highest value, indicated by the persistent, popular appeal of his work across Western nations, and beyond, over time.

A century before the reviews of his 1998 exhibition in Washington, D.C., similar observations already were being made about Van Gogh. Prior to his death in July 1890, Van Gogh was able to read: "What characterizes his work as a whole is its excess, its excess of strength, of nervousness, its violence of expression. ... a terrible and demented genius, often sublime, sometimes grotesque, *always at the brink of the pathological*" (Albert Aurier qtd. in Naifeh and Smith 805; italics in original). The year before, in 1889, a Dutch critic and painter described Van Gogh as an artist "who knows how to give form to his emotions, who invests his canvas with his life" (J.J. Isaacson qtd. in Zemel, *Formation* 14). The difference between these initial evaluations and those appearing a century later lies in their sources: the earlier assessments originate from the specialized perspectives of the select few – other artists and art critics. While Van Gogh's emotionality, even madness, were recognized by the time of his death, these were not yet linked to a general, popular accessibility exemplified by his work.

In her study of the early reception of Van Gogh's work, *The Formation of a Legend,* Zemel examines responses to the artist in four European countries (the Netherlands, France, Germany, England) from 1890, the year of his death, to 1920 by which time Zemel believes Van Gogh's status as a 'legend' is entrenched. As with other scholars I rely upon in this chapter, emotions are not Zemel's primary concern, but what she has to say has direct bearing on a consideration of emotionality and aesthetics. Van Gogh's critical fate – whether he is lauded, reviled, or ignored by members of the art field – varies from nation to nation. However, in *all* cases, discussion centers on the place of emotionality in art, based on the prominence of passion in Van Gogh's work and life. Zemel notes:

> more than any other aspect of his paintings, the issue of his emotionality or temperament permeated criticism of his art. There was hardly a writer who did not consider the paintings to be distillations of van Gogh's feelings. ... Whether moved or repelled by his efforts, many critics wondered if his art was the haphazard product of madness or the inspired but willfully formed expression of genius – or some combination of the two.
>
> (*Formation* 3)

Critical response to his work was largely positive in both the Netherlands and Germany. Two and a half years after his death, exhibits of his work were being mounted on a regular basis in the Netherlands (Ibid.). In this case, he suffered no long, or even minimal, period of neglect despite the myth of his struggle as a misunderstood artist, leading to delayed recognition of his accomplishments. By 1900, Van Gogh's legendary status was in place in his country of origin and, by 1905, the specific elements of Van Gogh's reputation were "firmly fixed" (Zemel, *Formation* 43, 33). Although the focus of discussion remained his "emotional intensity," resolution was reached in the Netherlands by accepting it as key to the critical understanding of his work which, then, could be favorably interpreted as "based on self-expressive factors and visionary concerns" (Ibid. 33). Thus, emotionality was central to Van Gogh's elevation as an artistic master in the Netherlands.[5]

Critical reaction to Van Gogh was at least as enthusiastic in Germany, although Zemel points out Van Gogh's work also engendered the most vocal opposition there (106). In particular, he was hailed as an example by members of the Expressionist movement across the arts, who saw in his paintings, letters, and the contours of his personal life, "the harbinger of a modernist spirit" (105). Drawn by his story of madness and suicide, they perceived in his "audacious style," a "liberating and visionary sensibility" (Ibid.). In other words, the countries in which he found the earliest favor were those that managed to link his life story and his intense emotionality to his formal artistic style. In Germany and the Netherlands, his paintings were interpreted as the remarkable aesthetic expression of "powerful passions" of "despair," coupled with an intense "desire to create" (Ferdinand Keizer qtd. in Zemel 22). Van Gogh was a tragic figure who struggled heroically and, as such, is already the tortured soul of accounts a century later. Initially, Van Gogh was most appreciated by other artists and critics who were able to reconcile the style of his work with the emotionality of his life.

In contrast, Van Gogh's reputation did not fare as well in France, the country in which he created his most famous and admired paintings. Yet critical reception, although reaching a different conclusion than in the Netherlands and Germany, did so on the basis of the same conceptual terrain: how to reconcile the emotionality of Van Gogh's work and life with the aesthetic standards of the day. In the years immediately following his death, a number of artists and critics sought to establish for Van Gogh "a heroic image of struggle, perseverance and self sacrifice" which resulted in both his "tormented nature and visionary art" (Zemel 60, 78). However, by the time of two major Van Gogh exhibitions in 1908, French commentators were having difficulty with Van Gogh's excessive, disordered emotionality which seemed "irreconcilable with the formal accomplishments" of the emerging, most valued aesthetic style of the era (Ibid. 93). Under the influence of the contemporaneously dominant aesthetics of "balance, order, stability," Van Gogh's work, in either "anguished or ecstatic" form, was found wanting (Ibid. 94).

Zemel explains that the same traits of passion and spontaneity, which rendered his work so appealing in the Netherlands and Germany, for French critics, "seemed to preclude any coherent system of forms. Some writers simply doubted his lucidity" (103). Instead, in France it wasn't his art that took hold, but rather the narrative of Van Gogh's life. The story of his difficult, impassioned nature, his madness, his social isolation and, despite all, his determination to keep creating, fit well with the dominant conceptualization of the modern artistic genius as "a man apart, beset by social and cultural resistance and committed to a lonely struggle for his art" (Ibid. 104). Thus the French art establishment, in the early years of the twentieth century, resolved the dilemma of emotionality by bifurcating Van Gogh's art from his life. The former went into decline (for example, no major exhibit of his work occurred for a decade after 1909), while the legend of his person flourished.

In England, Van Gogh met with the harshest response of the four countries studied by Zemel. Again, the problem focused on his emotionality and the inability to reconcile it with the demands of contemporaneous aesthetic standards. Post-Impressionism received its first major exhibition in England in 1910, and by 1912 influential art and cultural critic, Roger Fry, had dismissed Van Gogh as "not primarily an artist" but, as the direct result of his tempestuous personality, merely "an inspired illustrator" (Fry qtd. in Zemel 147). For Fry and other English critics, emotionality could not be integrated with the purely formalist aesthetics they espoused. The result was that his style of "total self-abandonment" and dramatic feeling existed at the expense of a more considered and aesthetically significant development based on a system of formal design (Fry qtd. in Zemel, Ibid.). The irrationality of both emotions and mental illness presented themselves in opposition to "the demonstrable clarity of formal issues and aesthetic concerns" (Zemel 153). Thus, as was the case in France, Van Gogh's work was seldom shown in the decade after 1913 and the critical response to his first major exhibition in 1923 was, in Zemel's word, "lukewarm" (146). Unlike France, however, where an aspect of his legendary status was established through his embodiment as "the exemplar of the tragic, starving modern artist," to borrow the description from 1998, in England he was largely consigned to playing "a marginal part [in] Post-Impressionist and modernist history" (Zemel 148).

High Modernism and Troubling Emotion

Of course, all the specialists who voiced their opinions on Van Gogh's place in art history did not pronounce solely on an individual artist but used his case to forward their own aesthetic principles with regard to what they believed modern art was or ought to be, in modernism's still formative years. And although no clear consensus was reached, all who participated in the debate surrounding Van Gogh's position in art history confronted the issue of his emotionality, including the passion of his paintings, whether "anguished or ecstatic," as well as the madness and suicide that seemed to dominate his life story. If there was no consensus on what to make of Van Gogh's emotionality, all who addressed his work were forced to acknowledge it. Some, represented by Fry in England, dismissed Van Gogh's work by arguing that his excessive emotionality rendered him a non-artist or, at any rate, an artist of little significance. Others, such as the dominant school in France, rejected his art on the basis of its emotionality but retained Van Gogh's figure as symbolic exemplar of the difficulties confronting the modern artist. Still others, such as his proponents in the Netherlands and Germany, saw his intense emotionality, in both his work and his life, as indicative of visionary, artistic genius. But none could comment on Van Gogh's role in modern aesthetics without coming to terms with the function of emotions in his work. Both his work and his person, then, became an avenue for arguing the meanings and value of emotions, and emotional disorders, in the world of art, whether in affirmation or repudiation.

Although I began this chapter with the observation that emotions commonly are perceived as permissible in or even requisite to artistic practices, their role in aesthetics is not wholly secured but always changing and, in certain instances, deeply troubling. Further, at any specific moment usually only a particular range of emotions is capable of being recognized or valorized. In Van Gogh's case, these are most especially the compilation of emotions that render the artist as tragic figure. While frequently associated with suffering, violence, and despair, his work is far more rarely considered in terms of joy or delight although, arguably, these emotions can also be found in his images. Van Gogh becomes such a compelling, mythic figure in the art and culture of the twentieth century precisely because of his capacity to feel, express, and apparently share this very specific range of emotions.

Despite a lack of critical consensus on Van Gogh and, indeed, some heated opposition to him in Europe, Zemel contends that by 1920 "the presence of his paintings in public collections [and] their growing market value ... testified to his international success" (149). Zemel arrives at her conclusion after outlining considerable polarization in critical accounts. On the one hand, when judged solely on the aesthetic merits of his work, Van Gogh was found wanting, as indicated by Fry's and others' dismissal of his techniques. On the other hand, he was valorized by those who proved successful in conceptually linking his temperament and life story to his work. Yet his mixed reviews from members of the art field well into the 1920s fails to explain his "international success" by 1920. As the title of her book, *The Formation of a Legend* suggests, and despite the quite serious aesthetic concerns she has raised, Zemel never doubts Van Gogh's early legendary status. However, the specifics of her study concerning the responses from experts in the art field leaves some element unaccounted for in the leap from mixed reviews to legendary status.

Zemel also contends that even earlier, by 1912, "in all countries, the stylistic issues raised by Van Gogh's paintings had been settled and his impact as a painter, whether limited or far-reaching, had been declared. But even as his stylistic influence subsided, his reputation continued to grow" (152). If his place in the narrative of modern art had been "settled" by 1912, and all critical positions on the issues raised already staked out – primarily concerning the role of emotionality and emotional disorders not only in his work but in art in general – then on what basis does Van Gogh's reputation continue to grow? The hardened nature of opinion on all sides of the debate regarding the merits of Van Gogh as an artist would suggest that his growing, positive reputation occurred beyond the staked-out positions of various critical schools, that is, beyond the specialists' parameters she identifies as having been established by 1912. Neglected in Zemel's account is the impact of Van Gogh's popularity among the non-specialized public, based not solely on the artist's life but also on the accessible emotionality of his work, as the 1998 reviews emphasize.

In contrast, Saltzman's account, which traces Van Gogh's posthumous career through the provenance of a single painting, *Portrait of Dr. Gachet* (1890), better addresses the artist's popularity beyond the art field. In 1990, *Portrait of Dr. Gachet* sold for the record-breaking sum of $82.5 million, surpassing Van Gogh's own previously set record for *Irises*, which was purchased for $53.9 million in 1987.[6] Like Zemel, Saltzman locates the origin of "the tragic myth of Van Gogh" in the days immediately following his suicide. In France, symbolist writers and critics, such as Albert Aurier, embraced Van Gogh and his circle (Gauguin, Bernard) precisely because they used "color, shape, and line to inscribe particular ideas and emotions into the fabric of the picture" (Saltzman 28). Moving away from either verisimilitude or the optical studies of the effects of light associated with the Impressionists, symbolism advocated an art founded in inner experience, focusing on "ideas, feelings, sensations, and states of mind" (Ibid. 27). Largely concurring with Zemel, Saltzman believes Van Gogh's reputation and popularity were firmly established in Europe during the 1920s.[7] From here, Saltzman turns her attention to the development of Van Gogh's standing in the United States.

Briefly, Van Gogh's presence in the US was established by such highlights as the 1929 Museum of Modern Art's inaugural exhibit in New York which featured the work of those designated as the most significant Post-Impressionists (Cezanne, Gauguin, Seurat, and Van Gogh); the 1927 publication of the first English edition of his letters; the publication in 1934 of Irving Stone's *Lust for Life* which became a bestseller; and a solo retrospective of Van Gogh's work at MOMA in 1935 which was highly praised by critics.[8] Van Gogh's reception in the U.S. was so enthusiastic, argues Saltzman, that by the late 1940s he "was probably the most well known artist in America" (234).

However, the rise in his popularity came with a simultaneous decline in his status as a painter among some art historians, who cast considerable doubt on his technical and formal skills. For example, the very influential Clement Greenberg, best known as a leading proponent of New York's Abstract Expressionist movement, raised questions about Van Gogh's "craft competence," whether he had "a professional command of his art," or if he could even be considered a great painter (Greenberg qtd. in Saltzman 237). Saltzman argues that the negative recalibration of Van Gogh's reputation in the US echoed a similar occurrence in Europe in the 1920s among art critics, as a result of the artist's accelerating public recognition. With regard to the US, Saltzman clearly links the reassessment of Van Gogh's standing in the art world to his popularity beyond the art world: "the success of the Van Gogh legend in America's mass market culture unsettled art professionals" (237). Under the dominance of formalism, art critics and historians called into question Van Gogh's talents as a painter because his work "seemed driven by emotional rather than aesthetic issues" (239). One result of critical dismissal was the absence of major Van Gogh exhibits in New York for over two decades, until 1971. Even then a show was mounted at the Brooklyn Museum of Art, not MOMA or the Met.

As noted, long-standing doubts concerning Van Gogh's skills co-existed alongside his continued rise in prominence. Even such supporters as Fred Leeman, a curator at the Van Gogh Museum in Amsterdam, delineated in the early 1990s the limitations he perceived. Describing the influence of Van Gogh's painting, "Madame Roulin with Baby Marcelle" (1888), on Picasso's "Mother and Child" (1901), which share striking similarities in composition, Leeman comments:

> Although it lacks the splendid coherence and expressive sophistication of his own *Mother and Child*, Picasso seem to have borrowed quite a few ideas from Van Gogh's work. (46)

Similarly, regarding a Van Gogh-influenced Matisse: "His [Matisse's] firm control of the decorative arrangement is in sharp contrast to Van Gogh's uncertain handling of space" (54). In a comparable manner, Zemel refers to Van Gogh's "difficulty rendering the figure, the area where his lack of training was most obvious," and she further suggests that his move toward posed portraits, which usually featured only the face and upper body of a subject, "allowed him to evade the difficulties of figure painting without eliminating human subjects from his *oeuvre*" entirely (*Van Gogh's Progress* 78, 90).[9]

However, despite critical denigration and the lower profile of his work in terms of museum exhibitions, "the price of his pictures rose with his public popularity" (Saltzman 239). Thus, regardless of critical word or action – what was written as well as what was, or was not, shown – Van Gogh's attractiveness to a broader public beyond art professionals continued to strengthen. Of most significance for this discussion, critical resistance formed around the intense emotionality of Van Gogh's work that continued to be viewed as reflections of his "troubled psyche":

> Assuming the paintings to be psychological illustrations lead certain critics to question van Gogh's ability as a painter.
>
> (Saltzman 237)

The same dichotomies that had occurred in Europe between the emotional and the cerebral, between the psychologically disordered and the formally ordered, were now being voiced in the US. Effectively, these assertions suggested that the paintings could not be simultaneously emotional and intellectual, the product of measured consideration and intense feeling, or the display of irrational mental illness with the reasoned clarity of aesthetic concerns.

Ultimately, the problem for members of the art field who advocated against Van Gogh's formal and technical skills is that their position could not be maintained. In the face of Van Gogh's seemingly ever-ascending popularity and the accompanying rise in prices for his work, and in an era that encompassed "blockbuster exhibits" devoted to him in Europe, North America, and Japan (Puente 1A), which museums depend upon to sustain them economically, the art field simply could not afford to dismiss him. Van Gogh exhibits set records both for attendance and for the sale of Van Gogh-related merchandise, from books and posters to clothing and household items (Schiermeier 99; Kasumi 409–410).

Thus arose the constitution of what Saltzman dubs "the new van Gogh," although clearly neither Van Gogh nor his work had changed (260). Instead, in her account, analyses by art experts altered drastically between 1984 and 1990, in an effort to reclaim Van Gogh for high art by reinventing him. Not coincidentally, this coincided with the period of a series of record-breaking sales for his paintings.[10] Saltzman dates the inauguration of "the new Van Gogh" to two "groundbreaking exhibitions" at the Metropolitan Museum in New York in 1984 and 1987, which were "part of an effort by art historians to dismantle the persistent Van Gogh legend and replace it with more accurately drawn historical information," including the conclusion that his mental illness "had little to do with his accomplishments as a painter" (254).[11] Here Saltzman states, in accordance with scholarly reevaluation and despite, as she acknowledges, sparse historical evidence, that the accurate account lies in the fact that Van Gogh's illness had little, if anything, to do with his artistic output or subsequent success.[12] Critical reevaluation from experts in the art field necessitated that Van Gogh be distanced from both his excessive emotionality and his madness. "Freed" from the limitations of his emotional and disordered psyche, Van Gogh became suitably fit for reinstatement in the pantheon of modern art, as "an intellectual leader of the Postimpressionist generation" and "a consummate craftsman and a cerebral painter" (Ibid. 254, 255, 265). However, in the process of reconstituting Van Gogh's reputation, the polarization between emotionality and aesthetics remained intact. The equation was simply inverted so that his emotionality and mental instability became negligible factors, permitting his aesthetic prowess, although previously long-questioned, to come to the fore.

In similar wording, and again referencing critical opinion, Saltzman describes the intentions of the 1984 exhibit at the Metropolitan as striving:

> to set the documentary record straight, to sweep away romanticized images of van Gogh, and to replace the notion of the artist as an emotionally volatile, gifted amateur with a factually grounded account of the artist as a consummate professional, producing at full throttle. (260–261)

Here Saltzman concurs with the 'new' critical assessment that the reconstruction of Van Gogh's image is a function of setting the "record straight" in a factually accurate manner. Additionally, the "romanticized images" she cites as requiring abolishment – which elsewhere she refers to as the "melodrama" of his story – are grounded in the emotionality of both his person and his work (261). While I certainly do not wish to quarrel with assessments of Van Gogh as a consummate professional in formal and intellectual terms, evidence remains that he also was always "emotionally volatile." To omit this surely is to neglect an important aspect of his work and life and, therefore, to ignore a significant source of the meanings and value he, and other artists, hold for audiences.

Further, with regard to the critical and scholarly reevaluation of Van Gogh's place in modernism and in art history, Saltzman writes that during the 1980s, art historians "purged the lingering doubts about van Gogh as an artist of the highest order" (255). The unformulated question here is exactly whose doubts are being put to rest? Certainly neither the record-setting audiences of the 1980s attending exhibitions of his work nor the people who were buying his paintings at record-breaking prices.[13] Instead, the lingering doubts belong to members of the art field, Bourdieu's set of specialized agents engaged in the production of meanings and value, who were striving to catch up to the perceptions of a wider, much-admiring public. Again from Saltzman:

> In the course of the 1980s, van Gogh not only withstood the demanding inquiry of historians, but emerged as a painter of far greater intellectual substance than before. … in a way that would convince a skeptical late-twentieth-century audience of his true stature. (271)

To reiterate, the late-twentieth-century skeptics certainly were not the broader, art-viewing public, such as those who attended the 1998 "blockbuster" exhibition with which I began my discussion of Van Gogh. Such attendees weren't skeptics but avid fans. And they weren't fans because suddenly the veil of historical misinformation had been lifted to reveal Van Gogh's greater than previously believed "intellectual substance."

None of the reevaluation that occurred within the art field altered Van Gogh's already extensive popularity with a broader public. Nor did reassessment by art experts change the reasons for the widespread popularity of Van Gogh's paintings. Those reasons remained attributable to the emotionality of his work, coupled with the ostensible "melodrama" of his biography, together formulating Van Gogh's "accessibility," as recognized in the 1998 reviews. No sudden public growth in Van Gogh's popularity occurred because of his newly revealed formal skills or intellectual qualities. Instead, adjustment came from within the art field, working to synchronize itself with a much wider-held public view.

However, some members of the art field felt they could not make this move without a justificatory system based on pure aesthetics. In the course of trying to synchronize up to strongly favorable public perceptions, art experts sought – and largely failed – to reconstruct the collectively held meanings of Van Gogh's work. As discussion surrounding the 1998 exhibition reveals, Van Gogh's public value remains vested in a dominant view of him as a painter of emotion.

Emotions in the Vernacular Modernism of Cinema

Defining modernism as a range of aesthetic and cultural practices that "reflects upon the processes of modernization and the experience of modernity," film scholar Miriam Hansen argues for the importance of recognizing alternative forms of modernism beyond 'high art' (333). Modernist aesthetics, as a reflection of the experiences of modernity, also encompass "mass-produced and mass-consumed" aesthetic practices, which she identifies as "vernacular modernism" (Ibid.). Vernacular modernism incorporates the popular and the quotidian, recalling Bourdieu's references to the 'ordinariness' of popular aesthetics. Prominent among these vernacular forms is Hollywood cinema, which emerged and developed contemporaneously to "'high' or 'hegemonic modernism'" (332).

Hansen's point is that cinema, "as an industrially produced, mass-based" medium, and as a means of representing the "particular historical experience" of the late nineteenth and twentieth centuries, qualifies as a legitimate, extensive, and highly significant modernist mode, operating parallel to the high modernism of the formal and political avant-gardes (337, 341). In this analysis, mass produced or reproduced culture is a critical attribute of modernity and modernism, and not a series of cultural events working to undermine and embarrass the cause of high art.

The latter view, that popular culture works toward the goal of undermining the pure aesthetic or, at the very least, fails to grasp its import is exemplified by Dutch sociologist Christine Delhaye, writing in the early 1990s. She describes "the cultural elite in both the Netherlands and abroad" being dismayed by the popularization (tourists overwhelming the Van Gogh Museum in Amsterdam) and commercialization (endless merchandise being snapped up) of all aspects of the Van Gogh legacy (16). The result is a "sense of embarrassment" felt with regard to all forms of "cultural expression" featuring or associated with Van Gogh (16). As a consequence, popular culture "appropriations" of Van Gogh have made it difficult "to read Van Gogh's art independently of all the negative connotations with which popular culture has burdened it" (16). These statements demonstrate an ongoing need for high art to exist in distinction, in Bourdieu's terms, from the masses, suggesting a continuation of the cultural divide between high art and popular culture that has typified much of twentieth century modernism. Struggle over cultural ownership is raised by Delhaye in the notion of 'appropriation,' which assumes that Van Gogh, the modern artist, properly belongs to high art but has been removed from his rightful position. Further, popular culture's effects serve only to obscure, but can never clarify, the meanings and value of Van Gogh's work, rendering it difficult, perhaps impossible, to accurately interpret or properly appreciate his art. Finally, in this view, popular culture's contributions to the Van Gogh legend are wholly "negative," functioning only as a burden, never an asset. In these statements, we find exemplification of Bourdieu's arguments that high art's mandate rests in distinguishing itself from a mass or everyday culture against which the pure aesthetic is formulated.

In contrast, Hansen points out that cinema was perceived as the "incarnation of *the modern*," the "very symbol" of modern times (as in the Chaplin film which bears that title), succeeding in becoming a "global vernacular" that served as an "international modernist idiom" (337, 341; italics in original). The particular experiences of modernity conveyed through cinema encompassed "its moments of abundance, play, and radical possibility" as well as serving as a means by which the traumas, difficulties, and disappointments of modernity could be exercised or exorcised (341).

Popular film (and in the latter half of the twentieth century, television) performed these functions in large part through the "sensory-affective" aspects of the viewing experience (337). That is to say, mass-mediated modernism operated by enabling its audiences to *feel* their way through the era's radical possibilities and traumas, although Hansen speaks principally in terms of sensory experience. I wish to emphasize vernacular modernism's role as emotional event, that is, moving pictures that move us emotionally. She cites Walter Benjamin's 1928 description of the cinema as the place where "people whom nothing moves or touches any longer learn to cry again" (Benjamin qtd. in Hansen 343). Or perhaps come to laugh or scream.

The importance of Van Gogh and other modernist artists is understood to reside in the attempt, in their work, to make sense of the experiences of modernity. Esner argues that from an early date certain commentators viewed Van Gogh as giving "voice to a distinctly modern view of the world," citing a Dutch critic in 1904 who described Van Gogh's art as an "expression of the 'neurasthenic sensation' of his times," linking his work with the turn-of-the-century emotional disorder, neurasthenia, widely viewed as one of the effects associated with the dislocations of rapid modernization (Esner 142; R. Jacobsen qtd. in Esner 142). A century later, in a 2010 publication, art historian Griselda Pollock considers Van Gogh's works as "indices of a specific historical moment of modernization and modernity," although she ultimately finds him lacking on this count due to his retreat into an idealized Romanticism ("History" 54).

Understanding film, television, and other mass-mediated aesthetic practices as fully modernist, rather than simply part of the broad, vague, largely undefined category of 'popular culture,' remains a pressing critical issue. Bourdieu, for example, suggests the latter course when he speaks of the popular or everyday aesthetic as that which high modernism was formulated against. Failing to incorporate important strands of twentieth century popular aesthetics as part of a vernacular modernism runs the risk of comprehending popular culture as separate from the manifestations of modernism, a throwback to or lingering effect of earlier epochs. Thus in its reliance on emotions, twentieth century popular culture can be mistaken as a continuation of nineteenth century Romantic sentimentality, as Pollock appears to do in Van Gogh's case. While twentieth century vernacular modernism was certainly influenced by Romanticism, among other sources, especially in their joint emphasis on emotionality – just as high modernism was affected by Romantic notions of the tragic the artistic genius – much of twentieth century popular culture, following Hansen's arguments, is an original response to transformed cultural circumstances, including technological, economic, political, social, and other changes.

As alternative, often competing, modernisms, vernacular aesthetics and high art forms all participate in the late nineteenth and twentieth century struggles over the meanings of modernity. It is this struggle, I believe, that the art field was engaged in, as late as the 1980s and largely unsuccessfully, in their efforts to reinvent Van Gogh in order to reclaim him *for* high modernism *from* vernacular modernism. I am arguing that the struggle over modernism was fought, to a significant degree, over the role, meanings, and value of emotionality. Grossberg contends that popular culture consistently works to represent emotions and to retain its association with emotional experience (*Gotta* 79). In contrast, as we saw, Bourdieu outlines high modernism's disdain for the naivety and vulgarity of everyday aesthetics, including its "passions, emotions, and feelings," positioning ordinary culture as the enemy of the pure aesthetic (*Distinction* 4, 34–35).

Hansen observes that as the site of mass, communal consumption of stories and shared emotional experiences, cinema functioned as a specifically modern public sphere. I would suggest that Van Gogh, along with artists such as Picasso and Jackson Pollock, whose work is mass-produced through reproductions and mass-consumed through their extensive, popular appeal, have become, in practice, a part of vernacular modernism, functioning in an alternative public sphere to that of high art. Or, perhaps, we can understand them as playing simultaneous, but different roles in both modernisms. Among their overlapping vernacular purposes, cinema and Van Gogh share in common the incorporation and negotiation of emotionality and emotional excess – even if the former favors 'happy endings' while the latter alternates between the "anguished or ecstatic."

Effectively, then, the 'other' of high art distinction is the everyday indistinction of emotionality. However, I believe Bourdieu is incorrect about who emerged as dominant or, at any rate, about the extent of the domination, in the competing claims of high versus vernacular modernism. It is the right to accessible emotionality that a general, non-specialized public has sought and continues to seek in their reception of Van Gogh, on their own terms. A number of the conflicts and contradictions of modernism and modernity are encapsulated in the figure of Van Gogh. As a person, painter, and legend, he has served as a ground upon which to argue, and to struggle over, the meanings of art, emotionality, and mental illness. To contend that high art was victorious in the twentieth century debate between two modernist movements, one elite and the other vernacular, and that the former survives as the 'dominant,' 'official,' or 'hegemonic' form of modernism, is to over- look Van Gogh's popularity as a painter of emotion.

Madness and Moodiness

Before leaving Van Gogh, I address the specific role of mental illness to his legend and legacy. As we have seen, Bourdieu and Pollock contend that the function of modern art, and modern art history, is the creation of the artist-figure who, through his/her personal genius, serves as source of meaningfulness. Pollock argues that the purpose of madness – why it has been so closely linked to artistic genius – is to bolster this same version of subjectivity. Thus, "the meaning extracted from an artistic text" produces "an authorial subject, the artist" ("Artists" 65). Both genius and madness secure a particularly constituted subjectivity in which talent and excess are simultaneously interwoven "articulations of a personality" (Ibid. 81). From the contours of an artist's personality, the correspondence of artistic genius and madness create "a unity of life and work" which, in a circuit of recip- rocal verification, is presumed to "make visible the organizing subjectivity of the artist" (Ibid. 73). The work, as the result of genius, and the life, as the exemplification of madness, together ensure the 'artist' as the autono- mous, coherent center of meaning through the creativity he/she represents as inspired but tormented. Within this line of reasoning, madness participates in providing the necessary coherency of personality. It is a coherency based on damage, illness, and misery but, nonetheless, a useful structure for the organization of meaning attributed to the artistic personality in which, as we have seen, the work exists not to reveal the world but to make apparent the artist as transcendent creator.

While Pollock's arguments seem convincing regarding the link between artistic genius and madness, in which the mad subject is used to bolster the coherency of the artistic genius, I would like to consider, more closely, opera- tive definitions of 'madness' as they are applied in the case of Van Gogh. The most intense period of Van Gogh's difficulties begin in Arles, in the south of France, in December 1888. This period's onset is signaled by the infamous act of cutting off a portion of his left ear. Over a year and a half, Van Gogh experienced hallucinations, disorientation, severe agitation and anxiety, and intervals of amnesia that required three periods of hospitalization as well as a year-long stay in an asylum (from May 1889 to May 1890).[14] During these attacks, he moved "in and out of coherence" for stretches at a time (Naifeh and Smith 707). He "lashed out violently," "trusted no one, recognized no one ... took no food, could not sleep, would not write, and refused to talk," or if he did, his "words came out in an incoherent babble" (Ibid. 708, 725).

Additionally, in the midst of these bouts, he could not paint or draw. His biographers, Naifeh and Smith, describe six instances of such attacks but they also point out that, progressively, they become more intense: not a single attack but a series of occurrences which dissipate only to return, and the bouts persist for longer periods of time, for example, for a month or a month and a half instead of a week.[15] These psychotic episodes are the ones most closely associated with Van Gogh's madness, although much current opinion believes these were manifestations of a form of epilepsy (for example, Naifeh and Smith 749–751, 762–763; Pollock "Artists" 74).[16]

On the basis of these psychotic/epileptic episodes, Pollock argues that given their limited duration and the fact they were confined to a two-to-three year period in his mid-thirties, it is inaccurate to profess that this "condition determined what or how he painted. [Van Gogh] cannot be positioned as mad in the sense of a continuous or progressive alteration of mental states" ("Artists" 75–76). Similarly, Saltzman describes Van Gogh's multiple episodes as "intermittent" attacks that were "periodic in nature" (59, 25). In the determination that his illness manifested in a sporadic, limited manner, in terms of both episodic duration and time period in his life, scholars have felt justified in maintaining, as we saw earlier, "whatever his illness may have been … the fact [is] that it did not directly affect his work" (Ronald Pickvance qtd. in Saltzman 254).

Some years later, in a contradiction of her own statement that Van Gogh's illness did not determine the nature of his work, Pollock characterizes the critical distance put between Van Gogh's art and his madness – enabling his recalibration to a cerebral, diligent, and consummate professional – as a "sanitized" event, in the sense of rendering him "sane" ("Crows" 219). This same process of sanitization makes it possible for Zemel to interpret a painting such as *Self-Portrait (Dedicated to Paul Gauguin)*, painted in September 1888 (three months before wounding his ear), as predating "the record of any destabilizing episode" (*Van Gogh's Progress* 158). The choice of this particular painting on Zemel's part is interesting given that Van Gogh's troubled relationship with Gauguin has long been perceived as triggering his psychotic episodes and, specifically, the act of cutting off a portion of his ear. However, Zemel's ability to claim that the *Self-Portrait* predates destabilizing episodes, as with any scholar who maintains that Van Gogh's illness did not affect his art, rests on a very selective understanding of madness or mental illness or, indeed, of what constitutes a "destabilizing episode." For instance, according to Naifeh and Smith in their extensive biography, already in his childhood Van Gogh was "a boy of inexplicable fierceness" who, throughout his life, pursued all his activities "in a fury," that is, with extreme urgency, rapidity, and fervent single-mindedness (4). Although often interpreted as a sign of the psychotic/epileptic behavior that plagued his final two years, the frenzy with which Van Gogh painted was not indicative of his latter-day illness but part of a life-long pattern – and certainly a feature of his stylistic habits throughout the ten years in which he practiced art.

Well before he determined, in 1880, to become an artist, Van Gogh lived through significant periods of anger, despair, and what Naifeh and Smith describe as "bizarre excesses of behavior" (210). His bizarre behaviors included extended lengths of time during which he failed to eat or sleep, maintained a disheveled appearance in both hygiene and clothing, engaged in frequent combative encounters with other people, and pursued physically punitive activities such as walking extraordinary distances. For example, in England in 1876, when the school where he worked changed locations, Van Gogh walked more than fifty miles to the new site, although inexpensive transportation was readily available (Naifeh and Smith 122). From his new location ten miles outside of London, Van Gogh often walked into and returned from the city within a single day and, sometimes, more than once per day (Ibid.).

His biographers record "breakdowns" everywhere he lived (Naifeh and Smith 434). And throughout his life, he demonstrates social ineptitude resulting in isolation. His relations with acquaintances, friends, and family, including his brother Theo, were typified by prolonged arguments and habitual upheaval. In an apparent attempt to minimize Van Gogh's interpersonal difficulties and, therefore, the question of his mental stability, Zemel in an understatement, describes him as "hardly remembered for close personal relationships" (*Van Gogh's Progress* 17). More bluntly, reporting on one occasion of many, Naifeh and Smith characterize the tone of contact between Vincent and Theo, the person with whom he maintained the closest, most enduring relationship, as suffused with "acrimony," during which Vincent, in his letters, "unleashed a torrent of abuse" on his brother (414).

Van Gogh describes his existence as beleaguered by "temporary fits of weakness, nervousness and melancholy" (Vincent Van Gogh in 1883 when living in The Hague qtd. in Naifeh and Smith 289). Other people, throughout his life, regarded him, at best, as odd or eccentric and, equally often, as "crazy," treating him – or shunning him – as mad (Naifeh and Smith 418, 434).[17] Clearly, all of Van Gogh's interactions with friends did not end in psychotic episodes; however, the tenor of his relations with Gauguin do not represent an unfamiliar departure from other social interactions in his life, which often followed a pattern of heated, lengthy arguments, an insurmountable strain that limited contact and, ultimately, a breaking off of the relationship.

An alternative view to understanding Van Gogh's illness as periodic, intermittent, and confined to his mid-thirties, is to consider his difficulties constitutive of "a life of struggle, poverty, and psychological pain" (58), which is the position attributed by Saltzman to numerous art critics, from the period shortly following the artist's death until the reformulation of his image in the 1980s as "the new Van Gogh." Regarding Van Gogh as subject to life-long psychological troubles entails viewing some form of mental illness as part of his existence prior to the onset, in December 1988, of psychosis, possibly associated with epilepsy.

Evidence exists that Theo Van Gogh perceived his brother's worsening condition, resulting in hospitalization, as a continuation of previous and ongoing problems. In a letter to his then-fiancée, Jo Bonger, following Vincent's first hospitalization in December 1888, Theo writes: "the attack was the culmination of a variety of things that had been pushing him in that direction over a long period of time" (Theo Van Gogh, Jan. 1, 1889 qtd. in Naifeh and Smith 712). In the following excerpts from another letter to Jo Bonger written around the time of Vincent's second hospitalization in February, 1889, when he was faced with the decision of putting Vincent in an asylum, Theo attempts to explain the impossibility of having his brother live either with the two of them in Paris or with his mother and sister in the Netherlands:

> From his style of dress and demeanor you can see at once that he is different and for years everyone who sees him has said *C'est un fou* [he's a madman]. Even those with whom he is the best of friends find him difficult to get along with.
>
> There's no such thing as a peaceful environment for him. … He spares nothing and no one. (Theo Van Gogh, Feb. 14, 1889 [qtd. in Naifeh and Smith 733])

Theo saw his brother only once during his hospitalizations (and never during his asylum stay) for a matter of hours on December 25, 1888, immediately following Vincent's first attack (Naifeh and Smith 706). This suggests that a number of the specific details in Theo's descriptions, above, are based on his brother's behavior outside the bounds of the episodes for which he was hospitalized.

If we accept that Theo is referring to an ongoing but intensified set of circumstances rather than an entirely new situation in his description of his brother's health, then it becomes highly questionable to maintain, as Saltzman does in her statement cited earlier, that the 1980s art historical revision of Van Gogh served to "sweep away" the romanticized view of him as "an emotionally volatile, gifted amateur" in favor of a more accurate image of the artist as a "consummate professional" (260–261). What cannot be so easily swept away in the recalibration of Van Gogh's illness, which attempts to confine it to his final year and a half, is the emotional volatility he experienced for much of his life and expressed in much of his work. An instance of the tendency to ignore emotional volatility in appraising Van Gogh's work is Zemel's previously mentioned analysis of *Self-Portrait (Dedicated to Paul Gauguin)*. The painting can be said to precede any destabilizing episode experienced by Van Gogh only if one expressly ignores or negates the evidence of emotional volatility that consistently accompanied much of his life.

Even if we take into account the notion that Naifeh's and Smith's biography falls into the category of romanticized renditions of Van Gogh as tormented genius, to which art historians such as Pollock strongly object, their (and other biographers') detailing of events in his existence indicate social and emotional disorders – emotional volatility – too numerous, specific, and consistent to dismiss. Yet Naifeh and Smith, after itemizing a lifetime of difficulties and disorder ("In the princely Hague they spat on him; in Neunen, they banished him; in Arles, they threw stones at him" [748]), conclude by summarizing Van Gogh's existence as "years of failure, penury, guilt, loneliness, and finally madness" (858). Compiling his life difficulties in this sequence and manner suggests he was mad only at the end ("finally") and that his madness occurs as a result of other events in his life, including failure, penury, guilt, and loneliness.[18]

The emotionality that holds such a prominent position in the legend of Van Gogh's life and art becomes subjected to attempts at displacement at least twice. First, elimination of emotionality occurs in efforts to render him a worthy modernist figure, in which he resurfaces as a consummate professional, an artist of the highest order befitting the echelons of high art. In this initial displacement, instead of exhibiting a style driven by emotional intensity, he is refigured as a painter of formal and intellectual substance in the cause and accomplishments of a pure aesthetic. In the second displacement of emotionality, his madness is dismissed as barely a factor in his creativity or aesthetic successes. In the process of sanitizing his madness, his emotional volatility also is ostensibly vanquished so that no form of disorder directly affects his work. Which is to say, if one manages to dismiss or limit the madness (psychosis), assumptions exist that issues of moodiness (emotional disorders) also are alleviated. An important component of what occurs in the debates over Van Gogh's legacy involves the specific formulation of madness as psychosis. As discussed in Chapters One and Two, psychoses tend to be regarded as serious, severe, or major mental illnesses while neuroses – reformulated contemporarily as mood and anxiety disorders – are perceived as minor, milder, or less harmful. Such a view enables the reduction of certain emotional disorders to simple unhappiness, problems of living, or malaise, as occurs in the case of 'the new Van Gogh.'

It is critical to emphasize that psychoses have intense emotional aspects. These are not circumstances in which issues of rationality can be neatly excised from emotionality, despite efforts to do so. In Van Gogh's instance, his psychotic episodes encompassed severe anxiety, agitation, "outbursts of temper," "brooding silence," paranoia, panic, and other mood swings (Naifeh and Smith 701, 708, 749). Further, symptoms of temporal lobe epilepsy may well include irritation, anger, rage, "easy excitability, furious work habits," apathy, depression, impulsiveness, aggression, and other forms of "profound mental suffering" and labile moods (Ibid. 751, 760–761, 750). However, Van Gogh's legacy represents an overarching cultural displacement of emotionality in which, if madness as psychosis can be dismissed, then the need to address any emotional disorders attached to his temperamental volatility, can be dispensed with or minimized as well. In these terms, the effort to explain away Van Gogh's madness as intermittent and occurring only in the last year and a half of his life assumes that the 'problem' of his emotional turmoil is gathered up and dealt with via the same explanation. Thus, once the issue of madness as psychosis presumably is put to rest, concerns about his emotional volatility also disappear as if satisfactorily resolved. Emotional volatility is recognized as disturbing when it exists in conjunction with a failure of lucidity, but often treated as minor or normal vicissitudes when appearing in stand-alone fashion.[19] Yet, 'madness' is not equivalent to, nor does it capture, all that is extended in the notion of 'moodiness.' While Van Gogh's form of epilepsy or psychosis may have lain dormant for long periods of time between episodes, as Naifeh and Smith point out, his social and emotional difficulties did not (750).

Finally, the emotions sought and lauded in artists such as Van Gogh represent a particular, narrow range out of the spectrum of all possible feelings. These often include states such as anguish, self-destructiveness, mental suffering, and isolation, characteristics most readily associated with tormented genius. Pollock observes that the myth associated with Van Gogh is "a violent one" ("History" 59). Saltzman notes that Seurat died of diphtheria at the age of thirty-two in 1891, in the year following and five years junior to Van Gogh. At the time, the pointillist was the far better known and admired painter. Yet, Seurat's illness and premature death were not connected to his reputation or to the meanings of his work, in the same way they were in Van Gogh's case (58).[20] This discrepancy in the treatment between Van Gogh and other artists such as Seurat has been attributed to public fascination with Van Gogh that resides in an excessive attraction to the emotional 'melodrama' of his life, at the price of attention to his body of work. However, this explanation seems insufficient in that Van Gogh's life story is embodied by his paintings, which people go to museums to see or buy reproductions of, in record numbers. It remains equally questionable whether aesthetic experts are capable of objective, disinterested assessments of his work, segregated from the renowned turbulence of his life and personality, as is also claimed.

Referring to *Lust for Life*, Pollock observes that the task of a biography, whether written or filmic, lies in creating "a coherent personality" by manufacturing a unity of all the disparate elements belonging to any given human existence ("Crows" 225). As we have seen, these are also the terms in which she understands the primary occupation of modern art history: the production of the coherent, individual artist "as the exclusive source of meaning" ("Artists" 58). Arguably, the production of a coherent personality also stands as the primary aim of the psy fields, a topic examined more closely in the next chapter. Pollock certainly views the emergence of psychiatry in the same historical period as modernism as complicit in sustaining the reification of the artist as both an inspired and a disordered individual (Ibid. 70). She also intimates, I believe correctly, that aesthetic history's production of the artist as a particular kind of subjectivity – the mad genius – is little different from they way figures like Van Gogh are venerated in popular culture, as brilliant but, or because, mad (Ibid. 61). Although the public at large may be repeatedly criticized for its apparent fascination with Van Gogh's life over his work, a theory of the modern artist based on the "charismatic ideology of 'creation,'" as Bourdieu describes it, or the coherency of the inspired artist as genius, effectively provides the theoretical and intellectual justification for just such a popular approach. In this instance, aesthetic theory, the psy fields, and popular culture all work, not in opposition but in conjunction with one another, to create a coherent personality of the artist as exceptionality, whether exceptional in terms of intellectual and aesthetic knowledge or emotional depth of feeling. Within this frame, it remains an open question whether popular cultural judgments on the arts can be considered "the exact opposite" of the pure aesthetic (Bourdieu, *Distinction* 4–5). In the final analysis, that of which popular culture is so often accused, of emphasizing personality over all other concerns, resembles the activities of aesthetics in establishing the artist as a particular form of coherent subjectivity: inspired but insane, brilliant but damaged, the source of all meaning but unable to withstand the emotional strains of this world.

In Chapter Four I return to psychology, focusing on the category of mental illness known as personality disorders. In particular, I consider how they took shape, on the one hand, as part of recent developments in the pivotal *Diagnostic and Statistical Manual of Mental Disorders* and, on the other hand, in the context of the emergence of social identity movements.

Notes

1. For a fuller account of the contrasts between theatrical melodrama and dramatic realism, particularly as they concern emotionality, see Chapter Two.
2. "Van Gogh's Van Goghs: Masterpieces from the Van Gogh Museum, Amsterdam" took place at the National Gallery of Art in Washington and comprised over seventy of his paintings. "Jackson Pollack: A Retrospective" was held at New York's Museum of Modern Art.
3. As for Jackson Pollock, "letting the paint leap off the end of a stick … allowed his deepest feelings to go directly into his pictures" (Plagens 80).
4. The subtitle reads in full: "A Blockbuster Exhibit by the Epitome of the Tragic Artist, Van Gogh, Could Be One of the USA's Biggest Cultural Attractions Ever" (Puente 1A).
5. This is not to suggest that Zemel argues critical viewpoints were ever unanimous or monolithic in any national context. Instead, they were subject to contestation and negotiation. In the Netherlands, for instance, where Van Gogh was largely welcomed and praised, one could also read: "the sick condition of his mind, that led to such a tragic end, prevented him from thinking and feeling soundly." (David van der Kellen qtd. in Zemel, *Formation* 21). The tendency exists, in a given national context, for a certain perspective to become more and more widely accepted over time and, therefore, ultimately the predominant view.
6. The record for *Portrait of Dr. Gachet* was not surpassed until 2004 with the sale of Picasso's *Garçon à la pipe* for $104.2 million.
7. Where Zemel specifies 1920, Saltzman argues Van Gogh's reputation solidified by 1931 (155).

8. These were followed by a retrospective of Van Gogh's work at New York's Metropolitan Museum in 1949 and the release of the film version of *Lust for Life*, directed by Vincent Minnelli, in 1956.

9. Naifeh and Smith speak of Van Gogh's "broadened buttocks, misaligned limbs, enlarged feet, crooked faces, or quivering contours" as well as "his lifeless faces and grotesque hands" (514, 679). Despite rendering a largely unsympathetic portrait of Gauguin, Naifeh and Smith nonetheless make it clear they believe Gauguin to be the better, more skilled draftsperson and painter, in technical and formal terms (679).

10. *Wheatfield with a Rising Sun* sold in 1985 for $9.9 million; *Vase with Fifteen Sun-flowers* sold in 1987 for $39.9 million; *Irises* also sold in 1987, for $53.9 million; *Portrait of Joseph Roulin* went for $58 million plus an exchange of works, along with *Bridge at Trinquetaille* for $20 million, and *Portrait of Adeline Ravoux* for $13.75 million, in 1989; 1990 saw the sale of *Self-Portrait (Dedicated to Charles Laval)* for $26.4 million and *Portrait of Dr. Gachet* (1890) for $82.5 million.

11. "Van Gogh in Arles" in 1984 and "Van Gogh in Saint-Rémy and Auvers" in 1987.

12. For example, Saltzman quotes British art scholar and author of the catalogue for the 1984 Metropolitan exhibit, "Van Gogh in Arles," Ronald Pickvance: "In van Gogh's case, there was what has been seen as a preordained progression from asylum (with the implied assumption of madness) to suicide, which has fueled the myth of the mad genius. But whatever his illness may have been … the fact [is] that it did not directly affect his work" (Pickvance qtd. in Saltzman 254).

13. In 1987, *Vase with Fifteen Sunflowers* was sold to a Japanese insurance company. *Irises* was sold to an Australian "tycoon" (Saltzman 277); when the tycoon couldn't cover the sale price of $53.9 million it was resold to the Getty Museum in California. *Portrait of Dr. Gachet* was bought by the head of a Japanese paper company. That these paintings sold to people beyond the art field is worth noting. Saltzman points out that in the past there may have been only twelve to eighteen potential buyers, all known collectors. By the 1980s most sales went to auction in order to reach the more than 200 potential buyers who had both the money and the interest to purchase such paintings (286–287).

14. The period of Van Gogh's psychotic episodes lasted from late December 1888 to April 1890, after which he left the south of France. There is no record of further bouts during his stay in Auvers from mid-May 1890 until his death in late July of the same year.

15. Pollock references seven "fits" between 1887 and 1890 ("Artists" 74). Naifeh and Smith believe there is evidence of two other, earlier episodes: one in September, 1883 in Drenthe, in the Netherlands, and the second during his stay in Antwerp, Belgium, in January and February 1886 (356, 702).

16. Turning to psychiatric accounts for elucidation on Van Gogh's illness remains precarious given the extensive number of differing diagnoses that have been made. Blumer, in 2002, indicates more than 150 physicians have written on the subject and 30 distinct diagnoses have been conjectured (519, 522).

17. Here, Naifeh and Smith refer specifically to events that occurred while Van Gogh was living in the Netherlands, the first in Drenthe in 1883 and the second in Neunen in 1885.

18. The inclusion of penury is particularly puzzling because Naifeh and Smith repeatedly point out that the money Theo provides Vincent on a monthly basis is more than adequate. His monthly stipend while in The Hague was more than the average

workman supported an entire family on, and in the south of France his financial contribution from Theo was twice as much as a teacher's earnings (271, 300, 579). Further, they portray Van Gogh as a "spendthrift" on items such as drawing and painting supplies, models, home furnishings, and his collection of prints (271).

19. Here, Van Gogh's letters play an important role as they often are taken as proof of lucidity throughout his life and, consequently, support contentions that question whether he ever suffered from mental illness, with the exception of his latter-day psychotic/epileptic episodes, during which he either could not write coherently or could not write at all. The letters are accepted as evidence of lucidity and, therefore, lack of illness, even in the sections where he is describing emotional distress.

20. Part of the explanation for the difference in historical treatment rests with the notion that Van Gogh's death was self-inflicted while Seurat's was 'natural.' However, Naifeh and Smith build the case, in considerable detail, that Van Gogh's gunshot wound was not suicide but an accidental shooting by a teenager who spent time with the artist in Auvers, often in order to taunt him (see their Chapter 43 and Appendix).

4 Personality Disorders, Biopsychiatry, and the Problem of Social Identity

In a 2001 essay, Manning asks why such a "very rapid elaboration of the category of personality disorder" has occurred since 1980, when it first appeared as a separate, detailed classification set in the *Diagnostic and Statistical Manual of Mental Disorders (DSM-III)* (76). Beginning with *DSM-III,* personality disorders were designated as a distinct category or axis of disorders – Axis II – intended to distinguish them from the more familiar Axis I diagnoses which include psychoses (such as schizophrenia), mood disorders, and anxiety disorders. Although used as a term for psychopathology since the early twentieth century, Manning observes that 'personality disorder' underwent wider application as a theoretical concept from the early 1960s, particularly in the United States. He conjectures that the cultural changes starting in the 1960s served as a "key stimulus" for their development (86). By 1980, personality disorders had received sufficient legitimacy to be included as a stand-alone classification of mental disorders, on a discrete axis, in the American Psychiatric Association's highly influential encyclopedia of psychopathological classification, as a distinct form of "severe or long-term nonpsychotic distress" (L. Brown 209).

The *DSM* functions as the most widely used guidebook for mental disorders on an international scale, pivotal for purposes of clinical diagnosis, insurance reimbursement, research funding, public mental health policy, and as 'proof' of the very existence of a psychic illness. Routinely referred to as psychiatry's bible, the *DSMs* reflect established positions within psy, although it is crucial to keep in mind that much of what is codified therein remains highly contentious, including among those who participate in authoring the *DSMs.*

DSM-III, the 1980 edition that established personality disorders as a discrete class of mental dysfunctions, was itself considered a watershed moment in the history of psychiatric classification or nosology. The transition to explicit, descriptive diagnostic criteria was both conceived and received as a more scientifically rigorous approach to mental illness, in comparison to previous *DSMs (I* and *II)* and their heavily psychoanalytic influences. Psychodynamic therapies came to be viewed as providing an etiological classification system, based on purported causes of respective illnesses that were vague, conjectural, and unverifiable. By the era of *DSM III,* biomedical perspectives had grown to dominant perspectives within the American Psychiatric Association and across psy fields in general.

The biomedical approach borrows from anatomical medicine's system of organization based on "specific disease entities," referring to the designated types or kinds of mental illness, which are then identified, for diagnostic purposes, in terms of their symptomology (Horwitz 2). Hence, the biomedical approach is referred to as descriptive psychiatry – designated by symptoms – in contrast to the etiological process associated with psychoanalysis and its subsequent psychodynamic variations, which tend to identify mental illness through, often unconscious, explanations of cause, such as repression. The movement to biomedical psychiatry was intended, through its links to scientific and medical methodologies, to provide the psy disciplines with the credibility many perceived them to be lacking. Scientific psychiatry's mission was to find "stable foundations that might restore a long lost sense of certitude to the discipline" because "the emancipatory promise of psychological knowledge," the promise to discover, explain, treat, and cure mental illness has remained largely unfulfilled (Brown and Stenner 21; Greco and Stenner 15). Thus, personality disorders in their contemporary form emerge alongside the increasingly biomedical and scientific context that shaped *DMS III*.

However, Manning's question about the timing of their appearance in social terms is intriguing. As discussed in Chapter Two, Rose argues that:

> Over the first 60 years or so of the twentieth century, human beings came to understand themselves as inhabited by a deep interior psychological space, to evaluate themselves and to act upon themselves in terms of this belief.
>
> ("Disorders" 480)

If this is the case, how do we account for the fact that personality disorders – the indicators of malfunctions in our "deep interior psychological space" – came to be solidified only in the latter part of the century, after an initial sixty years or so of psychological interiority defined as personality? Indeed, personality disorders do not emerge in a substantial, albeit contested, configuration until a time period in which Rose also suggests that the deep interiority of the human psyche may be beginning to "flatten out" or disappear, with the rise of the neurochemical self stressed by emerging brain and genetic sciences ("Psychology as Social Science" 447, 460). Theorists like Rose argue that characteristics of normality and pathology may no longer apply even to physiological states. Rose points out that at the genomic level there exists no 'normal' but only variety and dissimilarity ("Normality" 73–74, 80). We are all unique or idiosyncratically different. There is no genetic zero point from which we depart when we become ill, no 'standard' genetic makeup to compare ourselves to, no singular efficacious or adaptive genetic model. Normality at the biogenetic level, as "a statistical average, a judgment of desireability, and an idea of health and illness" is chimeric (Ibid. 74). We are all aggregations of multiplicity, complexity, and variation.

As we saw in Chapter Two, Rose specifically links the constitution of an interior, psychological space to the concepts of individualism and personality, among other factors. Thus psychology, at its outset, served as a "technology of individualization" concerned with the management of people through the formulation of "personality" ("Psychology as Social Science" 447–448; 451–452). Yet following Manning's timeline, personality disorders as concepts of psychic abnormality took on more expansive and specific shape amidst the cultural changes of the 1960s and 1970s, to emerge only in that era in the form in which we currently understand them. As such, personality disorders do not belong with the development of psychological interiority and personality in the first sixty years of the century. Instead, they are more contemporaneous with the social identity movements of the '60s and '70s, including civil rights, feminism, and gay rights. Therefore, in temporal terms, they are more congruent with the turn to political and theoretical concerns surrounding 'identity' in the decades that saw out the twentieth century and welcomed in the twenty-first. In this chapter, I argue that personality disorders can be understood, in part, as a response to late-twentieth-century preoccupations with social collectivities as constitutive of individual identities. Although perhaps not as immediately identifiable as belonging to the category of 'emotional disorders' as those in the mood or anxiety classes, I turn to the example of personality disorders, as "severe or long-term nonpsychotic distress," because of the embeddedness of felt emotional experience as well as interpersonal and socioemotional expression in the concept of properly functioning personality as well as to its malfunctions.

Biopsychiatry

Disciplines gathered under the relatively recent labels of biological or scientific psychiatry are extensive, and include genetics, evolutionary biology, neuroscience, biochemistry, psychopharmacology, and empirical-based cognitive sciences. The credibility of scientific psy resides in the hope that "the brain will yield what psychiatry has long sought: a taxonomy of disorders validated by biochemical findings" or other irrefutable physiological proof of mental illness (Greenberg, *The Book of Woe* 352). The brain currently is believed to hold the key because the uncovering of its, thus far, mysterious workings might resolve long standing accusations of psychiatry's lack of a valid scientific basis in diagnosing and treating mental illnesses. While such organic proof does not yet exist, many in the biopsychiatric disciplines stake their claim on the assertion that science and medicine will progress to the point of having the capacity to thoroughly and accurately understand the origins and, thereby, effectively treat or cure mental illness, an outcome that has historically and to date largely eluded the psy fields.

In the short run, biopsychiatry lodges its current and future reputation on finding biological markers, material signs or indicators of the verifiable presence of mental illness, for instance, through neuroimaging, discussed in Chapter Five. Many believe that locating such biological markers will lead, in the long term, to establishing the anatomical causes of mental illness (for example, a gene or genes for schizophrenia; the biochemical neurotransmitters responsible for or the brain circuitry that malfunctions in mood or anxiety disorders). Darrel Regier, vice chair of the APA's task force responsible for *DSM-5* (2013), maintains that the route to such discoveries lies in establishing "better syndrome boundaries," that is, clearly distinguishing among various mental disorders, with the ultimate goal of determining "the statistically valid cutpoints between normal and pathological" (Regier qtd. in Greenberg, *The Book of Woe* 128). The immediate task at hand, in this analysis, is to continue to pursue "the threshold" between normality and abnormality, the long sought holy grail of the psy fields (see Chapter Two) (Regier qtd. in Greenberg, *The Book of Woe* 175).

1980's *DSM-III*, with its divergence to biomedical models of disease and symptomology was celebrated, on the one hand, as a major achievement for scientific psy, in its inauguration of a "biomedical revolution" in the field (Kirk, Gomory, and Cohen 176, 148). On the other hand, the *DSMs*, beginning with *DSM-III*, have been widely blamed for the current crises besetting psychopathology, as explicitly charged in the titles of influential books, such as *Making Us Crazy: DSM: The Psychiatric Bible and the Creation of Mental Disorders* (Kutchins and Kirk), and *The Book of Woe: The DSM and the Unmaking of Psychiatry* (Greenberg). Kirk, Gomery, and Cohen allege that from its third edition, *DSM* has become "a massive compendium of human troubles," merely masquerading as reliable or valid scientific progress, which falsely claims to be moving "ever closer to finding causes and cures" for mental illnesses (126, 1).

In particular, *DSM-III* and subsequent editions have been held almost single-handedly responsible for the proliferation of mental disorders, believed to have directly caused the current state of global epidemic which, as we saw in Chapter Two, threatens to undermine the very foundations of psy as viable disciplines. *DSM-I* in 1952 itemized approximately 100 different disorders, *DSM-III* indicates 265, and the current *DSM-5* suggests in the range of 300. The attribution of blame to the *DSM* follows the reasoning that their significant expansion in types of mental disorders has enabled the dramatic increase in the number of people who, by its standards, legitimately can be diagnosed as suffering from a mental illness. For *DSM-III's* many critics, the majority of new disorders were not valid medical or scientific determinations but, as discussed in Chapter Two, the erroneous medicalizing of simple unhappiness, problems of living, normal misery, or ordinary "human troubles." The *DSMs* have reframed "troublesome problems in living" or "the management of misery and misbehavior" into biomedical illness (Kirk, Gomory, and Cohen ix, 2). In this view, an inseparable link occurs between the increased number of existing disorders and the proliferation of those said to be suffering from mental illness.

Thus, according to differing accounts, *DSM-III* heralds or can be blamed for a significant turning point in the history of psychopathology. Although the *DSMs*, since version three in 1980 and most recently *DSM-5* issued in 2013, are routinely held responsible for psy's current crises, in particular the global epidemic of emotional disorders, I consider these difficulties to belong to psy on a larger scale. Which is to say, the *DSMs* are more symptomatic of psy's problems than their causes. Certainly, a portion of the current difficulties can be attributed to the contemporary pervasiveness of medical, biopsychiatric, and neuroscientific approaches, now dominating the psy fields, discussed further in this chapter and in the next. However, the crises also can be attributed, in part, to occurrences taking place before 'the biomedical revolution,' such as the much broader inclusion of emotionality since the advent of neuroses, a significant factor in the proliferation of people who have come to be considered mentally disordered (see Chapters One and Two). Finally, as we will see, sociocultural changes in the decades just prior to, and since, 1980 can also be interpreted as undermining the contemporary psy fields' stability and sense of purpose. In this chapter, I turn to personality disorders in order to approach some of the current problems surrounding the *DSMs* and facing psychopathology more generally.

Personality and Its Disorders

> Personality *traits* are enduring patterns of perceiving, relating to, and thinking about the environment and oneself, and are exhibited in a wide range of important social and personal contexts. It is only when *personality traits* are inflexible and maladaptive and cause either significant impairment in social or occupational functioning or subjective distress that they constitute *Personality Disorders*.
>
> (*DSM-III*, 305; italics in original)

The conceptualization of 'personality' is deeply personal. Personality, as dominantly culturally constituted in the West, enshrines each individual as not only unique but idiosyncratic. Therefore, any given personality trait is also always potentially idiosyncratic and, as such, difficult to measure in terms of normality/abnormality. It is precisely our personalities as expressions of individuality that render the notion of a commonality of traits – or symptoms – so difficult to account for within the paradigm of 'personality.' In common understanding, every individual is an assemblage of multiple traits, some of which may be considered beneficial and others detrimental to optimal functioning. Such multiplicity and variation are fundamental conditions required for the existence of personality as the marker of a unique individual. Traits, the entities that serve as the building blocks of personality, "can combine in virtually an infinite number of ways – which accords with our day-to-day sense that all individuals have their own unique personalities" (Skodol et al., "Personality Disorder" 15). And a good many of the traits that constitute personality are emotional in nature. Like emotions with which it is so closely aligned, personality is a complex, fluid network that we use to identify who we believe we are as selves.

As noted above, one strategy advocated by influential figures in contemporary psy is to continue the search for "the threshold" between normality and abnormality. However, like emotionality, personality has been difficult to accommodate within binary notions of healthy versus pathological. 'Abnormal' in psychology and psychiatry has been described, variously, as aberrance, irregularity, maladaptation, or disease. In response, 'normal' can be configured in a number of ways: as the average (a statistical mean), the common (the majority), the adaptive (effective), and/or the healthy (applying a physiological analogy). Each of these, however, bears evident limitations when applied to personality.

A statistical average is useful for situations in which outliers serve as misrepresentative, as in the instance of quantitative analysis. For human functioning, however, outliers can be highly valued, whether they are outstanding athletes, artistic geniuses, or intellectual 'aberrations.' Indeed, a few pre-*DSM* schemas for character disorders included desirable social anomalies, such as talent, precisely because they were, nonetheless, abnormal (Berrios 433). For example, Kurt Schneider in 1921 incorporated "eminently creative and intelligent individuals" as a separate group in his classification of characterological types because they represented "statistical deviations from an estimated average norm" (Sass and Herpetz 639–640).

Normal personality can also be considered that which is common, reflecting the majority population. Such a criterion is then based on social norms and conventions in which those who conform are normal. However, personality as a multifaceted network means that every individual may conform in terms of some traits but deviate idiosyncratically in others (Millon and Grossman, "Evolutionary Model" 8). Even in the cases of reliably diagnosed severe personality disorders, only certain traits are dysfunctional. Conversely, some traits in every individual can be considered to deviate from social norms. In other words, personality is not a coherent unit but a complex, variegated system composed of nearly limitless aspects.

In order to guard against the limitations of normality based on statistical averages or majority convention, the criterion of adaptive or functional behavior is often simultaneously applied. An adaptive or maladaptive criterion refers to "the effectiveness or ineffectiveness of a person's behavior" or personality traits (Maddux, Gosselin, and Winstead 6). Yet, here too, problems abound because "even behaviors that are statistically rare and therefore abnormal" can be adaptive (Ibid.) or, conversely, widespread social norms might be quite maladaptive. Additionally, actions that are adaptive in one set of circumstances may prove maladaptive at another moment in time or in an alternate context (Millon and Grossman, "Evolutionary Model" 8). For example, what does 'average' or 'adaptive' trust look like? What might be considered an optimal, effective amount, degree, or type of trust versus suspicion? The same attribute, in only slightly altered social conditions, can be considered 'trusting' as a positive quality or 'too trusting' as a flawed tendency.

And of course, mental and emotional experiences also have long been theorized through analogies to physiological health versus illness or disease (see Chapter One). This is an assumption made in *DSM-III* and following editions, as indicated by their utilization of a biomedical paradigm. As discussed, the publication of *DSM-III* in 1980 was considered a significant turning point in the development of personality disorders. For the first time, they were presented as a distinct class of disorders, on Axis II, and itemized in terms of the eleven personality disorders on which agreement for the validity of their existence could be reached.[1] Additionally, they were grouped into three clusters, based on similarity of characteristics: cluster A, designated as odd or eccentric behavior, cluster B considered dramatic, emotional, or erratic in type, and cluster C, identified as anxious or fearful in tenor.

Cluster A personality disorders (paranoid, schizoid, schizotypal), although identified by the behavioral criteria of odd or eccentric, feature prominent emotional characteristics in their symptomatology.[2] The remaining two clusters are identified overtly by emotions. Cluster B, the dramatic, emotional, and erratic grouping, encompasses borderline, antisocial, histrionic, and narcissistic personality disorders.[3] Cluster C personality disorders (avoidant, dependent, compulsive and passive-aggressive) are also identified by emotions, in this case along the anxiety and fear spectrum.[4]

The effects of *DSM-III* were immediate and profound, resulting in a significantly increased number of diagnoses of personality disorder as well as a sizable augmentation in research studies devoted to this class of mental illness (Lenzenweger and Clarkin 7; Strack xx; Pilkonis et al. 69; Emmelkamp and Power 363; Oldham 7). A number of studies have indicated that the prevalence rate for personality disorders is strikingly high. The most common figures cited point to between 9 percent and 15 percent of the general population who fit the diagnostic criteria for at least one of the personality disorders.[5] In discussing their only recent establishment as a sanctioned, related group of illnesses, I am not suggesting that the phenomena to which personality disorders point are either imaginary or irrelevant. Both their substantial prevalence and the often extreme misery experienced by those thus diagnosed merit serious attention. As early as 1938, Adolph Stern noted of character disorders:

> There is no doubt that such patients suffer much. ... They hurt themselves in their business, professional, social, in fact all affective relationships. (475)

At the same time, a widely held opinion exists that the prognosis for personality disorders is poor and treatment options limited (Dolan, Warren, and Norton 274, 275; Coker and Widiger 202; Fowler, O'Donohue, and Lilienfeld 11; Tyrer, Casey, and Ferguson 463, 468; Stern 467, 473, 475; Manning 76). Tyrer, Casey, and Ferguson call the personality disorders "a diagnosis of despair," in part because they fare so badly within the capabilities of contemporary psychopharmacology or psychotherapies (463). In an article titled, "Personality Disorder: The Patients Psychiatrists Dislike," Lewis and Appleby argue that the entire category of personality disorders should be jettisoned because, according to their study, "psychiatrists form pejorative, judgemental, and rejecting attitudes" to those thus diagnosed (47). Such patients are viewed as difficult, manipulative, attention-seeking, annoying, unsympathetic, noncompliant, and less deserving of time and treatment than patients with other mental disorders (Ibid. 44, 47, 48). Even those in the discipline who object to such a negative view of the prognosis for personality disorders hardly paint an optimistic picture. Coker and Widiger suggest that treatment of personality disorders "can produce clinically and socially meaningful changes;" however, "the development of an ideal or fully healthy personality structure is unlikely" (202).

As the excerpt from *DSM III* at the beginning of this section makes clear, a symptom is a sign of disorder in descriptive psychopathology. Diagnoses for personality disorders are made on the basis of a requisite number of such symptoms. In contrast, a trait comprises the "conceptual unit of analysis" that, aggregated with an individual's other traits, constitutes a properly functioning personality (Berrios 423). Thus traits are adaptive features of personality, while symptoms reference their maladaptive versions. This raises the question how, precisely, do traits and symptoms differ given pervasive variation among individuals? Is the difference between an adaptive trait and a maladaptive symptom only a matter of degree, as Tyrer, Casey, and Gall suggest? (407). Yet Maddux, Gosselin, and Winstead remind us that every "so-called normal personality" embodies what could be considered maladaptive facets (6). If so, at what point and in which ways does a person who is viewed as suspicious or distrustful 'by nature' become someone with paranoid personality disorder? (Wedding, Boyd, and Niemiec 74). Can the same behavior be regarded as a trait in one person but a symptom in another? Might an individual display a trait in one context that is assessed as a symptom in a different set of circumstances?

Such difficulties were exacerbated by the fact that *DSM-III* failed to provide guidelines by which to distinguish "normal personality variation" from personality disorders, or personality traits from symptoms (Tyrer, "What's Wrong" 284; Berrios 419). Thus, it remained unclear at what specific degree personality traits came to signify pathology versus functionality, or how to account for trait variations and personality differences across individuals, some of whom must be 'normal,' 'average,' or 'healthy.' Allen Frances, who served on the *DSM-III* work group responsible for drafting the section on PDs, admits "the personality disorders are not at all clearly distinct from normal functioning or from each other" (Frances qtd. in Greenberg, *The Book of Woe* 263). Frances would later become chair of the task force that created 1994's *DSM-IV*, an edition that did little to rectify the substantial problems associated with *DSM-III's* new codification of personality disorders.

Social Origins of Personality Disorders

The essential feature of a Personality Disorder is an enduring pattern of inner experience and behavior that deviates markedly from the expectations of the individual's culture and is manifested in at least two of the following areas: cognition, affectivity, interpersonal functioning, or impulse control.

(DSM-IV, 630)

McCallum locates the origins of character disorders in the latter half of the nineteenth century, indicating that they arose in the attempt to distinguish insanity and mental deficiency from criminality and other forms of social deviancy (55, 60). The development of a dichotomous notion of "the bad or the mad" fit well with the late nineteenth and early twentieth century distinction between 'chronic' versus 'acute' cases (McCallum 60, 64–65). Chronic cases, like the criminally deviant, held less appeal for psychiatry "as there was little it could do in terms of treatment, compared with the more interesting and prestigious acute patients" (Ibid. 64). The contemporary category of mood disorders, as an example of acute illness, is by definition temporary or transient. The notion of 'mood' signifies a departure from one's habitual or premorbid state of existence. In contrast, the chronic criminal deviant, who was incapable of distinguishing either legal or moral right and wrong, represented a class of persons whose behavioral problems could not be ameliorated through either treatment or punishment. Dallaire et al. point out that 'badness,' referring to "motivated criminal or delinquent acts" and illness as "a 'no fault' state" demand different social consequences: "punishment/control toward intentional deviance, and treatment/care toward deviance without responsibility" (133).

Further, lifetime criminals as chronic cases departed from the mentally ill in that their ongoing condition was not connected to a diminished rational capacity, the principle factor defining other classes of insanity, such as psychoses. However, the criterion of rationality proved to be an insufficient explanation for the range of total human motivations, leading to the broader conceptualization captured by personality as an internalized, complex form of subjectivity. In 1905, for example, Alfred Binet made a distinction between two categories of defect: those lacking in intelligence and those who are unstable. The unstable group "do not necessarily manifest inferiority of intelligence"; instead, "they are turbulent, vicious, rebellious to all discipline" (Binet qtd. in McCallum 67). Emergent from the category of instability was the 'psychopathic' person whose formulation, in turn, helped enable the psychology of personality (McCallum 68). By the 1920s, the notion of personality as an interiorized form of subjectivity composed of multiple facets was established within the psy disciplines. Encapsulated in the concept of personality were other elements beyond intellect or rationality that factored into successful or unsuccessful human functioning, including temperament, personal traits, emotional makeup, and so on. Thus, by the middle of the twentieth century, "psychiatry came to supervise a range of phenomena known as 'psycho-pathological' that previously had been seen as moral and criminal problems" (McCallum 60). The psychopath exhibited traits that were enduring and stable – lifelong attributes – requiring the social response of control, normally in the form of imprisonment (Ibid. 68).

The specific term 'psychopathic' was introduced in 1891, although it referred to a wider series of "chronic characterological disorders" than those represented in the current usage of either psychopathy or antisocial personality disorder (Patrick 112). In its earlier forms, psychopathy was akin to the contemporary term, 'psychopathology,' referring to any type of mental disorder (Sass and Herpetz 635; Berrios 429). 'Sociopath' was added to the psychiatric lexicon in 1909, with the intention of indicating the social and environmental causes of chronic characterological disorders, in contrast to the presumed physiological origins implicit in 'psychopath' (Patrick 112). The two terms, psychopathy and sociopathy, now are used largely synonymously.

The concepts of psychopathy and sociopathy were employed in Europe and the US throughout the 1920s and 1930s but, in all versions, incorporated elements that would fall both within and beyond today's understandings of either psychopathy or antisocial personality disorder. In 1923, Kurt Schneider defined such patients as: "Abnormal personalities who suffer through their abnormalities and through whose abnormalities society suffers" (Schneider qtd. in Tyrer, Casey, and Ferguson 465). Berrios reports that Schneider's book, *Psychopathic Personalities,* was so popular that, "by opting for the term 'personality,' he rendered ' character' and 'temperament' obsolete" (431).

As is true for the majority of personality disorders, the role of emotions was central to the concept of psychopathy/antisocial personality, in this case in terms of their absence. Patrick credits psychiatrist Hervey Cleckley in 1941 for narrowing the definition of psychopathy to a state of malfunction more closely approximating its current configuration, as well as with characterizing it as primarily "affective in nature (i.e., a core deficit in emotional reactivity)" (Cleckly qtd. in Patrick 112).

> Although the psychopath can react verbally as though he understood love, pride, grief, shame, or the other emotions, he has no real experience of these human values or connotations.
>
> (Cleckly qtd. in Sass and Herpetz 637)

Another pivotal precursor of contemporary personality disorders is the borderline state, also historically a form of affective insanity. If psychopathy/ sociopathy/antisocial personality disorder grew out of overlapping issues between psychiatry and the judicial system, borderline owes much of its lineage to the interaction between psychiatry and psychoanalysis. Now referring to a particularized personality disorder, borderline began as a broad term encompassing many of the personality disorders as we currently understand them. It became used to describe patients who could not be considered psychotic because they exhibited "intact reality testing" (Higgitt and Fonagy 24), but whose emotional and behavioral problems were notably more severe than neuroses. The term was employed for a wide range of patients who existed on the borderline or in the borderland between neuroses and psychoses (Wilson 400; Knight 159; Frosch 264). Thus borderline came to designate severe neurotics who displayed emotional instability and emotional excess on an enduring and stable basis.

By the 1970s, borderline increasingly referred to patients who suffered from impulsiveness, anger, irascibility, hostility, depression, self-destructive behaviors, and turbulent relationships. These emotional symptoms appear as the narrower, more specific manifestation of borderline personality disorder in *DSM-III* in 1980. If antisocial personality disorder has been recognized as a "core deficit" in the ability to feel certain emotions, the borderline personality disordered suffer from an excess of emotional experience and expression.

One of the central markers of personality disorders is that they are ongoing, stable aspects of an individual, that is, chronic rather than acute conditions or states. The *DSM* citation at the head of this section describes them "as an enduring pattern of inner experience and behavior." As a result, the Axis II personality disorders are viewed as ego-syntonic or "consistent with self-concept" (Maddux, Gosselin, and Winstead 2). In contrast, the majority of Axis I illnesses are regarded as ego-dystonic or "perceived as originating from outside the self or unacceptable to the self" (Bartz, Kaplan, and Hollander 326). Personality disorders are ego-syntonic because they encompass deeply embedded personal traits or symptoms that are enduring, stable patterns for the individuals in question. In contrast, ego-dystonic Axis I disorders are perceived as "more ephemeral," comprising temporary or transient mental states, as in the cases of mood or anxiety disorders (Tyrer, "What's Wrong" 287).

Herein lies the source of some of the greatest conceptual difficulties posed by personality disorders, especially surrounding their definition as inner experiences of distress or behavioral impairment, rather than social deviancy. The dilemma of personality disorders reflects the distinction between 'the mad' as a no fault state, or deviance without responsibility, versus 'the bad' as involving motivated or willful "criminal or delinquent acts," that is, intentional deviance. Personality disorders are more likely to be experienced by the patient as "unpleasant but logical and inevitable for them," that is, as a familiar, inherent facet of who the person 'is' (Stern 474). Personality disorders, like personality itself, function as part of an individual's core identity. Meanwhile, mood or anxiety disorders tend to be recognized by those to whom they occur, and in professional conceptualizations, as departures from the person's optimal or usual state of existence, an imposition originating "from outside the self or unacceptable to the self." The symptoms of personality disorders represent commonplace functioning for those experiencing them rather than a divergence from a previous or desired norm. Greenberg notes, "An Axis I disorder is what you *have*. An Axis II disorder is who you *are*" (*The Book of Woe* 260; italics in original). Therefore, personality disorders indicate the transition from affective forms of mental illness as a temporary inhabitation to their appearance as ongoing, stable parts of identity. Personality disorders signal a cultural move from having an illness to taking up an identity, a reflection of social concerns at the time they attracted growing attention, in the 1960s and 1970s, and helping to account for their solidification in 1980's *DSM-III* and over the years that followed.

Those with personality disorders tend to be regarded as "treatment resisting" while those with Axis I illnesses comprise the more satisfactory "treatment seeking" patients (Tyrer, "Diagnostic" 373). This helps account for the personality disordered as 'the patients psychiatrists dislike,' because they find them difficult and noncompliant as personalities and as objects of treatment. Those whose adversities feel dystonic are far more likely to seek treatment because, in their departure from normal or optimal functioning, they are already admitting to having 'a problem.' In contrast, the syntonic personality disordered may not view their circumstances in terms of either impairment or distress, the threshold requirements for any mental disorder. For example, for those with schizoid personality disorder, the "lack of social interaction is likely to be more worrisome to relatives or colleagues than it is to themselves" (Coker and Widiger 212). In the case of antisocial personality disorder, there may well exist a marked *absence* of subjective distress, given that lack of guilt or remorse are defining features (Maddux, Gosselin, and Winstead 7; Samuel and Widiger 178).

Those diagnosed with or suspected of having a personality disorder often regard their difficulties as caused by other individuals or an intractable social world. As a consequence, ineffective interpersonal and social relations commonly are considered to be the most significant manifestations of this group of disorders, evidenced through "the position of the patient in his or her relationship with society over a long period" (Tyrer, "What's Wrong" 285; Tyrer, Casey, and Ferguson 465; Rutter 453; Higgitt and Fonagy 25; Rivera 232). Stemming from this, personality disorders are viewed as exacting a heavy toll on society. This is the thrust of Schneider's widely cited 1923 definition of the personality disordered as: "Abnormal personalities who suffer through their abnormalities and through whose abnormalities society suffers." As a result of its significant, deleterious social repercussions, "personality disorder must always be judged by its effects on others, be they friends, relations or others in close contact with the patient, or society as a whole" (Tyrer, Casey, and Ferguson 465). Because the person diagnosed with a PD is not necessarily who "suffers the most," a diagnosis "should include markers for the social burdens" imposed by these patients on the public (Pilkonis et al. 78). Thus, professionals in the psy fields appeal directly to a social world in diagnosing personality disorders. If the perception of disorder occurs primarily from the standpoint of family members, interpersonal relationships, psychiatric professionals, or "society as a whole," rather than as a measure of personal distress or impairment, then judgment from a social world about deviancy is, indeed, being rendered.

Sociality and Psychopathology

Whatever its original cause, [a mental disorder] must currently be considered a manifestation of a behavioral, psychological, or biological dysfunction in the individual. Neither deviant behavior (e.g., political, religious, or sexual) nor conflicts that are primarily between the individual and society are mental disorders unless the deviance or conflict is a symptom of a dysfunction in the individual as described above.

(*DSM-IV*, xxi–xxii) (*DSM-IV-TR*, xxxi)

DSM-IV (1994) and *DSM-IV-TR* (2000) include in their overall definition of mental disorders, as cited above, the specific exclusion that deviant behavior occurring between the individual and society cannot be considered an instance of mental disorder, unless it specifically manifests as a behavioral, psychological, or biological dysfunction within the individual. Thus the determination of mental disorder versus deviancy hinges on the difficult distinction between behaviors that occur in the interaction of individual with society versus actions that can be attributed chiefly to internalized, personal states. But as Maddux, Gosselin, and Winstead query:

How does one determine whether deviant behavior or conflicts are primarily between the individual and society?. ... Is it possible to say that a psychological or behavioral dysfunction can occur in the individual apart from the sociocultural and interpersonal milieu in which the person is acting? (10)

The *DSMs* have continued to rely on distinctions between internal versus external, or personal rather than social that, in an era deeply influenced by social construction understandings of human functioning, have become increasingly difficult to sustain. As argued in recent decades, psychiatric illnesses, as well as personality in general, can never be solely biomedical, psychological or personal but also always falls within social, political, legal, and other forms of culturally negotiated, if not determined, experiences. For instance, changing circumstances such as the disappearance of hysteria and neurasthenia in their nineteenth and early twentieth century forms, or the rise of post-traumatic stress disorder and personality disorders in more recent years, "are not comprehensible with the medical framework" of the *DSMs* but must be accounted for in historically variable sociocultural terms (P. Brown 404).

The conceptualization of 'identity,' in contrast to 'personality,' is precisely that which is constituted between the individual and society. Yet as quoted above, for the *DSMs*, the individual and societal largely remain mutually exclusive categories, in which intentional social deviance or conflicts primarily between the individual and society do not constitute mental disorders. Whatever its originating cause, a mental disorder must be "a manifestation of a behavioral, psychological, or biological dysfunction in the individual." The 'threshold' between individual and society is another impasse that, to date, has not been satisfactorily addressed by the *DSMs* but with which I believe the personality disorders were intended to engage. This helps explain their appearance, following Manning, in extensive codified form only in the wake of the 1960s social and political movements, rather than in an earlier era of a deeply interiorized self, pace Rose, signaled by the development of uniquely individuated personalities.

The personality disorders that officially emerge in 1980 take up the question of identity and emotionality in that PDs serve as a transition from the perceived temporary or acute status of ego-dystonic illnesses, such as mood and anxiety disorders, to more enduring, stable states. Personality disorders reflect a concern with ego-syntonicity: ongoing features that correspond more closely with identity. Like personality, personality disorders function as part of individuals' core identities – who they are rather than what they have. In this sense, the personality disorders as configured from 1980 on, represent an attempt to think through personality and its disorders in light of broader cultural concerns surrounding the notion of social identities. Further, for some in psy, personality disorders provide a means to think more inclusively about social categories such as race, gender, and sexuality that, following the political identity movements of the 1960s and 1970s, became more widely accepted as core parts of personality. Although these reasons may have helped motivate the development of the Axis II personality disorders, in practice their emergence largely served to make visible the *competing* claims and difficulties of what it means to think in terms of 'personality' in light of concepts of sociocultural 'identity.' The upsurge in attention devoted to personality disorders from around 1980 sought to reconcile incongruities between personality and identity but, instead, have revealed those conflicts to be largely intractable.

One such difficulty becomes apparent in the ways the *DSMs* employ the notion of 'deviance,' which has direct bearing on how personality disorders are diagnosed. The *DSMs* specifically exclude political, religious, sexual, criminal, and other conflicts as forms of social deviancy indicating, in and of themselves, mental dysfunction. However, as outlined earlier, mental disorders by definition are a form of deviance measured against social norms. Widiger describes psychic illness as: "Aberrant, dysfunctional, and maladaptive thinking, feeling, behaving, and relating" to others (63). Such a definition implicitly assumes a model of normal, functional, and adaptive thinking, feeling, behaving, and relating to others against which the aberrant, dysfunctional, and maladaptive can be gauged. The very ability to imagine a concept of mental disorder necessitates the recognition of individuals who display conduct that is "inconsistent with socially accepted and culturally sanctioned ways of thinking, feeling, and behaving," in comparison to those who abide by standards deemed socially appropriate (Maddux, Gosselin, and Winstead 7). Personality disorders as "an enduring pattern of inner experience and behavior," which exist as markers of permanent or long term unacceptable feelings or actions, become difficult to conceive of *except as* judgments of social deviancy.

Further, the notion of 'deviancy' must also address the distinction made between social versus cultural deviation. Whereas social deviancy refers to the norm-departing actions of individuals within a matrix of socially agreed-upon standards, cultural deviancy designates the divergent, sanctioned norms among varying societies. Thus, the general criteria for personality disorder states that the disordered person's behavior must deviate "markedly from the expectations of the individual's culture" (*DSM-IV*, 633). This criterion is intended to guard against psy professionals from one national, racial, or ethnic background diagnosing upon the basis of what may be quite acceptable behavior within the terms of the patient's cultural context (Samuel and Widiger 170). That is, the cultural deviance exclusion acknowledges cultural variations in what is considered 'normal' and, therefore, in what can accurately be judged as pathological. To be diagnosed as personality disordered, individuals must diverge from the social norms of their respective cultures, operationalizing a complex, unstable notion of normal versus aberrant behavior, in order to meet the requirements for both social and cultural deviancy.

The dynamics of culture, as theorized in recent years, pose other fundamental contradictions for psychology, psychiatry, and personality disorders. For example, studies have indicated that as many as half of the male prison population meet the diagnostic criteria for antisocial personality disorder (Coker and Widiger 202; Coid 584).[6] Furthermore, because the antisocial variant has the worst prognosis of all personality disorders, it is often assumed that "lengthy incarceration may be the most effective 'treatment'" (Coker and Widiger 209). Does this presume that African Americans and Latinos, who are disproportionately overrepresented among prison populations in the United States, have a significantly higher overall prevalence rate for antisocial personality disorder? Both Patrick and Coid point out that, in fact, no significant differences exist in the prevalence of antisocial PD "across White, African-American, and Hispanic groups" (Patrick 120; Coid 587–588), leaving no satisfactory explanation for the reported rampant prevalence of antisocial PD within prison populations.[7]

In a comparable manner, Levy et al. note debates concerning the relationship of narcissistic personality disorder to Western, especially American, cultural values (257–258). Are the traits of grandiosity, a sense of self-importance, entitlement, arrogance, and the expectation of preferential treatment qualities valorized in a highly individualistic, competitive, capitalist culture or are they the symptoms of narcissistic personality disorder within an individual? Does class play a role here? For example, are members of the upper classes treated with greater privilege and preference because they are viewed as more important? If so, are they more – or less – likely to be diagnosed with narcissistic personality disorder?

Similarly, Warner observes that many of the symptoms for antisocial personality disorder are very close to, if not identical with, "culturally valued" features of masculinity, including "toughness, aggressiveness, unemotionality, worldiness, skillfulness in business dealings, reduced concern for the opinions or feelings of others, and limited expression of tender feelings"

(841). Nuckolls provides the same example of masculinity and antisocial PD but links it to the aspect of class, so that "the poor man who robs gas stations and the rich man who robs pension funds may be equally 'antisocial'" but they do not face incarceration at comparable rates (46). "Indeed, wealthy and successful men with strongly antisocial characteristics may more often be upheld as models" (Ibid.). Ernst concurs, arguing that in certain circumstances the antisocially disordered have been culturally validated in Western society and can be found among its heroes and leaders (648). He cites the quality of aggression as particularly suitable for certain military activities to which, in some situations, could be added the necessity for a diminished sense of remorse, guilt, or empathy in order to endure circumstances without, in turn, incurring mental disorders such as PTSD.

The symptoms of personality disorders also may be valorized as ideological representations. Wedding, Boyd, and Niemiec argue that a number of the loner cowboy figures found in Western films meet the criteria for schizoid personality disorder (62). Presumably, this also would apply to other highly individualistic mediated characters, such as cops and detectives. Yet, the loner lawman is a culturally heroic figure; in Hollywood westerns he is linked to settling and civilizing the nation. To what degree, then, can it be said that American national identity is founded on the basis of a personality disorder, whether antisocial, narcissistic, or schizoid?

Perhaps no example serves better to exemplify the problem of culture for psy than the heated debates surrounding the earlier *DSM* inclusion of homosexuality as a psychosexual disorder. Prior to homosexuality's complete removal from *DSM-III-R* in 1987, the attempt was made in 1980's *DSM-III* to describe it as a mental disorder only when it was ego-dystonic, that is, when internalized in such a manner that it caused significant subjective distress (Samuel and Widiger 178). Reclassified as "Ego-dystonic Homosexuality," *DSM-III* states, "Homosexuality that is ego-syntonic is not classified as a mental disorder" (282).

> This category is reserved for homosexuals for whom changing sexual orientations is a persistent concern. Similarly, distress resulting simply from a conflict between a homosexual and society should not be classified here.
>
> (*DSM-III*, 282)

Thus, homosexuality judged as deviancy by social others did not constitute disorder in the recipient, unless such censure or disapproval became internalized, as a "behavioral, psychological, or biological dysfunction in the individual." Of course, difficulties arose in determining what 'belongs' to an individual versus that which is socially derived, or how social norms might be put into effect other than through 'internalization' as individual experience.[8] Millon and Grossman point out that the means by which social rules are transmitted "are often emotionally charged and erratic, entailing persuasion, seduction, coercion, deception, and threat" (Millon and Grossman,

"Sociocultural Factors" 224). To this list of emotionally charged means of social transmission, I would add love, admiration, trust, and other forms of pleasurable acculturation. Expectations of appropriate or inappropriate behaviors transmitted through emotions points, precisely, to some of the cultural functions of emotionality, which are lived as internalized, individual felt experience. And indeed, clinicians quickly discovered that much or most of the subjective distress for homosexuals in therapy resulted from "stigmatization, discrimination, and social condemnation" (Samuel and Widiger 178). The quandary lies in assessing 'distress' as simultaneously internalized *and* the result of social conflict, because this would be to undermine the definitional distinction of mental disorder as dysfunction within the individual, rather than between the individual and society. Ultimately, the dilemma surrounding homosexuality was 'solved' by eliminating it entirely from the *DSM* as a disorder in 1987. This enabled the specific 'case' of homosexuality to disappear, but failed to address the competing psychic/cultural claims from which the heated debates surrounding homosexuality within the context of psy emerged in the first place.

As Kantrowitz and Ballou stress, in most psy models "individuals are expected to improve their adaptive capacities" in order to match their functioning to existing social conditions (79). Generally, when conflicts between individuals and society become visible within psychopathology, individuals are charged with moving toward socially designated, appropriate behaviors rather than making assumptions that social norms should be altered to accommodate the exigencies of individual experiences. However, from the 1960s on, that position collides with many of the political arguments of social identity movements, which place responsibility on flawed cultural norms and expectations, rather than flawed individuals. This raises the difficulty of how, within the parameters of psy, flawed or limited social, rather than individual, conceptualizations, systems, and practices might be subject to reevaluation.

Further, it is unclear how personality traits that at least on some occasions represent effective, and often respected, cultural values, as in the examples provided earlier of valorized characteristics otherwise associated with antisocial, narcissistic, or schizoid PDs, can be viewed as symptoms of personality disorder given that they conform to, rather than deviate from, social norms. The process by which the adoption of culturally valorized emotional traits come to be perceived as failings of the individual or symptoms of disorder, despite the fact that such traits and values have been advanced, precisely, as social norms and ideals, awaits further elucidation. Given these dilemmas, it is no longer clear how to adjudicate illness *within* an individual. As Suyemoto suggests, "personality ought to be regarded, and in practice exists," as "an in-depth consideration of the individual in personal, social, historical and cultural context" (76). In doing so, however, the old notion of personality as the guarantor of individual uniqueness becomes more akin to conceptualizations of identity as not solely the 'personal' of personality but, also, a reflection of social, historical, and cultural factors.

In the next section, I consider more closely how specific emotional qualities come to exist, simultaneously, as valorized traits and symptoms of disorder. As we will see, in the difficult transition from 'personality' to 'identity,'
psychological deviancy transforms into a greater problem of *conformity to
social norms*, rather than an aberrational departure from them. I investigate the degree to which personality disorders represent a dysfunction of
'over-conformity' to, as much as a rejection of, social norms, by taking a more
focused look at gender trouble in the context of the personality disorders.

Personality Encounters Identity: The Case of Gender Euphoria

> Certain Personality Disorders (e.g., Antisocial Personality Disorder)
> are diagnosed more frequently in men. Others (e.g., Borderline, His-
> trionic, and Dependent Personality Disorders) are diagnosed more fre-
> quently in women. Although these differences in prevalence probably
> reflect real gender differences in the presence of such patterns, clini-
> cians must be cautious not to overdiagnose or underdiagnose certain
> Personality Disorders in females or in males because of social stereo-
> types about typical gender roles and behaviors.
>
> (*DSM-IV*, 631–632) (*DSM-IV-TR*, 688)

As we have seen, one of the predicaments that confront psychology and
psychiatry in the notion of cultural deviancy is that specific meanings of
what is normal, appropriate, or healthy vary across cultures. Such variations
exist not solely across cultures but within them as well. Our identities, our
personalities, are shaped by multiple cultural affiliations and experiences.
The 'problem' of social identity has brought such matters to the fore. We can
see the stumbling blocks in the encounter between the *DSMs* and cultural
identity through the specific example of gender, which has raised considerable concern in the field of personality disorders.

I focus on the cluster B dramatic, erratic disorders, in particular, because
they are defined in affective terms as either absence or surplus of emotions, in which patients are either "emotionally constricted" or "excessively
emotional" (Oldham, 58). Additionally, the cluster B personality disorders
have strongly gendered associations, in which two are linked dominantly
to masculinity (antisocial, narcissistic) and two with femininity (borderline,
histrionic), although the overall prevalence rate for personality disorders is
similar for men and women (Morey, Alexander, and Boggs 542). Cluster B
also represents the most common personality disorders, with an especially
high comorbidity rate among these four (Zimmerman, Rothschild, and
Chelminski 1916–1917; Bradley, Conklin, and Westen 170; Blagov, Fowler,
and Lilienfeld 207, 210; Levy et al. 246; Tyrer, "What's Wrong" 283; Rutter
452). Comorbidity refers to cases in which individuals are diagnosed with
more than one disorder at the same time. While occurring across the spectrum of mental illnesses, comorbidity among personality disorders exists
at a disturbingly high rate. Up to 80 percent of those meeting the criteria

for narcissistic personality disorder also reach the diagnostic threshold for borderline PD (Levy et al. 246). Such "problematically high overlap" within cluster B has led to suggestions that, for instance, histrionic and antisocial personality disorders are gender-distinguished manifestations of the same illness, that is, different emotional experiences and social behaviors surface for men and women, although the underlying illness is similar (Levy et al. 246; Blagov, Fowler, and Lilienfeld 217; Coker and Widiger 207).

The cluster B personality disorders are diagnosed quite markedly by gender. In the case of antisocial PD, men are diagnosed more often than women by a rate of three to one (Patrick 120; Coker and Widiger 207; *DSM-IV-TR*, 708). The inverse applies to borderline, with women making up three-quarters of those diagnosed (Wedding, Boyd, and Niemiec 67; Coker and Widiger 213; *DSM-5*, 666).[9] As in the case of race, ethnicity, and antisocial personality disorders among prison versus civilian populations, *DSM* diagnoses and other sociocultural factors exist in contestation. Given the sharp gender disparity for particular personality disorders, one might expect to find considerable overlap between feminine-associated borderline and histrionic PDs, and between the masculine-linked antisocial and narcissistic PDs, respectively. And, indeed, histrionic PD has the highest comorbidity rate with borderline (Blagov, Fowler, and Lilienfeld 210). Yet it is also difficult to distinguish the criteria for histrionic PD from those for narcissistic or antisocial PDs (Ibid. 210, 216). In light of the considerable overlap in diagnostic criteria, what then accounts for the acute extent of gender-differentiated diagnoses? That is to say, if Cluster B disorders are gender distinct to a significant degree, how can we explain the extensive comorbidity among those designated *either* masculine *or* feminine, for example, histrionic (feminine) with narcissistic (masculine) PDs? The two simultaneous states of gender distinction and gender comorbidity should be largely mutually exclusive. That gender distinction and gender comorbidity co-exist signals a point of conflict between conceptualizations of personality disorders and other sociocultural considerations, as we saw in the cases of homosexuality and prison populations.

'Gender trouble' appears borne out by studies that indicate when clinicians were presented with identical symptomatology but variations in patient gender (male, female, or unspecified) the diagnoses reached were inconsistent (Fowler, O'Donohue, and Lilienfeld 11). For example, when given a case history based on male-linked antisocial personality disorder, clinicians diagnosed it as such 42 percent of the time when the patient was identified as male and in 48 percent of instances when the patient's gender was not specified. However, antisocial PD was diagnosed in only 15 percent of the cases in which the patient was identified as female; 46 percent of the clinicians opted, instead, for a diagnosis of histrionic PD (Blagov, Fowler, and Lilienfeld 215).

A number of arguments from members of the psy disciplines suggest that such discrepancies reflect gender bias in diagnostic constructs and criteria and/or in clinical interpretations and applications, most of which could be ameliorated though greater professional rigor and vigilance. This position is exhibited in the excerpt from *DSM-IV* at the head of this section, in which clinicians are urged to neither "overdiagnose or underdiagnose" based on social stereotypes or personal bias. In contrast, I am suggesting that such gender disturbances represent irreconcilability in the fundamental principles and assumptions between personality, its disorders, and notions of social identity.

In principle, if personality disorders are dysfunctions within the individual that pinpoint deviations from social determinations of 'normality,' as the *DSMs* specify, then more men than women should be diagnosed with feminine-associated disorders (borderline and histrionic PDs) because they would be departing from social norms of appropriately 'masculine' subjective feelings and behaviors, and vice versa. And indeed, an often-cited study from the 1970s found that psychotherapists evaluated psychologically healthy women as those who conform to feminine stereotypes and mentally well-adjusted men as those who adhere to masculine roles and expectations (P. Brown 397; Sprock, Crosby, and Nielsen 44). This is known as the "sex role inconsistency hypothesis" in which "symptoms that are inconsistent with sex roles are viewed more negatively while sex role congruence results in more positive evaluations" of mental health (Sprock, Crosby, and Nielsen 44). Thus, more women than men should be diagnosed with antisocial personality disorder if they lack what are considered socially acceptable levels of feminine emotionality, or they should be found to have narcissistic personality disorder for failing to have sufficient empathy for others, core traits stereotypically required of women. In contrast, men should have greater latitude for displaying an absence of emotionality or reduced empathy in keeping with common stereotypes of masculinity. At the same time, more men than women ought to be diagnosed with borderline or histrionic personality disorder because excessive emotionality contradicts appropriate masculine behavior but remains consonant with expectations for femininity.

Yet, the opposite phenomena exist. Substantially more women are diagnosed with feminine-linked personality disorders and more men with masculine-associated PDs. In 1983, Kaplan published an important article titled, "A Woman's View of *DSM-III*." Her paper, written from a feminist perspective, initiated extensive discussion concerning gender bias in *DSM* diagnostic constructions and criteria. Here, I am most interested in one of her specific contentions. Building on the work of Phyllis Chesler, Kaplan argues that "women who overconform to sex role stereotypes" are routinely diagnosed with mental illness (787). Kaplan's statement raises questions about what exactly "overconforming," in contrast to simply conforming, might mean and how it differs from socially appropriate, validated, or mandated forms of compliance with social norms. However, her claim that patients are punished for 'overconforming' to gender roles helps explain the higher numbers of women diagnosed with feminine-designated personality disorders as well as the disproportionate ratio of men meeting the threshold for personality disorders perceived as masculine. In practice, one of the effects of personality disorders, as currently constructed, is to pathologize dominant stereotypes, traits, and values of femininity and masculinity, that is, marking as deviant or ill, gender *consistent* emotions and behaviors more than gender inconsistent ones.

To overdiagnose women with histrionic or borderline PD or men with antisocial and narcissistic PD suggests that there exists something inherently flawed with those aspects of female or male identity. If we accept the prevalence rates for cluster B personality disorders, a widespread problem exists with same-sex 'overconforming,' in which case the problems reside either in prevailing concepts of masculinity and femininity or with stunningly inadequate processes of gender acculturation. It is not the lack of appropriately gendered identity but, in greater proportion, the boundaries of perceived *excessive* femininity for women and *exaggerated* masculinity for men that are monitored via cluster B personality disorders. To say that significant numbers of people suffer from "hyperfeminization" or being "hypermasculine" (Morey, Alexander, and Boggs 553), is to indicate a social problem, not of insufficient gendered identity, but of its excess. Of all borderline patients, only one in four are 'overly feminine' men displaying a surfeit of emotionality, while three out of four are 'excessively feminine,' that is, excessively emotional women, despite the centrality of emotionality to women's prescribed social roles. Similarly, with antisocial PD, for every woman diagnosed as insufficiently emotional, three men are found to be 'overconforming' to the socially expected, masculine lack of emotionality.

In response to Kaplan's contention regarding the pathologizing of stereotypical or 'normal' gendered subjectivity, Sprock, Crosby, and Nielsen conducted a study in which they largely confirmed the validity of Kaplan's position. Their findings pinpoint a tendency for specific diagnostic criteria to be viewed as more maladaptive when *consistent* with gender roles, and they "failed to confirm previous findings of a gender inconsistency hypothesis" (Sprock, Crosby, and Nielsen 56). For the personality disorders, gender syntonic, not dystonic, emotional qualities are diagnosed as most problematic for each sex. Morey, Alexander, and Boggs refer to gender inconsistent behaviors and traits, in which men fail to conform to dominant qualities of masculinity or women diverge from stereotypical aspects of femininity, as "gender dysphoria" (553). By this criterion, excessive conformation to sex-appropriate behavior and traits, as evidenced with certain personality disorders, exist as a form of 'gender euphoria.'

Kaplan believes that the gender biased assumptions of *DSM-III* "are codified most explicitly in diagnostic criteria for Personality Disorders" (788). Her claim makes sense if we recall that, unlike many of the Axis I disorders which are regarded as temporarily invading a pre-existing, coherent personality, personality disorders are viewed as exemplifying who the person actually *is,* based on the assumption that traits and symptoms represent enduring, stable qualities. According to Brown, gender (and other identity formations) "constitute a series of core and enduring personality traits" (L. Brown 212). If this is the case, gender, as our example, is a fundamental aspect of personality, bringing contemporary understandings of personality into closer affiliation with notions of identity. At the same time, as far as personality disorders are concerned, we are looking at normative social identities framed as individual dysfunctions.

Addressing the question why so many more women than men receive diagnoses of borderline personality disorder, Skodol and Bender frame the answer as limited to two possibilities.

> The essential question is whether the higher rate of BPD observed in women is a result of sampling or diagnostic bias, or is it a reflection of biological or sociocultural differences in women and men?
>
> (Skodol and Bender, "Why Are Women?" 349)

Here, the explanatory permutations are restricted to *either* insufficient rigor in the application of existing, sound psychiatric criteria *or* 'real,' essential differences between women and men. Excluded from this framework is the possibility of understanding gender euphoria within the personality pathologies of individuals as incompatible with emergent notions of social identity. The thrust of arguments concerning gender and other identity formations is to maintain that identity as selfhood cannot function solely or even predominantly at the level of the individual. Identities are culturally constituted and reproduced forms of subjectivity. Thus, high levels of mental disorder within specific identity categories (women, prison populations, homosexuals) indicate, not that there might be something 'abnormal' or dysfunctional about certain individuals, or something amiss with the lack of gender-neutrality in *DSM* diagnostic structures, but that there exist fundamental flaws in the classes of social identity against which we determine the normality or pathology of individual personalities. While personality disorders originally were intended to pinpoint flaws in certain individuals, in many ways they effectively make visible contradictions and limitations within the categories upon which social norms of identity are based and through which personalities are constituted. As Kaplan remarks, it remains difficult to determine "when society should be labeled as *unjust* and when an individual should be labeled as *crazy*" (789). This is not to revert to older notions that it is society, not the individual, that is 'crazy.' Rather, it is to point out that 'mentally unstable' or 'just and unjust' are different, often competing sets of cultural practices that cannot be forced into equivalency.

In Manning's query with which I began this chapter, regarding the sharp rise of attention directed toward personality disorders since 1980, we can trace what occurs to the meanings of 'personality,' and its emotional components, as it shifts to address something more akin to 'identity' issues. I am arguing that increased attention devoted to personality disorders can be viewed as a response to political identity movements and developments in identity theory in the last decades of the twentieth century. Identity is a more 'public' or collective sense of selfhood than the traditional conceptualization of personality as individual, internalized, and autonomous. Identity theories demand recognition of the inseparability of the individual and the social. The personality disorders embody, for portions of contemporary psy, the meeting of inner experience and the constitutive social, which thus far has proven to be an uneasy encounter.

If the personality disorders reveal 'psy trouble' around issues of social identity, they also shed light on difficulties accompanying the turn to biological psychiatry. The following section returns to biopsychiatry, to consider some of the implications of that movement, and its relationship to recent psy crises, as reflected in the personality disorders.

Emotions as Inner Experience

In *DSM-III* each of the mental disorders is conceptualized as a clinically significant behavioral or psychological syndrome or pattern that occurs in an individual and that is typically associated with either a painful symptom (distress) or impairment in one or more important areas of functioning (disability).

(*DSM-III*, 6)

Having historically defined much of its terrain as internal, individualized mental experience, the psychological arena, including the psychopathological, has sometimes found it difficult to situate the cultural within its parameters, as the previous discussion on social identity makes evident. More surprising, however, given its claimed ground, is that the concept of 'inner experience' also has proven troubling for psychopathology, particularly for various formulations of scientific psy.

Berrios contends that the "incorporation of *subjective experiences* into the symptom-repertoire of [descriptive psychopathology] is, perhaps, the single most important contribution of the nineteenth century" (22; italics in original). This development opened up new avenues for understanding and treating mental illnesses and, more broadly, it enabled "the psychologization of the old notion of consciousness" (Berrios 23). The conceptualization of a deep, interior space within human functioning was made possible by the emergence of subjective experience as the realm of emotional life. In turn, subjective experience was created through the establishment of affect as an independent human faculty, distinct from reason or will (Ibid. 18).

Yet, despite the importance of this development, "the clinical disorders of affect struggled for recognition" at the end of the nineteenth and the beginning of the twentieth centuries, with affective disorders emerging as an accepted category only in the early part of the twentieth century (Berrios 297, 298). Before that time, those working in the psychiatric professions prioritized intellectual functions and dysfunctions. In his account, Berrios attributes this preference to the fact that:

'Feelings,' 'emotions,' 'moods,' 'affects,' and 'passions' are states whose experiential and behavioural components elude definition; to this day, for example, there is no agreement as to what should count as a valid report for an emotion. (289)

As a result, and as incorporated from *DSM-III* on, many in the field favor diagnostic profiles based on external, observable behaviors, such as appearance, actions, or patterns of speech. These can be recognized and measured by an outside analyst, such as a psychiatrist or other clinician, instead of using criteria based on subjective distress that rely on patients' less empirically verifiable, self-reported accounts of what they are feeling (Ibid. 296).

Berrios also contends that the prioritizing of "intellectualistic" symptoms and disorders (delusions, hallucinations, memory deficits), because they are considered more reliably measurable or observable, retain the most prominent position in contemporary psychiatry, citing as an example the recent turn to cognitive theory and therapies which give "primacy" to cognition over affect (289). So, despite Berrios' claim that, historically, the introduction of subjective experience may well have been the most significant psychiatric development of the nineteenth century, for certain psy researchers and clinicians, the realm of inner experience remains untrustworthy.

The *DSM-III* change in methodology to more measurable diagnostic criteria derived from overt patient behavior, that is, "easily observable symptoms" (Wilson 405), reflects a disciplinary desire to achieve greater scientific credibility, which patient self-reporting based on inner experience threatens. Emotions often have been considered unamenable to empirical description, regarded instead as "unscientific feelings" (Lloyd Williams 133). As quoted at the head of this section, the traditional *DSM* definition for mental disorder requires the presence of distress and/or impairment in the patient in order to meet the diagnostic threshold. A mental disorder must be a syndrome or pattern "that is typically associated with either a painful symptom (distress) or impairment in one or more important areas of functioning (disability)" (*DSM-III*, 6). While impairment may be amenable to clinical observation on the part of psy professionals in that it appears to point to behaviors, it is difficult to see how level or degree of distress might be determined without recourse to self-reports describing subjective emotional experience on the part of the affected individual. Yet the concept of subjective distress remains troubling because it relies, as noted above, on "unscientific feelings." Williams states that many investigators "judge subjective feelings to be private events inaccessible to science" and, as a result, turn instead to physical, autonomic evaluation criteria (Lloyd Williams 133). He cautions that "physiological arousal gets people's unscientific feelings out of the way, but at a high scientific price" (Ibid.). I would suggest the high price paid is not only to science but, equally, to attempts at understanding the entire realm of emotional experience.

Under contention in the debates on self-reporting, inner experience, and subjective distress are emotions for which, as Berrios points out, there remains a lack of consensus on how they should be described, defined, or quantified. If we recall Berrios' analysis, the development of inner experience and the life of emotions, as a distinct affective faculty, made the psy disciplines possible. At the same time, they call into question the field's legitimacy as a science. Although psy situates the realm of inner, personal experience as its own, it has difficulty accounting for emotions within the disciplinary and methodological parameters it has established. Livesley notes: "If the goal is to develop a scientific classification, the only thing that matters is empirical evidence" ("Disorder" 365). This raises serious dilemmas for scientific psy concerning conceptualizations of emotions and emotional dysfunctions.

DSM-5 and Counting

> A diagnosis of a personality disorder requires two determinations: an assessment of the level of impairment in personality functioning ... [and] an evaluation of pathological personality traits. ...
>
> The impairments in personality functioning and personality trait expression are relatively inflexible and pervasive across a broad range of personal and social situations [and] relatively stable over time.
>
> (*DSM-5*, 762)

Much of the debate surrounding personality and its disorders has focused on the distinction between categorical versus dimensional understandings of personality. This returns us to the problem of determining between a trait, presumed healthy or normal, versus a symptom which signals dysfunction. *DSM-III* employed a categorical approach to personality disorders, which implies that the symptoms representative of a disorder have identifiable boundaries separating them from proper functioning, that is, accurate thresholds between normality and pathology. A categorical model determines that a symptom and, therefore, a disorder as an accumulation of symptoms, either is or is not present. In contrast, a dimensional approach takes a specific aspect of personality, such as trust/suspiciousness, and assesses it by degrees from healthy or adaptive trait through stages of severity as maladaptive symptom. Many in the psychiatric and psychological fields have argued that a dimensional approach, based on a continuum from 'normal' to pathological, with varying degrees of abnormal functioning in between, better applies to personality and its disorders. However, one of the difficulties with a dimensional approach is that the number of potential traits to be measured is enormous, "covering virtually the whole range of adjectives that could be applied to people" (Rutter 450). Greenberg references that number of adjectives as approximately four thousand (*The Book of Woe* 266). The specific dimensions to employ has been much debated because diagnoses will vary, from which personality disorder a patient has to whether the individual is healthy or disordered, depending upon the specific trait criteria chosen.

Over the years, the majority of research studies on personality disorders has advocated just such a dimensional approach. The principal difficulty has been a matter of reaching professional, political, and ideological agreement on which specific personality dimensions or traits to analyze and how best to measure variations in degree, from normal to abnormal functioning (Oldham and Skodol 24; Fowler, O'Donohue, and Lilienfeld 7). Such political difficulties resulted in the personality disorders section of the *DSMs* from *III* (1980) to *IV-TR* (2000) to be left largely unchanged.

As discussed earlier, a number of those responsible for 2013's *DSM-5* believe that the way forward for psy lies in better determining the threshold between mental health and pathology. Many feel the best way of achieving those thresholds or cut off points rests with the adoption of dimensional rather than categorical models of illness. For the personality disorders, prior to the publication of *DSM-5*, its framers heralded the volume's advancements precisely because it introduced just such a dimensional approach. However, once again, agreement failed to be reached on which personality traits to focus on and how to measure degrees of severity.

As a result, *DMS-5* adopts two diametrically different 'solutions' for the classification and diagnosis of PDs. Under "Diagnostic Criteria and Codes," the largest segment of the book and "the core of *DSM-5*," personality disorders are acknowledged to be "virtually unchanged" from their categorical formulation in previous *DSMs* (*DSM-5*, 10, xliii). *DSM-5* also introduces another, dimensional system titled "Alternative *DSM-5* Model for Personality Personality Disorders" (761–781). Originally intended to replace the existing system for PDs, the alternative dimensional model was so immediately and heatedly contested, it was consigned to what is effectively an appendix of *DSM-5* (Skodol et al., "Proposed Changes" 5; Pilkonis et al. 68–69; Greenberg, *The Book of Woe* 270–271, 321–322). Although widespread lack of confidence in the categorical model for PDs continues, dissensus on the pros and cons of the proposed dimensional approach led to its relegation as an addendum (Porter and Risler 50; Emmelkamp and Power 363; Livesley, "Disorder" 364). Thus, *DSM-5* presents two largely conflicting, irreconcilable systems for diagnosing personality disorders.[10]

The alternative, dimensional system is complex; indeed, the model's complexity is one of the criticisms levied against it (Verheul 370; Livesley, "Disorder" 364). For purposes here, I focus on one major reformulation that directly affects this discussion on emotionality.[11] The alternative model places greatly augmented emphasis on "pathological personality *traits*" (*DSM-5*, 761; italics in original). A "trait-specified approach" conceives of specific qualities or attributes as the building blocks of personality (*DSM-5*, xliii; Skodol et al., "Proposed Changes" 15). In this view, individual personalities materialize as "different agglomerations" of these trait factors, in which the personality disordered result from a "lack or excess of particular factors" (Greenberg, *The Book of Woe* 265–266). The challenge in this approach is to determine which of the nearly limitless adjectives that can be applied to personality ought to be selected, and how their respective severity or 'normality' should be measured.[12]

To this end, resulting in charges of its unworkable complexity, *DSM-5's* alternative model specifies five broad trait domains, within which exist twenty-five more specific trait facets as subcategories for each domain. The five broad domains consist of: negative affectivity, detachment, antagonism, disinhibition, and psychoticism.[13] One difficulty with the trait-based approach concerns the delineation of specific traits, tacitly based on understandings of which emotions we do, and do not, acknowledge as existing at any historical moment or location, and how, collectively, we conceive of them. Berrios observes that the experiential and behavioral aspects of emotions continue to "elude definition," leaving psy with no consensus on "what should count as a valid report for an emotion" (289). In the case of the five domains, examples provided for the first, 'negative affectivity,' include anxiety, depression, guilt/shame, worry, and anger (*DSM-5*, 779). On what basis, then, are detachment, antagonism, and disinhibition construed as distinct domains in their own right, rather than further instances of negative affectivity? Are we to understand detachment, antagonism, and disinhibition as broader or more fundamental kinds of emotional issues than anxiety, shame, and anger?

Livesley, a strong opponent of *DSM-5's* dimensional schema, notes instances in which the definition of a specific trait facet varies from one personality disorder type to another ("Tradition" 86–87). For example, *DSM-5* outlines 'impulsivity,' one of the seven possible trait facets of antisocial personality disorder, in three descriptive phrases:

> Acting on the spur of the moment in response to immediate stimuli; acting on a momentary basis without a plan or consideration of outcomes; difficulty establishing and following plans.
>
> (*DSM-5*, 764)

Impulsivity also appears as an important trait facet of borderline personality disorder. However, in addition to the above items, impulsivity within the borderline category contains an additional fourth descriptive phrase: "a sense of urgency and self-harming behavior under emotional distress" (*DSM-5*, 767). Livesley's point is that different versions of impulsivity within the same diagnostic system "raise the legitimate question of whether the two definitions represent the same construct" ("Tradition" 86).[14] Are these then the same or differing emotions? *DSM-5's* alternative model was intended to provide a more empirically grounded schematic by diminishing subjective reports of distress in favor of more objectively assessable impairment. However, reformulation to 'pathological personality traits' restores emotionality's centrality, inserting back into the picture the traditional difficulties emotions pose for scientific psy.

Additionally, *DSM-5's* alternative model describes personality traits as existing "on a spectrum with two opposing poles," providing the example of the trait facet, callousness, whose opposite positive pole is empathy or kindheartedness (773). At one point, *DSM-5* indicates that kindheartedness, like callousness, can be maladaptive in certain circumstances, as in instances when the kindhearted "repeatedly allow themselves to be taken advantage of by unscrupulous others" (Ibid.). Shortly following, however, the manual again affirms that "healthy, adaptive, and resilient personality traits [are] identified as the polar opposites" of negative trait domains and facets, which includes kindheartedness as the inverse of callousness (Ibid.). Yet, if a positive pole can be maladaptive, this would suggest that any trait, even in its most negative manifestation, as well as at all stages on the spectrum between the poles, might on certain occasions or in certain contexts be adaptive, once again leaving no clear threshold between pathological or normal. Further, it is not at all clear that 'empathy' and being 'kindhearted,' as the opposites of callousness, refer to the same emotional quality. And doesn't 'callousness' have other conceivable opposites? Indeed, is 'callousness' even the most extreme, maladaptive variant for that spectrum, rather than cruelty or mercilessness, for example?

Attempting to situate emotions into systemic order contradicts how they are felt – experienced and lived – as nuanced, malleable phenomena for which, following Berrios, consensus on classification and demarcations continue to elude. Despite the intentions of *DSM-5's* alternative model, its increased emphasis on personality traits, and whether they are adaptive or maladaptive, serves to continue to obscure the distinction between normal and pathological rather than clarify it, largely because a trait-based approach remains firmly embedded in emotionality.

If traditional psy currently finds itself challenged by social construction and political identity theories from one important direction, it also confronts the demands and dilemmas posed by biopsychiatry on other flanks. Personality disorders attempt to address crucial aspects of human functioning but, as currently conceptualized, fail to satisfy the exigencies of either sociocultural or scientific psy theories. Instead, personality disorders underscore the complexity and fluidity of emotionality. Emotions are not adequately explained through the specific narratives of self provided by traditional psy's deeply interiorized subject, scientific psy's largely biological being, or the exteriorized entity formulated by social construction theories. Emotions are irreducible to inner experience, biological imperatives, or socially fixed categories. But neither can they be excluded from any of these domains.

Chapter Five continues discussion on the recent, widespread influence of biopsychiatry, turning specifically to the neurosciences. "Neuroscience and Other Narratives of Emotionality" also returns to the question of aesthetics, through the techniques of neuroimaging.

Notes

1. Additionally, from *DSM-III* an option became available to diagnose "personality disorder not otherwise specified" (PDNOS) for those who do not fit the specified PDs but, rather, tend to fall between them (Zimmerman, Rothschild, and Chelminski 1914). In their study Zimmerman et al. found that PDNOS was the single most frequently diagnosed personality disorder (1917).
2. Cluster A's emotional symptoms include: the suspiciousness, mistrust, hostility, and hypersensitivity to slights associated with paranoid personality disorder; apathy, flattened affect, and detachment found in schizoid personality disorder; and extreme discomfort in relationships in the schizotypal category (Wedding , Boyd, and Niemiec 59–62; Fowler, O'Donohue, and Lilienfeld 4; Bernstein and Useda 41–42).
3. Borderline is characterized as emotional dysregulation manifested in unstable relationships, abrupt mood shifts, anger, and impulsivity (Wedding, Boyd, and Niemiec 66; Fowler, O'Donohue, and Lilienfeld 4; Bradley, Conklin, and Westen

180, 182, 183). Antisocial personality disorder is marked by aggression, manipulation, and a conspicuous absence of shame, remorse, or guilt (Sass and Herpetz 635–636, 646). Histrionic, known as hysterical personality disorder until *DSM-III* in 1980, is defined primarily by excessive attention seeking, self-centeredness, and inappropriate seductiveness (Wedding, Boyd, and Niemiec 67; Fowler, O'Donohue, and Lilienfeld 4; Blagov, Fowler, and Lilienfeld 203–204, 207, 214). Narcissistic personality disorder is recognized by a constant need for admiration, an inflated sense of self-importance, and a lack of empathy (Wedding, Boyd, and Niemiec 68–69; Fowler, O'Donohue, and Lilienfeld 4; Levy et al. 233–234).

4. Avoidant personality disorder entails feelings of inadequacy, fears of rejection, hypersensitivity to criticism, and social inhibition (Wedding, Boyd, and Niemiec 70; Fowler, O'Donohue, and Lilienfeld 4; Herbert 279–280). Symptoms linked to dependent personality disorder involve submissiveness, passivity, clinginess, and an extreme need to be taken care of (Wedding, Boyd, and Niemiec 71; Fowler, O'Donohue, and Lilienfeld 4; Bornstein 307). Compulsive personality disorder was renamed obsessive-compulsive PD in 1987 (*DSM-III-R*). Those diagnosed with it exhibit inflexibility, perfectionism, and the desire to control situations and people (Wedding, Boyd, and Niemiec 72–73; Fowler, O'Donohue, and Lilienfeld 4; Bartz, Kaplan, and Hollander 325–326). Passive-aggressive personality disorder was eliminated from 1990's *DSM-IV*, reducing the total number of PDs to ten.

5. Lenzenweger and Clarkin state 9% to 13% (9); Manning indicates about 10% (83); Fowler, O'Donohue, and Lilienfeld provide a figure of 13% (5); Coker and Widiger specify 10% to 15% (202); Oldham, Skodol, and Bender state about 12% (xvii); and Rose cites the number at 9% to 13% in Britain and 15% among Americans ("Disorders" 471).

6. In a meta-analysis of studies done in North America, Europe, and Australia, Coid cites 47% of male prisoners and 21% of female prisoners with antisocial personality disorder. Coid also indicates that 65% of all male prisoners and 42% of all female prisoners were diagnosed with some form of personality disorder (584).

7. The prevalence rate for antisocial personality disorder in the general population of Western nations is estimated at between .6% and 3.7% (Coid 586).

8. *DSM-5* (2013) explicitly states: "Mental disorders are defined in relation to cultural, social, and familial norms and values" in which those norms and values "are internalized by the individual" (14).

9. It should be noted that debate exists about the accuracy of sharp gender diagnostic distinctions (Morey, Alexander, and Boggs 544).

10. Among the most visible modifications in *DSM-5* overall, the multiaxial system is eliminated entirely so that personality disorders no longer are constructed as a distinct class or trajectory of mental illness (*DSM-5*, 16). Additionally, in the alternative model, grouping of PDs by clusters A, B, and C ceases (Ibid. 646).

11. More accurately, the alternative model attempts to follow a "hybrid" approach, seeking to straddle the categorical concept, in which each disorder is "categorically separate" from both states of health and other disorders, with a dimensional system based on a continuum that ranges from "maladaptive variants of personality traits that merge imperceptibly into normality and into one another" (*DSM-5*, xliii, 12, 646). Concession to the categorical approach in the dimensional system is evident in the retention of distinct personality disorder types, although these are reduced in number. The new schema recognizes

six discrete personality disorders: avoidant, antisocial, borderline, narcissistic, obsessive-compulsive, and schizotypal. Conversely, paranoid, schizoid, histrionic, and dependent PDs have been excised.

12. The new system emphasizes traits over symptoms. Instead of transforming at some point into symptoms, the traits themselves range from wholly adaptive to severely maladaptive (*DSM-5*, 762). This is determined by a five-point rating scale, which ranges from little or no impairment to extreme impairment. Thus, a trait is no longer solely the adaptive portion of a specific personality feature. Although this is intended to circumvent the problem of determining when, and why, a trait transitions into a symptom, effectively it shifts the same dilemma to the distinction between adaptive versus maladaptive trait.

13. The facets are as follows.

    Negative affectivity: emotional lability, anxiousness, separation insecurity, submissiveness, hostility, perseveration, depressivity, suspiciousness, lack of restricted affectivity.

    Detachment: withdrawal, intimacy avoidance, anhedonia, depressivity, restricted affectivity, suspiciousness.

    Antagonism: manipulativeness, deceitfulness, grandiosity, attention seeking, callousness, hostility.

    Disinhibition: irresponsibility, impulsivity, distractibility, risk taking, lack of rigid perfectionism.

    Psychoticism: unusual beliefs and experiences, eccentricity, cognitive and perceptual dysregulation. (*DSM-5*, 779–781).

14. Livesley provides the additional example of 'hostility,' which for borderline personality disorder is defined as: "Persistent or frequent angry feelings; anger or irritability in response to minor slights and insults" ("Tradition" 87). But to the definition of hostility as a factor of antisocial personality disorder the phrase, "mean, nasty, or vengeful behavior," has been added (Ibid.).

5 Neuroscience and Other Narratives of Emotional Disorders

Neurosciences, focusing on the role of the brain in human thoughts, feelings, and behaviors, received mounting attention during the latter decades of the twentieth century, coming to predominate in psychology and psychiatry by the twenty-first. Increasingly influential in the study of emotions and emotional disorders, neuroscience has generated related disciplines, such as neuroimaging, a key topic for this chapter. "Neuroscience and Other Narratives of Emotional Disorders" explores how scientific research on emotions incorporates aesthetics, arguing that the two operate conjointly in the study of emotionality.

Because emotions and their disorders pose specific challenges as objects of study, science and aesthetics often function in tacit partnership. To this end, Chapter Five takes the examples of neuroimaging, affective computing, and experimental physiology in order to explore how the study of emotions in scientific contexts often necessitates engaging with aesthetics.

In its narrower usage, aesthetics references creative, usually artistic, practices. More specifically, it indicates the modes of expression or formal techniques available to various art forms. In broader understandings, aesthetics concerns the creative conduct of life. With regard to emotionality, part of living creatively entails the ways we deal with life's pains and pleasures, including the experiential suffering that accompanies emotional disorders. Aesthetics in this sense pays attention to ways we experience life's emotional valences, how we conduct ourselves in their midst, the means we have fashioned for entangling with suffering or feeling pleasure. Aesthetics, more broadly understood, encompasses qualitative evaluations of experience.

The chapter then returns to neuroimaging to investigate aesthetics, in its more specific meaning. PET scans involve visualizing the brain through applications of aesthetic values, such as color, in order to render images that 'make sense.' Thus, processes like neuroimaging create explanatory narratives, in this instance, visual stories about the brain and emotions.

Chapter Five contends that one of the values of emotionality rests with its potential to resist dichotomization, including pairings most familiar to us as mind/body, science/aesthetics, biology/social construction, individual/society. Cultural approaches to emotions imagine them functioning as webs of connectivity as they move among, and negotiate between, various modes of existence. I conclude with a return to the current global epidemic of emotional disorders and how we might address, in more nuanced ways, the range of phenomena contemporary strands of psy characterize as normal misery.

Considering Aesthetics

As noted above, in its more specific usage, aesthetics concerns the modes of expression available to various art forms. Raymond Williams describes this implementation as referring to visual appearance and effects, to which must be added audio, linguistic, textural, performative, and other modes of expression (*Keywords* 32). Aesthetics, in this sense, designates specific genres of artistic activity including painting, literature, music, theatre, film, and so on. It also references the means or manner of expression, the formal properties, that make particular arts forms possible, whether color and brushstrokes for painting, the tonal qualities of music, or modes of storytelling found in film and theatre. Aesthetics, in its narrower treatment, aligns with Foucault's assertions, in the latter part of *Mental Illness and Psychology* and in *History of Madness,* that exceptions to the silencing of madness in the modern world can be found, if only sporadically, in the work of mad artists (Chapter One). The more specific notion of aesthetics also conforms to my analyses of theatrical melodrama and dramatic realism in Chapter Two, as well as painting and cinema as forms of high art or vernacular modernism in Chapter Three.

In its broader connotations, aesthetics considers some of the properties associated with the arts, such as beauty, sensuality, or pleasure, as they might be applied to life in general. In this version, aesthetics refers to ways of life or to an 'art' of living. Such an aesthetics is concerned with how we *conduct* our experiences, with attention to qualitative aspects of existence, such as the sensual, ethical – or emotional. Brown and Stenner maintain that psychology largely has overlooked aesthetics in these terms, quoting Whitehead that "the Art of Life" means not just to survive, as in evolutionary psychology, but to "(i) to live, (ii) to live well, (iii) to live better" (Whitehead qtd. in Brown and Stenner 201). In order to strive for aesthetics in the more encompassing sense, qualitative evaluations of what constitutes living well or living better are required.

As qualitative evaluations of life experiences, aesthetics, in both narrow and broader usage, are culturally and emotionally meaningful events. Cultural activities, including scientific ones, cannot proceed without rendering such qualitative evaluations. In other words, they engage with aesthetics. As the following examples of neuroimaging, affective computing, and experimental physiology demonstrate, the study of emotions in scientific contexts – or attempts to eliminate emotionality's affects from those environments – necessitate the incorporation of aesthetic explanations.

Neuroimaging

In his study of positron emission tomography (PET) functional brain imaging, Joseph Dumit explores how this specific neuroscientific development must rely on particular understandings of brain, mind, subjectivity, identity, and other aspects of "personhood" in order to make sense of that which it renders visible. PET images are not self-evident, faithful reproductions of the brain but depend on particular interpretations of the subject matter under investigation in order to both create and make interpretable the final visual product. PET scanning is a complex technological process that results in images of brain activity (memory, attention) or states (depression, schizophrenia). Because the science and technology of PET render brain activities or states, it is considered functional, rather than anatomical, imaging.

Referring to the cultural understandings that underpin PET imaging as metaphors of personhood, the most troubling issues arise when Dumit turns to mental illness and its emotional aspects. In the case of depression, in order to grasp the results of PET scans – to be able to interpret the voluminous gathered data – "histories and cultural categories of moods and emotions, and sadness [in contrast to] depression must be investigated" (174). PET imaging is a comparative process, between 'normals' and other categories like 'the depressed.' Brain scans of individuals determined to fall into either one or the other category are averaged together. Dumit points out that we do not "see" mental illness (or mental health) in the brain (118). Rather, variations among brains become visualized through the PET scanning process, which is then correlated to states like normalcy or morbidity. In order to arrive at such determinations, people must first be pre-grouped into representative samples; for example, those who are normal controls versus those experiencing depression. The test groups' averaged scans, either normal or depressed, are then assumed, in a tautological manner, to provide evidence of depressed or non-depressed brain functioning for persons who were pre-selected as representative of those categories in the first place. Thus, neuroimaging is dependent upon already constituted categories of personhood, often derived from a normal versus pathological distinction.

Similarly, in order to visualize a normal brain state from one that is depressed, assumptions about the differences between sadness and depression, for example, must be operative prior to the creation of scans, in order to establish entities for comparative purposes. Dumit's point is that the PET process depends intrinsically on assumptions about different kinds of subjects and, in the case of the complex field of emotionality, hinges on making difficult distinctions among feeling states that are presumed to be discernible (175). Such procedural demands pose challenging questions. For instance, what are the differences between a 'normal' brain and a 'sad' one? In what ways does sadness diverge from depression? Exactly what emotional state or states define normality – that is, neither sad nor depressed? The same range of questions confronts any series of emotions: happiness, euphoria, and mania to cite another grouping. In this manner, attempts to measure feeling states scientifically cannot help but invoke layered "histories and cultural categories of moods and emotions" (174).

Another attendant complexity arises because neuroscience largely has been based in "microprograms of cognition," such as attention, memory, perception, and language functions (Dumit 178, 206). Helen Mayberg, a neurologist whose research involves the brain imaging of 'mood,' describes successful cognitive neuroscience as that which has been able to break down brain functions into component, measurable parts. In contrast:

> Emotions experiments are just harder to put into the cognitive neuro-science model. Emotions don't easily fit into these constructs.
> (Mayberg qtd. in Dumit 178)

Thus, the terms of cognitive psychology make it difficult to study emotions in the brain and, I would add, elsewhere. Indeed Mayberg, who describes her research as attempting to plot "the distributed network that regulates mood," argues that doing so necessitates separating "the cognitive compo-nent" from what she calls "the experiential component" (Mayberg qtd. in Dumit 173, 175). Here, mood or emotions are depicted as something that may overlap with cognition but, equally, exist as a type of life experience that lies beyond thought processes.

However, the difficulties related to such studies do not arise merely as a consequence of the parameters of cognitive psychology. Rather, cognitive psychology as a discipline is enabled by dominant cultural metaphors or models that are themselves cognitively based. Dumit cites current, promi-nent understandings of the brain in terms of computational functions, such as information processing, interrelated systems or circuits, and coding or coding errors (179, 183–4; also Orr 66–69; Angel 343).[1] In describing these as metaphors of personhood, Dumit does not point to them simply as illus-trative analogies but, instead, as constituting our fundamental knowledge of the phenomena such metaphors seek to describe.

Although Dumit speaks in terms of metaphors, I prefer to understand that to which he refers in terms of narrativity: stories about the brain, tales concerning proper human functioning, chronicles of what and how we feel. Narrativity encompasses a more complex network of unfolding events, reversals, contradictions, and resolutions than does metaphor. The notion of narrative involves a developmental process, often winding or weaving to create paradoxes and intersections, made possible through its multiplicity of components or 'moving parts.' Finally, metaphors normally operate lin-guistically while narratives can be conveyed by words, visuals, audio, and performance techniques (nonverbal communication).

For the most part, contemporary narratives of brain functioning lack complex, culturally shared renderings of emotions. One result of computa-tional narratives to describe neurofunctioning is that:

> We can imagine intelligence working like a computer, but we cannot imagine a program for sadness. In fact, the computer is often pointed to precisely as the embodiment of emotionlessness.
> (Dumit 179)

Author Brian Christian discusses the Turing test, an annual competition whose participants vie to make computers think like humans (4–5). Judges 'converse' with a concealed computer and an unseen person by posing a series of questions to each on any topics they wish. The judge then decides which conversationalist he or she believes is human versus computer. The computer program that convinces the greatest number of judges it is a person receives the Most Human Computer award, the sought-after victory in the Turing competition. Parenthetically, the person who the greatest number of judges deems human garners an award for Most Human Human.

Charles Platt, 1994's Most Human Human, identifies his winning strategy as "being moody, irritable, and obnoxious" (Platt qtd. in Christian 5). If we cannot imagine a computer program for sadness or other emotions, as Dumit suggests, then a dominant, contemporary cultural paradigm for the human mind, indeed, is emotionlessness. Conversely, if a person can be distinguished from a computer by being moody, irritable, and obnoxious, then emotions remain a key marker of the human subject, believed to be and "experienced as the deeply authentic, existential ground of who we are" (Freund 213).

Following Dumit, we need to ask what the consequences might be of neuroscientific knowledge that relies on narratives of personhood that largely posit emotionlessness. How do neuroscientifc researchers deal with emotions when their dominant disciplinary and social models assume emotionlessness? Due to the ill-fit of emotions to neurobiology and cognitive science, Dumit argues that, "emotions are more easily conceived of by the analogy to a disease – a change in the state of a person – than by the analogy to a computer network" (179). While narratives based on computer networks provide explanations for human cognitive functioning, emotions continue to pose a problem, making more sense within the traditional, narrative paradigms of disease or aberration, normality or abnormality, rather than as common, healthy aspects of brain/mind activities.

Despite these limitations, PET scans have become increasingly influential

> as visual evidence of brain differences between those with mental illness and those without it. PET often enters as proof of the biological existence of mental illness in the brain.
>
> (Dumit 18)

Neuroimaging studies largely are based on cognitive conceptualizations of brain/mind lodged in disciplinary parameters dependent upon discrete, measurable cognitive components rather than emotional ("experiential") networks of mental functioning. The existence of predominantly cognitive models of mental functioning, in turn, depends upon narratives about the brain as primarily emotionless even when emotions, and the emotional aspects of mental illness, exist as the subject matter under investigation. Exploring scientific interpretations of personhood and emotionality, then, must focus on that which is missing as well as what stories they are able to tell.

Affective Computing

Affective computing follows two avenues of investigation. First, it attempts to discern, through computer mediation, the specific emotions human subjects are experiencing or expressing. Second, it works to recreate or simulate human emotions in 'artificial intelligence agents,' similar to but more elaborate than the programs entered into the Turing test, as described by Christian.

In his analysis of affective computing, Frances Dyson also understands emotions as core markers for "being human" (262, 247–48). He indicates that affective computer researchers describe what they are after as "'mind-reading' functions" (257). Mind-reading functions involve the ability to infer or imply socioemotional meanings conveyed through nonverbal forms of communication, for instance, facial expressions, eye contact, gestures, posture, tone of voice, intonation, and so on.[2] This realm of human expression necessitates the invocation of 'mind,' not just 'brain,' because it involves the generation of meanings in social contexts, rather than solely the work of brain functions as anatomical processes. The intangible "emotional content" transmitted through forms of nonverbal communication sometimes is referred to as "back-channel feedback" (Dyson 258, 256). Yet it exists in the pivotal, forefront of human experiential and social relations. However, within the parameters of cognitive functionality, emotional meanings become located as back-channel properties.

In the quest to simulate the 'mind-reading' functions of human emotion within the field of affective computing, Dyson describes emotional content as "elusive," bearing an "ambiguous status, with ill-defined meaning" (258, 259). While this may well be the case in rational, empirical, cognitive, linguistic, and computational terms, emotions are significantly less elusive and ill-defined in the context of other frames of reference, including performative aesthetic or nonverbal communicative modes. In the aesthetic practice of nonverbal communication, as Dyson's study outlines, people are quite familiar with, apply or perform, and interpret emotional content in a multiplicity of ongoing, ordinary ways on a moment-to-moment basis in daily life.

And indeed, Dyson purposefully turns to aesthetics to explain the 'elusive' material that affective computing attempts to capture. Dealing specifically with the nonverbal component of tone of voice, an element of paralanguage, he notes that tone can "run as a lyrical or musical correlate to what is spoken" and, as such, might be "better understood through the musical meaning of tone and the performative meaning of intonation" (259). At the level of affective or emotional meaning (Dyson uses 'affect' and 'emotion' interchangeably), the fields of music and performance serve more productively than computational concepts as explanatory narratives, even within the computational arena.

With regard to affective computing, Dyson describes the substantive content of the voice alongside the uses of tone as the merger of "the computational and the aesthetic" (262). Here, content can be equated with computational procedures, the field in which Dyson operates, but the emotional practices of tone can only be explained by turning to aesthetic terms. Again, aesthetics cannot easily be separated from certain technological or scientific processes. The computation of affect concerns "mapping the acoustics of tone onto the contours of algorithms that have themselves been charged with the impossible task of defining emotion" (265). To reiterate, the task of comprehending emotions is only rendered "impossible," or at least inadequate, within certain conceptualizations, such as cognitive or computational terms, when used to the exclusion of others, like the aesthetic. Dyson already has shown that the emotional content of nonverbal communication, such as the functions and meanings attached to tone of voice, can be approached by associating tone with music.

Dyson outlines a specific project undertaken at MIT: Recognizing Affect in Speech, which creates a computerized "conversational agent," rendered as a female figure presumably due to women's historical and cultural associations with emotion (200). The subsequently projected figure is "capable of speech with intonation, and facial and bodily gestures" (Ibid.). 'She' interacts with humans, much as entrants in the Turing test do, but with a projected visual and audio presence (260). The Recognizing Affect in Speech project can be considered a venture into 'artificial emotionality' rather than artificial intelligence. One of the tasks assumed by the computerized conversational agent is to make small talk with humans because doing so "establishes trust" (261). Although Dyson has discussed affective computing in terms of emotional content and emotional meanings, the conversational agent who attempts to establish trust with human interlocutors holds significance because it underscores that 'content' and 'meaning' exist as interrelated but different entities with varying purposes. While substantive content is a function of emotional expression, intended to convey responses of anger or delight for example, a conversational agent engaging in small talk does not do so primarily to transmit informational content. Instead, small talk here is a relational activity, meant to develop feelings of trust between the conversationalists, computerized and human, in which how something is said matters more than specific substance. Thus, 'content' is not equivalent to 'meaning.' Meaning exceeds content in the processes of socioemotional interaction. As in the instance of establishing trust through small talk, significance rests not in what is being said, but in how something is expressed, to whom, in order to relay certain feelings and to provoke reciprocation of certain kinds of relational qualities. Functions of emotions that exceed the substantive, as in the realm of relational meanings, may be particularly dependent upon aesthetic interpretations in order to comprehend them.

However, although Dyson specifically invokes music as a form of aesthetics, necessary to understanding the functions of tone of voice, he does not make the link that what he investigates – the nonverbal, performative, and emotional aspects of artificial intelligence – are markedly aesthetic as well. We noted earlier that Mayberg, the neurologist of moods, argues emotions do not apply well to cognitive neuroscientific categories or methodologies. Others have argued that emotions and emotional disorders fit poorly within scientific paradigms more generally (Chapter Four). For example, Ussher observes that "if a phenomenon cannot be objectively observed and measured using reliable, standardized techniques," as in the case of psychological symptoms, then it becomes difficult for those phenomena to be recognized, acknowledged, or accounted for within positivist science (210; also Kirk, Gomory, and Cohen 38; Leys and Goldman 675).

In these terms, that which poses challenges to being observed, measured, and otherwise quantified may well be better recognized and accounted for by aesthetics, broadly construed, as the realm of qualitative evaluation. Thus affective computing must rely on the aesthetics of nonverbal communication, a field which long has outlined the meaningfulness of bodily expression for sociality. When dealing with emotions, scientific and technological studies may well depend on aesthetics, even if tacitly, as the means of 'measuring' qualitative experience.

Experimental Physiology

The problem of 'emotionlessness' as empirical equilibrium when emotions are not the subject under investigation is explored in Otniel Dror's intriguing account of physiological experiments in the early twentieth century. Using dogs, cats, rabbits, and rats in order to determine objective, universally applicable knowledge about anatomical functions, such as blood pressure, glucose absorption, digestive operations, and so forth, scientists found that emotions altered the physiological processes of their animal test subjects in a myriad of ways that undermined the validity and reliability of their experiments. Experimental procedures, such as the way animal subjects were handled and spoken to, as well as the broader environment of the laboratory, including the presence and behavior of humans, other animals, background sounds, and so on, evoked emotions in test subjects that caused significant physiological variations within individual animals and across experiments, rendering replication from study to study problematic (207).

The range of emotions that could disturb the accrual of scientifically valid findings included, "fear, anger, jealousy, joy, apprehension, anxiety, and restlessness," because they caused emotional excitement in animals and, therefore, physiological changes (208, 226). Thus, one researcher in 1936 described himself as having become "a psychologist of cats," and another, in 1931, stated that it was "scientifically essential" to maintain rats in "fearless contentment" (qtd. in Dror 223, 227).

To counter the distorting effects of emotions on their scientific studies, "a series of correctives that targeted emotions and eliminated their destructive effects on the production of physiological knowledge" were instituted (Dror 216). Such correctives involved changes to an extensive range of experimental procedures and environmental aspects of laboratories, all designed to abolish states of emotional excitement in animal subjects.

However, the procedural and environmental correctives implemented were not sufficient to eliminate 'the problem of emotions' from experimental studies. Physiologists also discovered that the specific test subjects chosen presented emotional complications. Variations in the personalities, temperaments, or dispositions of individual animals contributed significantly to inconsistencies in study results. Noted physiologist, Walter Cannon, spoke of the considerable differences in his laboratory cats, who could range from savage, restless, or indolent to friendly, affectionate, serene, or playful (Cannon qtd. in Dror 219). The outcome of successful experiments, therefore, depended upon selecting "emotionally appropriate" test animals (Dror 219). Inevitably, ideal candidates were considered calm, contented representatives of their species, in which the "standard" affective state "was always, without exception, zero [emotional] excitement" (Ibid. 229, 222).

By attending to these considerations of process, environment, and temperament, Dror's physiologists believed it was possible "to control emotions and achieve replication, universal knowledge, and decreased variability" (229). But here, it is crucial to ask what kinds of knowledge were achieved and on the basis of what assumptions regarding emotions. In other words, narratives about emotions were necessary in order to arrive at certain forms of knowledge, yet such narratives about emotions affected the kinds of knowledge actually achieved.

Instead of being viewed as common, variable phenomena that required inclusion, emotions came to be perceived as impediments to the gathering of scientific knowledge. "The identification of emotion with disorder was widespread," resulting in characterizations of emotions as intrusive, unpredictable, and out-of-the-ordinary events, functioning as "a broad class of disruptive moments," and signifying loss of control in the accumulation of scientifically valid results (Dror 236–237). This recalls Dumit's contention that, due to their ill-fit with computational metaphors, cognitive models, and the demands of empiricism, emotions are more widely accepted, not as indicators of proper, regular functionality, but as markers of a "change in the state" of a being, whether as disease, disorder, disruption, or some other form of aberrational departure. Rather than 'normal' phenomena of lived existence, emotions tend to be understood as a change in natural equilibrium, an equilibrium which can only belong to an *unaffected* state of being. 'Emotionlessness' as lack of emotional excitement then becomes the standardized barometer.

Dror's physiologists believed it was both necessary and possible to eliminate emotions, particularly those that caused 'excitement.' Or, at the very least, that they could be minimized to "a constant and standard emotional state" of tranquility or "fearless contentment," as in the case of one researcher's rats (217). Through this belief, experimental physiologists proceeded with a standard of 'normal' emotionality that was ostensibly devoid of emotions but actually gave precedence to certain emotional states, such as contentment and tranquility. This "new emotion-controlled 'normal'" was then accepted as or equated with "nature's true physiological state" of emotional equilibrium or an unaffected state of being (Ibid.).

Thus, such experimental results were based on the narrative that 'normal' means to be 'emotionless' for both human and animal beings, universally applied as the natural, objective state of existence. Further, emotionlessness became equated with calm contentedness as the norm for sentient beings, although this is highly contestable in the course of much lived existence. It remains an open question whether most animals or human beings can or do exist in prolonged states of calm or fearless contentment. To accept this as the norm means that physiological responses when in emotional states of 'excitement' can be interpreted only as abnormalities or departures from that established standard. Therefore, the positive presence (in the sense of existing) of a great range of emotions comes to be regarded as aberrant.

Additionally, the physiological data gathered applied primarily to individual animals whose dispositions were interpreted as especially tranquil or to those who were carefully lulled into temporary states of calm. This provides no comparable baseline of measurement for states of fear or anger or joy. I have already noted it is open to debate whether a baseline of tranquility can be judged as the habitual state of sentient beings. Yet the reasoning by which calm contentedness was assumed to be the most minimal emotional state remains unclear, rather than boredom or indifference, for example. In the case of many humans, contentment appears to be a relatively rare, if much-desired mode of existence, towards which considerable time and effort is exerted in the hopes of achievement. Similarly, it remains unresolved whether tranquility, calmness, contentedness, serenity, docility, being good-natured, or any of the other descriptors used to label emotionally appropriate test subjects, can be considered a singular emotional state, all pointing to a similar set of experiences. Finally, as Dror points out, the effort at "purging" emotions led to the introduction of "qualitative emotional descriptors into the quantitative language" of experiments (236, 207). Attempting to assess the personality types or dispositions of dogs, cats, rabbits, or rats necessitated judgments based on non-objective appraisals, including descriptors such as sensitive, excitable, timid, nervous, restless, serene, or resistant. The assessment of what emotional state test animals were feeling at any specific moment, whether fear, anger, jealousy, joy, apprehension, or anxiety demanded interpretive evaluations of emotional states that could not be measured or otherwise empirically ascertained.

Such qualitative evaluations were themselves impossible to excise from experiments because they "captured and negotiated aspects of laboratory life that the rigorous language of numbers and curves failed to articulate" (208). No means were found to eliminate emotions from objective, empirical work without introducing qualitative emotional concepts and criteria as part of the assessment process. Emotions ostensibly could be eradicated but only through their inclusion into the operations of the lab. Discussing an earlier moment in experimental physiology, the vivisection debates of the 1870s, Paul White provides an account that complements Dror's. White argues that attempts to *control* emotions – in this case, experimenters' rather than animals' feelings, in which physiologists were portrayed as striving to discipline their own humane emotions of sympathy or pity for animal test subjects in the name of scientific knowledge – was not equivalent to the *effacement* of emotions (118). Instead, the effort surrounding the ostensible "control of emotion within the experimental setting could itself be described as a highly affective process" (Ibid.). Emotional effects, as aspects of life that numbers and curves fail to capture, had to be taken into account in terms that were not strictly scientific but, rather, qualitative or aesthetic, in order to then make the claim that they had been neutralized.

Dumit, Dyson, and Dror tell different stories about emotions and science. But what these narratives share in common is recognition of the ill-fit of emotions in various quests for objective knowledge. Their accounts suggest that this cannot be done easily or, perhaps, at all. I have been arguing that aesthetics, in its broader understanding as qualitative evaluations that involve meaningfulness, is a necessary addition to making sense of emotionality and, specifically, emotional disorders. I return now to neuroimaging, in order to discuss it in the more precise sense of aesthetics, as a means of *visualizing* brain activity. However, to do so is to find, via emotions, that we are led again to aesthetics in its more expansive forms.

The Visual Aesthetics of Neuroscience

An analysis of neuroimaging must take into account the kind of 'visual evidence' brain imaging constitutes, when rendering both the mind's normal and abnormal functionings. Representations of PET results are rendered in aesthetic terms, as images. Neuroimaging technologies like PET – including CT (computed tomography), SPECT (single-photon emission computed tomography) and fMRI (functional magnetic resonance imaging) – are based on the principles of tomography, the analysis of an object to be scanned, such as the brain, section by section or in 'slices.' Information for the location and intensity of activity in minute, multiple subsections of each slice are rendered as numerical data, in the case of PET by following radioactive tracers in the blood flow through the brain that result from specific cognitive activities or emotional states.

Subsequent stages involve tomographic reconstruction, in which the numerical data are fed into computer programs and, via one of a number of existing algorithms, are processed as relative values of distribution (location and intensity) throughout the brain. Produced by means of computer analysis is a "brainset," "an apparently stable set of numbers that represent the flow rate of the tracer" and, therefore, stand for a presumed reliable record of activity in the brain (Dumit 81). The resulting complex of statistical evidence that constitutes the brainset could be reported as numbers. The difficulty, according to Henry Wagner, one of the founders of nuclear medicine, is that PET scans yield "a tremendous amount of data," too much quantitative information to comprehend (Wagner qtd. in

Dumit 90). In contrast, "images are a very, very nice way of abstracting quantification" (Ibid. 91).

At the point of "abstracting quantification," the process has moved to also encompass aesthetics. For 'abstracting,' in this instance, is a form of representation in which pictorial information comes to stand for numerical data. Of course, numerical information is itself a mathematical form of abstraction for biological activity. Thus, images of brain activity already involve at least two layers of representation.

The process of visualizing statistical data concerns transforming quantitative information into qualitative images of brain functioning. Importantly, PET functional imaging is not a photographic process. Its results are created without a camera and, therefore, its formal properties and procedures are closer to CGI than live action photography or film. The appearance of the final product not withstanding, PET scans are not direct reproductions of the brain.

Instead, constructing images based on data derived from brain scans requires "careful measurement and complex physiological modeling" (Dumit 27). PET results are often plotted onto CT or MRI derived anatomical landscapes upon which the statistical evidence of functional events is layered. In this manner, PET data arrive at the brightly colored, computer-generated still images of the brain 'in action' that have become iconic in popular culture. These are usually presented as a series, for comparative purposes, either depicting differing functions in opertation in a brainset,[3] or the varying physiological responses of the same activity on the part of different categories of test subjects.

A number of narrowly aesthetic issues come into play with these pictorial abstractions, one of the most complex and ambiguous of which concerns the uses of color. PET-generated data can be rendered visually on a gray scale, in which lighter and darker variations identify the location and intensity of a specific mental activity or state (Dumit 80, 91). Such an approach is more conducive to a notion of gradations in brain functions, rather than discretely located areas of activity. However, variations in shades of gray are not easily perceived by the human eye, thus color "was introduced to make subtle distinctions visible," and its use now has become standardized (Ibid. 91). But colors, like many aesthetic elements, are qualitative, relational phenomena, which becomes apparent in brain imaging procedures in a number of ways. Depending on which aspects are emphasized and which minimized via color, scans can be rendered to look quite different even when using the same single brain or brainset (91). Michel Ter-Pogossian, professor of radiation sciences and one of the founders of PET imaging, explains that the colored images can be made to "signify whatever you want them to signify" (Ter-Pogossian qtd. in Dumit 93).

The use of color is arbitrary in a number of ways. First, it bears no direct relationship to its referents. Indeed, the colors employed in PET images are referred to as "pseudo-colors" due to the fact that they do not reflect actual colors of the brain (Dumit 92). Second, the relationship between selected colors is ambiguous. For example, what does yellow next to red signify? Do the two colors measure more or less of the same activity or are two different events being depicted? Third, one of the ways color exaggerates information is by appearing to create boundaries in the brain where none exist. When colors change, from yellow to red for example, a visually distinct border between regions of the brain appears, even though the line between the colors may represent only "a small change in numerical value" (Dumit 93). Thus, color tends to magnify gradations or "subtle distinctions" into discrete locations, although such discrete locations do not exist in the brain, which functions in a far more integrated, cross-network, and intracommunciative manner (Ibid. 79).

I would like to pursue, in greater depth, comments made by Ter-Pogossian because they raise particularly interesting aesthetic concerns. He notes, "the pictures [of PET brain scans] that are particularly attractive that you have seen in general are fairly heavily doctored, in the sense of making them more attractive than they should be" (Ter-Pogossian qtd. in Dumit 94). This observation provokes consideration about the role of 'attractiveness' in the process of imaging data, and in scientific knowledge more generally. What is the role of attractiveness in providing persuasive or compelling scientific accounts? Should such images be made attractive at all? If so, based on what criteria and to which ends? Why would one suppose that 'unattractive' images represent quantitative data more accurately?

Ter-Pogossian continues: "It is misleading to just use aesthetic values" (Ibid.). What does it mean to use solely aesthetic values? How can that occur when imaging is based on scientifically accrued data? In a situation of "just aesthetics" where do the scientific aspects recede to? What degree or kind of aesthetics nullifies the science? enhances it? What is the acceptable ratio of aesthetics to science in cases, such as PET imaging, in which aesthetic values cannot be eliminated? Ter-Pogossian's statements introduce complex matters belonging to the realm of aesthetics as much as to science.

For Dumit, the visual representation of data cannot avoid "a necessary addition of supplementary meaning" (93). This is so because an aesthetic rendering functions as a further layer of metaphor against which the data inevitably are interpreted. Such supplementary meanings are both visual and narrative – PET scans tell a story: in Dumit's example, of different categories of brains between those who are depressed and those who are not, that is, narratives of normality versus depression. And as with all narratives, some become more compelling than others at particular points in time and place.

Technologies of representation, such as neuroimaging, "are deployed by scientists and others to build persuasive accounts about the structure of natural and social worlds" (95). Dumit refers to the process of building persuasive accounts as one of aesthetics, in which renderings data become interpretable because of the narratives that can be drawn from a particular set of data. In the instance of PET scans, it becomes apparent that aesthetics, in both its more narrow and wider implications, cannot be absent from the techniques and technologies of neuroimaging.

None of this is to suggest that aesthetics somehow 'trumps' scientific explanations or that it is a sufficient explanatory system in and of itself. As Chapters Two and Three show, aesthetic representations of emotions may well be as limited or constraining as neurobiological or cognitive interpretations. Rather, it is to say that aesthetics serves as another explanatory complex: an extensive series of cultural conceptualizations about knowledge and experience, as intricate as physical science or social science accounts. And although aesthetics may not, in itself, provide a sufficient or exhaustive series of explanatory mechanisms, some of the complexities and ambiguities that arise within scientific disciplines concerning emotions can only be resolved in terms other than the 'purely' scientific. We saw this, for example, in Dror's study of experimental physiology in which emotions could only be considered neutralized when actually encompassed through qualitative terms, through qualitative terms, such as describing the personalities of animal test subjects. The inclusion of aesthetics doesn't negate scientific forms of knowledge but the two may well be inseparable. Ultimately, aesthetics as a web of potential meanings may be necessary to the production of explanatory narratives concerning 'qualitative data' – phenomena difficult to measure, such as emotions and emotional disorders, as well as other aspects of self, identity, and sociality. What we seek, then, are additional explanatory forms that help us explore the cultural impact and processes of emotional experience and expression.

Yet currently, scientific psy and, in particular, neuroscience exist as the West's most compelling narratives on human emotional functioning. An ongoing "desire for a certain kind of revelation that science will be able to satisfy" about brain, mind, emotions, and mental illness continues (Papoulias and Callard 36–37). For example, Radden speaks of the entrenched belief that biological psychiatry will provide "fully causal accounts of pathological depression" so that "modern science will conquer and, with time, expunge" the extensive, now-global public health problems posed by emotional disorders (108, 18). Faith in the full explanatory power of neurobiology and neuropsychiatry regarding emotional disorders expresses the belief that emotions can be rendered fully comprehensible, in empirical terms. Yet there remains little reason to suppose, were neuroscience able to provide more complete physiological and psychological explanations, that the conceptual and lived complexities surrounding mind, emotion, and mental illness would simply dissipate. Although neuroscientific knowledge certainly alters the nature and experience of emotional disorders, especially in terms of prevention or remediation, it doesn't account for how we might seek to live our emotional existences, again calling for an aesthetics as well as a science of emotionality.

The Aesthetics of Experience: "Every Second of Being Alive Hurt Me"

Managing emotions when they are experienced by individuals has been widely regarded as belonging to some formulation of 'the personal.' The difficulty is that emotions, due to their equivalently individual and socio-cultural nature, belong simultaneously to 'the personal' and 'the public.' Indeed, the personal/public dichotomy, as it relates to emotions, remains unsustainable. An alternative possibility is to regard biographical emotions as a matter of aesthetics, in the expansive sense, as ways of living. Here, biography references any individuated, narrative account, written or oth-erwise, including stories that remain unspoken. Emotions as an aesthetics of living describe ways of existing, of moving through and experiencing the world, of making sense of it, which is to account for the meanings we attribute to our emotional conditions. However, in this rendition, aesthet-ics are never unbounded; they remain subject to limitations of possibility as much as to breadths of desire. Emotionality in these terms has little to do with ideals of personal freedom or self-realization. Aesthetic forms of living always exist within constraints, often severe, whether biological, psychological, social, economic, political, or combinations of these and other factors.

The benefit of an aesthetics of emotionality lies in the ability to conceive of emotions as part of the circumstances through which the individual is operationalized as subject/self/personality, in a complex process that renders the individual and the cultural as relational events. Lived experience can then be understood, via emotionality, as the linking or mediating of social insti-tutions, cultural practices, and individual existences. The individual never occurs in an hypothesized, separate realm of 'the personal.' Rather, through the collective, shared meanings provided by the practices of emotional aesthetics, 'the individual' and 'the social' interact in mutually constituting relations.

As example, I turn briefly to a written biographical account of the lived experience of depression. In his book, *Noonday Demons*, which details Andrew Solomon's experiences with severe depression, he expresses his frus-tration with the inadequacy of neurochemical explanations. Solomon com-plains that being told one has a neurochemical disorder located in the brain clarifies very little about existing in a state of depression or, for that matter, about feeling other emotions, such as happiness or guilt. "Everything about a person is just chemical if one wants to think in those terms" (22). Physio-logical or neurobiological accounts provide specific kinds of knowledge but they don't tell people how they ought or might go about conducting their emotional states. Thus, Solomon maintains, "anyone who lives through this [severe depression] knows that it is never as simple as complicated chemis-try" (81). For Solomon, brain functioning is an incomplete means by which to fully or even adequately explain one's diagnostic identity. Yet, he turns to such accounts, if ultimately to reject them, in an effort to give shape to the experiences he encounters in his life.

Those "whose lives are significantly defined by psychiatry" (Lucas 156), must turn to available cultural narratives, including psychobiomedical ones, to attempt to make sense of their psychiatric identities and emotional lives.

Solomon does so, although he ultimately finds neuroscientific accounts deeply lacking towards the explanations he seeks. Lucas points out that the mentally ill in the study he conducted sought out aesthetic forms, especially instances of popular culture such as books, films, television, and music, as the most available and helpful means of giving shape to their diagnostic identities and experiential existences. They directed their attention to popular narratives precisely because the coherent, useful explanations they sought appeared only as 'gaps' or missing elements in prevailing psychiatric accounts. In its place, popular culture becomes "the very vehicle by which schizophrenic experiences were apprehended by [study] participants and then conveyed in communications" (Lucas 158). Such apprehension and communication through aesthetics, narrowly defined, helps delineate an aesthetics, in its expansive meanings, as ways of conducting one's lived existence.

Solomon reminds us of the urgency of this process because: "Every second of being alive hurt me" (19). The exigency of such felt states demands that we not lose sight of the experiential aspects of emotional disorders or emotions overall. Scholars have argued that certain forms of social constructionism, as well as biospychiatric and other psychological accounts, fail to make room for the legitimately intense pain and suffering experienced by the mentally ill and, therefore, such approaches ignore vital aspects of the meanings of emotional disorders (Blackman 185). In other words, social construction theories may constitute a form of cultural reductionism. In contrast, emotions can serve as remediation for analyses in recent decades that have linked culture too closely with identity, as well as with ideology, language, and other cognitive social processes. Similarly, pain and suffering experienced emotionally, rather than as physiological functions, have been accorded diminished status in what have been widely criticized as contemporary forms of biological or neuro reductionism.

Biographical accounts are never merely 'personal' or 'subjective.' They reveal something of import about the cultural parameters of emotions and the circumstances emotionality creates in our lives. In this sense then, emotions could be considered subjective in that they participate in determining the specific subjects we can or cannot become. Emotions, like the ability to suffer or to feel pleasures, may well serve as markers for being human. However, we lack sufficiently complex accounts of how emotionality moves us, from one emotional state to another and from one social circumstance to the next. Such accounts remain a pressing issue, as many writing on emotional disorders make clear. The very real pains of felt experience demand attention because every second of being alive could well mean acute suffering and despair.

Reductionisms

In his much-cited 1884 essay, "What Is an Emotion?," William James refers to "the *aesthetic* sphere of the mind," which he explicitly links to the mind's "longings, its pleasures and pains, and its emotions" (244–245; italics in original).

Alberti contends that a principal motive for James in writing his essay was to counteract an overly cognitive understanding of the brain (*Matters* 7, 147). And indeed, James begins the essay with precisely this complaint. Physiologists "exploring the functions of the brain, have limited their attempts at explanation to its cognitive and volitional performances" (244). James asserts that focusing so much on the cognitive, rational elements of human existence omits something vital, leaving us with what is only "pale, colourless, destitute of emotional warmth" (248). In order to allow for an aesthetics of emotion, his solution is to seek an integration of the cognitive and corporeal. In attempting to synthesize mind and body, one can certainly argue that James' proposal is an overcorrection of the contemporaneous physiological studies he finds wanting, in which he favors the corporeal to redress the strongly cognitive imbalance. But arguments have been made that it was not James' intent to disavow mind entirely for the sake of body (Barbalet 1999).

Burkitt, too, observes that James wrote "What Is an Emotion?" to counter the Darwinian view that "facial expressions and bodily gestures are only the *expression* of emotion, while the emotion itself is "a state of 'mind'" (52; italics in original). In his overall work on emotions, James was searching for a fuller, more integrated notion that encompassed body, mind, social situations, and the meanings attached to those situations. According to Burkitt, in James' view integrating the embodied meanings of emotions stood as necessary to the "full experience" of life which, as we saw, also encompasses an aesthetic, emotional sphere of mind (53). In these terms, "meaningful experiences must be *felt*" as well as thought, thus linking an aesthetics of emotion as well as embodiment to experiential existence (Burkitt 73; italics in original).

In her exploration of the historical development "away from the heart of feeling and towards the brain of feeling," an occurrence she labels "cranio-centrism," Alberti emphasizes that the development of scientific medicine, beginning in the nineteenth century and continuing today, has enabled the sharp dichotomizing of mind from body (*Matters* 7). She argues that the rise of 'mind,' the relocation of emotions to the brain, and the separation of mind from body as distinct realms, are all quite recent events, resulting in the loss of a holistic, integrated concept of the human being.

In contrast, she believes that humoral theory, as it existed in various forms for two thousand years, held the capacity for such a systemically integrated account, uniting "the soul, the brain, the emotions, and the heart" (163). Alberti contends that one of the reasons humoral theory survived for so long was precisely because of its ability to provide an explanation for the integration of human functions. In its place, medical and scientific forms of knowledge have endowed us with explanatory models of autonomic reflexes, sensory impulses, and neurochemical transmitters, still leaving us without a satisfactory account of how emotions operate in sociocultural and experiential contexts or what their functions in those arenas might be. The legacy of scientific medicine is that it has "made the heart an organ of the body, the brain the source of ourselves, and the soul as redundant" (163). To which I would add, in the current climate of cranio-centrism, as evidenced in fields such as neurobiology and cultural affect theory, 'mind' in the recent brain/mind dynamic also risks being made redundant through the establishment of a brain/body unity, still consigning us to an inadequate account of emotionality.

Like Alberti, Dixon views a sharp mind/body distinction as a nineteenth-century development, exaggerating any division that might have occurred in previous eras. He regards a more rigorous polarization of mind and body as the result of the growth of psychology, including in its physiological, behavioral, neurological, evolutionary, cognitive, and psychoanalytic manifestations (*From Passions* 12). The emergence of psychology as a distinct set of disciplines altered the way we understand and experience the range of phenomena that includes "hope, fear, love, hate, joy, sorrow, anger" (Ibid. 4). Specifically, psychology as a distinct body of knowledge resulted in a shift in Anglo-American linguistic usage between 1800 and 1850, so that these phenomena became referred to inclusively as 'emotions.' Previously, and in contrast, they had been viewed as varying events or states that included passions, appetites, affections, and sentiments (249). Dixon's argument is that because passions, appetites, affections, and sentiments represent a wide range of experiences, encompassing what we would now consider the most bodily to the most cognitive phenomena, a sharp distinction between body and mind could not exist in the way we conceive of it today. Instead, it was the creation of the singular category of 'the emotions,' that made possible their subsequent "opposition to reason, intellect and will" (3). Thus, the reason-passion division following the Enlightenment, "was replaced in the nineteenth century by an even stronger intellect-emotion dichotomy" (17). In place of a range of emotive concepts that covered feelings from sensation through thought, a binary formula emerged distinguishing cognition from emotion.

In turn, Alberti suggests that in the cultural conceptual shift to brain/mind, "the role of the brain as cognitive centre" grew more pivotal (47). Although also the seat of emotions, the individual psyche that developed over the course of the nineteenth and twentieth centuries shaped a mind/brain with increased emphasis on cognition. Thus, while emotions were relocated to the brain, along with cognition, their importance in the new configuration receded in favor of the thinking human being.

Alberti and Dixon track important historical developments leading to current apprehensions about a growing tide of neuroreductionism. Some of the sharpest, most consistent criticisms of neuroscience, from both within and beyond the psy fields, assert that it has led, increasingly, to the dissolution of mind in lieu of brain. For example, Horwitz charges that biomedical psychiatry has relocated psychopathology, in a wholesale manner, to "the physical properties of brains, not in the symbolic systems of minds" (3). For her part, Martin cautions that a number of "contemporary modes of thought about the human mind are bent on reducing 'mind' to 'body' by interpreting psychological processes as neuronal ones," in which "neuro-reductionism appears to be invading the domain of culture and reducing it to electrical and chemical events" (190, 207). Thus she views neuroscietific develop-ments as threatening a more inclusive understanding of individuals in their cultural contexts.

In these concerns we can see that the mind/body dualism that Alberti and Dixon describe as intensifying in the nineteenth century has not abated. On the contrary, the mind/body dichotomy, which Blackman characterizes as so stubbornly "entrenched" within the psy disciplines (194), has spread to a variety of fields, for instance, from neuroscience to philosophical affect theory. One of Dumit's primary concerns, in his study of PET neuroimag-ing, resides in the prospect that such neurotechnologies, and the scientific theory upon which they are based, tend to reduce 'personhood' to the bio-logical functioning of the brain. In this view, 'mind' becomes equivalent to the brain, "brains have types, these types are people" of varying kinds, includ-ing the mentally normal and abnormal (141). The effect is to give the brain near-absolute explanatory power.

Paradoxically, despite his association with having bequeathed an influ-ential, strongly embodied understanding of emotionality, elsewhere James upholds as valuable the ambiguity of emotions as an indeterminate state of existence.

> [I]n practical life no urgent need has yet arisen for deciding whether to treat them [affectional experiences] as rigorously mental or as rigor-ously physical facts. So they remain equivocal; and, as the world goes, their equivocality is one of their great conveniences.
>
> (James 1912 qtd. in Leys 468)

As noted, James confronted a similar mind/body distinction in his time, spe-cifically the overvaluation of the cognitive and a concomitant exclusion of the corporeal. In the above quote, however, he advocates the advantages of *not* resolving this dilemma as far as emotion goes, citing its convenient equivocality as a strength rather than a flaw.

Leys' disquiet about current mind/body distinctions is that they only "posit consciousness and the body, with no third term," such as the psy-chic unconscious (Leys and Goldman 675). Leys argues that in an era in which mind has been reduced to conscious thought and cognition, and affect stands in for the body, a place for other potential realms of existence has been excised. Her particular concern is the loss, within the concept of mind, of a domain for the psychoanalytic unconscious, her third term. Of course, three is an arbitrary number. There may well exist multiple spheres beyond the polarization of a cognitive mind and an affective body. Further, as we have seen, multiple, overlapping forms of reductionism – mind to brain, mind to cognition, affect as purely embodied – can be operationalized simultaneously, often in an effort to unify opposing terms by effacing one in favor of the other.

I suggest that emotions as a third (or fourth or fifth) term hold theoretical value precisely because of their convenient equivocality, making them happily difficult to reduce to either mind or body, biology or social construction, individual or society, science or aesthetics. Emotionality carries the potential of moving between first and second terms, whatever they may be.

If emotions resist being either rigorously mental or rigorously physical, as James states, if they cannot be effectively collapsed or equated with one term over the other, then their removal from the struggle between proponents of body *versus* mind would be efficacious, so that we spend less time asking what emotions are, in preference for analyses of what they do as individual and cultural events. If mind has not been made redundant, like the soul before it, then openings remain for matters of pleasure and suffering, and explorations of how we ought to live them. Indeed, if existence includes "the perceiving, suffering, and reasoning mind," then all of these forces, including suffering, require investigation (Brown and Stenner 15).

To include emotionality in 'mind-reading' functions, per Dyson and affective computing, is to *keep in mind* the role of emotions in the generation of both linguistic and nonlinguistic meanings in sociocultural contexts. Keeping emotions in mind, not solely in body, establishes more experiential, aesthetic spheres of life. Because emotions possess convenient equivocality, they cannot effectively be dissolved into body or mind, cognition or affect, individuality or sociality. Our conceptualization of emotionality encompasses a broad range of experiences, taking up a relational position, moving between various realms, in order to circulate, integrate, and negotiate among them. Emotions are not events that infiltrate, intrude upon, disturb, or disrupt other, already existing modes of life. Rather, they are a means of enabling and creating ways of living.

Finally, this chapter circles back to the issue of the excessive psychomedicalizing of emotional disorders, resulting in the current global epidemic, where this book began. Because we also must ask what happens to the ways of life of those deemed *not* to be medically or psychologically ill but, rather, only erroneously diagnosed as such.

Normal Misery

I began this book with the present alarm over an escalating global epidemic of emotional disorders, in which the numbers of those diagnosed with mood, anxiety, and related forms of mental illness has increased exponentially, so that "the world is in the midst of an epidemic of depression of startling proportions" (Bentall 20). Repeatedly cited statistics indicate that "by 2020 depression will be the second leading cause of ill health worldwide," after heart disease, and is "already the leading cause of disability for 15-to-44 year olds" internationally (Radden 97; Horwitz and Wakefield 5).

As we have seen at various points throughout the book, many attribute the current epidemic to the overmedicalizing and excessive psychologizing of ordinary, everyday life (Rose; Miller; Kutchins and Kirk; Horwitz and Wakefield; Greenberg; Bentall; Kirk, Gomery, and Cohen; Radden). The consequences have been characterized, variously, as the medicopsychologizing of minor troubles, simple unhappiness, malaise, life's vicissitudes, generic human dissatisfaction, normal misery, and the suffering of ordinary people. Kutchins and Kirk charge there is "a growing tendency in our society to medicalize problems that are not medical, to find psychopathology where there is only pathos" (x). Here they point out the overlapping origin of pathos as emotion and pathology as disease or aberrance; but in doing so, their comments also raise the question, why should we view emotional pain as "only" pathos?

Like others writing on the subject, Radden calls for "conceptual distinctions separating the depressive states that are pathological from those that are normal and normative responses to misfortune" (97). She believes, as do others, that such a partition is useful, necessary, and in certain senses, 'real.' To this end, she advocates reserving 'pathological depression' for those instances in which a disturbance originating within the individual can be determined, per *DSM* criteria as discussed in Chapter Four. This requires the carving out of "a conceptual space for [emotional] distress that is not pathological," which she also refers to as circumstantial depression (99). However, Radden also acknowledges that circumstantial depression can be the result of a vast array of conditions, from ordinary misfortune to overt oppression. Therefore, she notes the "ubiquity and rapid increase of depression wherever war, want, and social upheaval are found" (97).

Radden's motive in working to preserve a notion of pathological depression, in contrast to circumstantial forms, has to do with the fate of the psy disciplines and the ongoing, viable existence of a psychic realm. If too many of life's aspects become psychologized, if virtually everyone is or can be subject to mental illness in the form of emotional disorders, a process begun historically with the development of neuroses, then the categories themselves (mental illness, emotional disorder) become meaningless through their prevalence. If abnormality exists as a differentiating mechanism by which to define normality then its sociocultural usefulness, in the case of mental health, would be undermined. The blurring of pathological and normal mental functioning destabilizes the foundation of the psychological disciplines as well as their value as social categories. For example, Horwitz and Wakefield argue that one of the benefits of distinguishing normal sadness, even when intense, from depressive disorder is that doing so "maintains the conceptual integrity of psychiatry" (21).

But Radden also recognizes that the attempt to draw conceptual differences between pathological and normal modes of depression is fraught with difficulties. Feelings and behaviors that result from pathological emotional disturbances within the individual often manifest as "indistinguishable" from the effects of human suffering caused by oppression, grief, loss of home and livelihood, or other forms of deprivation (20). The felt pain of those living with circumstantial rather than pathological depression can be as profound and debilitating; the effects on each existence may well render them similarly "dysfunctional" (103). Additionally, pathological mood or anxiety disorders exist that, by definition, originate circumstantially, as in the case of post-traumatic stress disorder. PTSD has been included in the *DSMs* since 1980 as an anxiety disorder, but only after heated debates precisely because of its social etiology (Young; Summerfield, "Invention").[4]

To complicate the situation further, those who have been diagnosed repeatedly with internally systemic mood or anxiety disorders can enter specific bouts through either identifiable, triggering circumstances or without immediate, discernible cause. Do we consider such patients as pathologically ill only when there is no determinable cause or triggering event? Do long-past events, such as childhood physical or sexual abuse, render the person's condition part of life's misfortunes rather than illness?

Despite these difficulties, Radden asserts that pathological versus circumstantial forms of emotional suffering "are marked by morally relevant differences: such conceptual boundaries must be affirmed and maintained" (20–21). One of the morally relevant reasons for affirming the distinction occurs because human condition disturbances require forms of remediation that psy disciplines cannot offer. For Radden, while pathological depression calls for varieties of psychological attention, whether psychopharmacological or psychotherapeutic, circumstantially provoked suffering demands larger social and political solutions. Thus she argues:

> The hapless inhabitants of refugee camps may suffer depression and may require medical intervention. But if that intervention comes at the cost of neglecting why they are there in the first place, and why they suffer – that is, the questions spurring social and political action – then it will be difficult to justify. (98)

In this argument, taken up by a number of commentators, the medicalization of emotional disorders caused by oppression, deprivation, and inequity risks providing individuated psychological attention *at the cost of* broader social and political actions. For this reason, human condition suffering ought to be maintained in distinction from pathological suffering, considered to originate within the individual.

> Collapsing these distinctions seems all too likely to forestall social and political action not only more fitting but, in directing itself towards the causes of much of this suffering, more effective. (Ibid.)

However, I would suggest that individuated and sociopolitical attention do not exist in mutual exclusivity. No justification is used for withholding psychotropic medication from those suffering from mood or anxiety disorders because the disturbances diagnosed within the individual were initiated by childhood physical or sexual abuse, that is, externalized, social harms which may have initially instigated the subsequent disorders. Why should the conditions provoked by "want, war, and social upheaval" be any different; why would they, too, not demand both individuated and sociopolitical responses? Equally, most of us would find it offensive to claim that child abuse no longer need be addressed as a sociopolitical issue because medical intervention exists that potentially alleviates the psychological effects of past abuse.

Arguments such as Radden's find basis in a fundamental but questionable assumption: that attention at one level – the psychic individual – undermines the likelihood of responsiveness at other levels. Such a view reinforces the dichotomization between individual and society. In contrast, greater focus on individuated forms of psychological pain, resulting from war and other kinds of upheaval or oppression, as well as attention paid to the resulting economic and social costs of such psychic distress, may well spur more sociopolitical action rather than less. To return to my example, arguably the long-term toll of childhood abuse on adult psychiatric patients has led to greater public awareness of the pressing need to redress, as a society, the sexual and physical mistreatment of children.

Radden quotes psychiatric anthropologist Arthur Kleinman, that harsh economic, political, and health deficiencies create:

> endemic feelings of hopelessness and helplessness, where demoralization and despair are responses to real conditions of chronic deprivation and persistent loss, where powerlessness is not a cognitive distortion but an accurate mapping of one's place in an oppressive social system.
> (Kleinman qtd. in Radden 100)

However, Radden understands the implications of Kleinman's comments differently than I do. She interprets them as necessitating the bracketing out of "the *medicalization of social problems,*" those cases in which hopelessness and helplessness are responses, in Kleinman's words, to "real conditions" (Radden 100; italics in original). In contrast, I would argue that Kleinman's sentiments call the sustainability of the psychobiomedical framework, as currently constituted, into question. He is a forceful advocate regarding the difficulty of drawing distinctions between mental health versus social policy needs. Especially in regions most affected by poverty and violence, "the medical, the economic, and the political may often be inseparable" (Kleinman 1519). This is so because places where "poverty, broken families, and a high risk of violence" are endemic also surface as "settings where depression, suicide, post-traumatic stress disorder, and drug misuse cluster" (Ibid.).

To exclude from psychological attention those whose feelings of "demoralization and despair" reflect "an accurate mapping" of their circumstances is a cruel form of abandonment, based on the reasoning that their difficulties are too daunting to be dealt with effectively so that the current psychobiomedical framework can provide little assistance towards ameliorating the emotional difficulties of their existences. Finding ways to conduct one's material and emotional circumstances might be ordinary in that we all must do so. However, chronic deprivation, persistent loss, and powerlessness in the face of oppressive social systems continue to be extraordinary conditions, not simple unhappiness, malaise, generic human dissatisfaction, or normal misery. Only from the bleakest, most dystopian perspective can we consider them routine. Good intentions notwithstanding, while sociopolitical crises, like war or displacement or dire economic inequities, could in principle be redressed, this seems highly unlikely in present circumstances. Additionally, natural disasters, accidents, or other unpreventable sources of human pain and suffering continue. What does it mean to say that people who have lost family members, homes, their means of livelihood, or their ways of life are responding normally, reasonably, or understandably, without sounding, or in fact being, dismissive? How might we better include the emotional costs of social, political, and economic exigencies?

Although some believe that the conceptual difference between pathological and human condition emotional disorders is a largely arbitrary *theoretical* judgment, very 'real-world' implications attach to such distinctions. At stake is whether individuals receive quite substantive attention and assistance. Medicopsychological status confers tangible efforts towards remediation that life's vicissitudes do not. As Ian Hacking observes: "To call something an illness, and not just madness, is to imply that there are experts to be called in, professionals who can attempt or achieve cures" (52). To the degree that we identify certain events as illnesses rather than madness, for reasons beyond discipline in Foucault's terms, that which we withhold from those designated with situational depression or similar emotional states is the promise of remediation or relief. Horwitz and Wakefield argue that, while "no one who is suffering should be denied access to services, separating nondisordered from dysfunctional conditions can focus the expertise of mental health professionals on true mental disorders and lead to a more efficient use of mental health resources" (21). Despite the disclaimer, what is being suggested here is precisely the holding back of resources from those not suffering "true mental disorders."

Greenberg describes the making of such distinctions in the following manner.

> Mental disorder, like all disease, is suffering that a society devotes resources to relieving. The line between sickness and health, mental and physical, is not biological but social and economic. It is the line between the distress for which we will provide sympathy and money and access to treatment, and the distress for which we will not. (*The Book of Woe* 356–357).

Disciplinary and conceptual boundaries determine whose suffering and distress will be dealt with, upon the basis of what criteria, and through offering which provisions. If the psy arena is not to be the only or dominant domain in which we locate emotions and their maladies, where else do they belong and in what configurations? Because maintaining distinctions between pathological and conditional forms of emotional suffering effectively prioritizes the reality and burden of biopsychological circumstances above social, political, or economic ones.

It is not my intent to debate the relative urgency of various sources of emotional disorders. On the contrary, in refusing the dichotomy between biomedical/psychic (pathological) and sociopolitical (circumstantial) forms of emotional disorders, it is to repudiate the schism imagined between 'the individual' and 'the social,' in favor of tracking how closely and complexly they are interrelated. One danger in clinging to notions of clear-cut psychopathological versus sociopolitical or 'ordinary' emotional suffering means we consign the paradoxically identified, normally disordered, to taking care of themselves in both material and conceptual respects. What becomes of the problem, in the current global epidemic, of the many who cannot be accommodated by psy? What kinds of aesthetic existences and explanatory narratives are made available to them? If psy is not the appropriate domain for the current proliferation of emotional disorders, how might people feel or conduct their emotional lives in terms other than psy?

At the same time that there is believed to be large-scale, erroneous overdiagnosing of mental illness, wide agreement persists that depression and other emotional disorders are "the cause of an immense amount of human suffering" (Horwitz 97). No one supposes that if certain forms of pathological mental illness are maintained while others are excluded, that the remaining vast number of people will simply stop feeling emotional distress or despair. The current global epidemic has usually been attributed to failings within psy, leading to rampant false diagnosis (Chapter Four). Held especially responsible is the pharmaceutical industry in its efforts to constantly increase market share for psychotropic medications. But to see the vast rise in numbers of people seeking relief from emotional suffering as due only or overwhelmingly to the manipulations of various elements within psy is to make dupes of the feeling public. Some portion of the intensely expressed need, on the part of the feeling populace, must be more than the response of pawns to the psy system. While many of those currently diagnosed with emotional disorders may well realize the limitations of psy, in its various forms, alternative ways to conceptualize and conduct the emotional exigencies of living remain frustratingly obscure, relegated quite literally to 'self-help' projects.

To what extent and when emotional pain should be addressed psycho-medically remains an open question. But alongside it we require other accounts, socioemotional, aesthetic, and so on. The challenge is to better understand emotional forms of life, as the current global epidemic of emotional disorders urgently requires. Emotions, and their disorders, can only be grasped in the profuse, cultural contexts in which they occur, and in the multifaceted forms by which they take shape. No single interpretation or set of narratives is sufficient to encompass the vast array of what we identify as emotional experience or the equally vast range of meanings generated by emotionality in all its manifestations. There will never be just one story about emotion, one narrative that encapsulates everything that can be expressed or felt about hope, fear, love, hate, joy, sorrow, anger. No singularly determining or sufficient way exists to visualize, hear, touch, perform, or otherwise create emotional relations.

Notes

1. On coding errors, neuroscientist Michael Phelps indicates that the task is to "understand the molecular regulations of the cell, identify the molecular errors of disease and develop molecular corrections. That is, if there is an error in the genetic code, knock it out" (Phelps qtd. in Dumit 184).
2. Nonverbal/nonlinguistic forms of sociality comprise well-established areas of study within the discipline of communications that have been neglected in recent decades as a result of the dominance of language, defined as verbal communication.
3. In this instance, a brain set entails an averaging of the scans of a group of 'like-minded' individuals, for example, 'normal' controls versus people with schizophrenia or depression.
4. Promoted initially by advocates for Vietnam veterans and later by women's groups concerned with victims of rape, incest, and other forms of sexual abuse, PTSD's inclusion in the *DSM* was resisted by many in the psy community (Young). Yet PTSD is now one of the emotional forms of mental illness that defines our era and, along with depression and other forms of anxiety, contributes to the current global epidemic.

Works Cited

Ahmed, Sara. *The Promise of Happiness*. Durham, NC: Duke University Press, 2010.
———. "Imaginary Prohibitions: Some Preliminary Remarks on the Founding Gestures of the 'New Materialism.'" *European Journal of Women's Studies* 15.1 (2008): 23–39.
———. *The Cultural Politics of Emotion*. Edinburgh: Edinburgh University Press, 2004.
Alberti, Fay Bound. *Matters of the Heart: History, Medicine, and Emotion*. Oxford: Oxford University Press, 2010.
———. "Introduction: Emotion Theory and Medical History." *Medicine, Emotion and Disease, 1700–1950*. Ed. Fay Bound Alberti. Basingstoke: Palgrave Macmillan, 2006.
Angel, Maria. "Brainfood: Rationality, Aesthetics and Economies of Affect." *Textual Practice* 19.2 (2005): 323–348.
Barbalet, Jack. "William James' Theory of Emotions: Filling in the Picture." *Journal for the Theory of Social Behaviour* 29.3 (1999): 251–266.
Barham, Peter. "Foucault and the Psychiatric Practitioner." *Rewriting the History of Madness: Studies in Foucault's Histoire de la folie*. Eds. Arthur Still and Irving Velody. London: Routledge, 1992. 45–50.
Bartz, Jennifer, Alicia Kaplan, and Eric Hollander. "Obsessive-Compulsive Disorder." *Personality Disorders: Towards the DSM-V*. Eds. William O'Donohue, Katherine Fowler, and Scott Lilienfeld. Thousand Oaks, CA: Sage, 2007.
Battersby, Christine. *Gender and Genius: Towards a Feminist Aesthetics*. Bloomington, IN: Indiana University Press, 1989.
Bentall, Richard. *Doctoring the Mind: Is Our Current Treatment of Mental Illness Any Good?* New York: New York University Press, 2009.
Bernstein, David, and David Useda. "Paranoid Personality Disorder." *Personality Disorders: Towards the DSM-V*. Eds. William O'Donohue, Katherine Fowler, and Scott Lilienfeld. Thousand Oaks, CA: Sage, 2007.
Berrios, German. *The History of Mental Symptoms: Descriptive Psychopathology since the Nineteenth Century*. Cambridge: Cambridge University Press, 1997.
Blackman, Lisa. "The Dialogical Self, Flexibility and the Cultural Production of Psychopathology." *Theory and Psychology* 15.2 (2005): 183–206.
Blagov, Pavel, Katherine Fowler, and Scott Lilienfeld. "Histrionic Personality Disorder." *Personality Disorders: Towards the DSM-V*. Eds. William O'Donohue, Katherine Fowler, and Scott Lilienfeld. Thousand Oaks, CA: Sage, 2007.
Blumer, Dietrich. "The Illness of Vincent van Gogh." *The American Journal of Psychiatry,* 159.4 (April 2002): 519–526.
Booth, Michael R. *Theatre in the Victorian Age*. Cambridge: Cambridge University Press, 1991.

Bornstein, Robert. "Dependent Personality Disorder." *Personality Disorders: Towards the DSM-V.* Eds. William O'Donohue, Katherine Fowler, and Scott Lilienfeld. Thousand Oaks, CA: Sage, 2007.

Bourdieu, Pierre. *The Rules of Art: Genesis and Structure of the Literary Field.* Trans. Susan Emanuel. Stanford, CA: University of Stanford Press, 1995.

———. "The Historical Genesis of a Pure Aesthetic." *The Journal of Aesthetics and Art Criticism,* 46 (1987): 201–210.

———. *Distinction: A Social Critique of the Judgement of Taste.* Trans. Richard Nice. Cambridge, MA: Harvard University Press, 1984.

Bradley, Rebekah, Carolyn Zittel Conklin, and Drew Westen. "Borderline Personality Disorder." *Personality Disorders: Towards the DSM-V.* Eds. William O'Donohue, Katherine Fowler, and Scott Lilienfeld. Thousand Oaks, CA: Sage, 2007.

Brooks, Peter. *The Melodramatic Imagination: Balzac, Henry James, Melodrama, and the Mode of Excess.* New Haven: Yale University Press, 1976.

Brown, Laura. "A Feminist Critique of the Personality Disorders." *Personality and Psychopathology: Feminist Reappraisals.* Eds. Laura Brown and Mary Ballou. New York: Guilford, 1992.

Brown, Phil. "The Name Game: Toward a Sociology of Diagnosis." *The Journal of Mind and Behavior* 11.3–4 (1990): 385–406.

Brown, Steven, and Paul Stenner. *Psychology without Foundations: History, Philosophy, and Psychosocial Theory.* Thousand Oaks, CA: Sage, 2009.

Buckley, Matthew. "Refugee Theatre: Melodrama and Modernity's Loss." *Theatre Journal* 61.2 (May 2009): 175–190.

Burkitt, Ian. *Emotions and Social Relations.* London: Sage, 2014.

Caputo, John. "On Not Knowing Who We Are: Madness, Hermeneutics, and the Night of Truth in Foucault." *Foucault and the Critique of Institutions.* Eds. John Caputo and Mark Yount. University Park, PA: The Pennsylvania State Press, 1993.

Cardinal, Roger. "Romantic Travel." *Rewriting the Self: Histories from the Renaissance to the Present.* Ed. Roy Porter. London: Routledge, 1997.

Castel, Robert. *The Regulation of Madness: The Origins of Incarceration in France.* Trans. W.D. Halls. Berkeley: University of California Press, 1988.

Christian, Brian. *The Most Human Human: What Artificial Intelligence Teaches Us about Being Alive.* New York: Anchor, 2012.

Coid, Jeremy. "Correctional Populations: Criminal Careers and Recidivism." *Textbook of Personality Disorders.* Eds. John Oldham, Andrew Skodol, and Donna Bender. Washington, DC: American Psychiatric Publishing, 2005.

Coker, Linda Anne, and Thomas Widiger. "Personality Disorders." *Psychopathology: Foundations for a Contemporary Understanding.* Eds. James Maddux and Barbara Winstead. Mahway, NJ: Lawrence Erlbaum, 2005.

Dallaire, Bernadette, Michael McCubbin, Paul Morin, and David Cohen. "Civil Commitment Due to Mental Illness and Dangerousness: The Union of Law and Psychiatry within a Treatment-Control System." *Rethinking the Sociology of Mental Health.* Ed. Joan Busfield. Oxford: Blackwell, 2001.

Delhaye, Christine. "Van Gogh and the National Canon of Dutch History." *Vincent Everywhere: Van Gogh's (Inter)National Identities.* Eds. Rachel Esner and Margriet Schavemaker. Amsterdam: Amsterdam University Press, 2010.

Diagnostic and Statistical Manual of Mental Disorders: DSM-5. Washington, DC: American Psychiatric Association, 2013.

Diagnostic and Statistical Manual of Mental Disorders: DSM-IV-TR. Washington, DC: American Psychiatric Association, 2000.

Diagnostic and Statistical Manual of Mental Disorders: DSM-IV. Washington, DC: American Psychiatric Association, 1994.

Diagnostic and Statistical Manual of Mental Disorders: DSM-III-R. Washington, DC: American Psychiatric Association, 1987.

Diagnostic and Statistical Manual of Mental Disorders: DSM-III. Washington, DC: American Psychiatric Association, 1980.

Diagnostic and Statistical Manual of Mental Disorders: DSM-II. Washington, DC: American Psychiatric Association, 1968.

Diagnostic and Statistical Manual of Mental Disorders: DSM-I. Washington, DC: American Psychiatric Association, 1952.

Dixon, Thomas. "Patients and Passions: Languages of Medicine and Emotion, 1789–1850." *Medicine, Emotion and Disease, 1700–1950*. Ed. Fay Bound Alberti. Basingstoke: Palgrave Macmillan, 2006.

———. *From Passions to Emotions: The Creation of a Secular Psychological Category*. Cambridge: Cambridge University Press, 2003.

Dolan, Bridget, Fiona Warren, and Kingsley Norton. "Change in Borderline Symptoms One Year after Therapeutic Community Treatment for Severe Personality Disorder." *The British Journal of Psychiatry* 171 (1997): 274–279.

Dreyfus, Hubert. "Foreward to the California Edition." *Mental Illness and Psychology*. Michel Foucault. Berkeley: University of California Press, 1987.

Dror, Otniel. "The Affect of Experiment: The Turn to Emotions in Anglo-American Physiology, 1900–1940." *Isis* 90.2 (June 1999): 205–237.

Dumit, Joseph. *Picturing Personhood: Brain Scans and Biomedical Identity*. Princeton, NJ: Princeton University Press, 2004.

Dyson, Frances. "Enchanting Data: Body, Voice and Tone in Affective Computing." *Emotion, Place and Culture*. Eds. Mick Smith, Joyce Davidson, Laura Cameron, and Liz Bondi. Farnham: Ashgate, 2009.

Emmelkamp, Paul, and Mick Power. "*DSM-5* Personality Disorders: Stop Before It Is Too Late." *Clinical Psychology and Psychotherapy* 19 (2012): 363.

Ernst, Waltraud. "Personality Disorders: Social Section." *A History of Clinical Psychiatry: The Origin and History of Psychiatric Disorders*. Eds. German Berrios and Roy Porter. New York: New York University Press, 1995.

Esner, Rachel. "Beyond Dutch: Van Gogh's Early Critical Reception." *Vincent Everywhere: Van Gogh's (Inter)National Identities*. Eds. Rachel Esner and Margriet Schavemaker. Amsterdam: Amsterdam University Press, 2010.

Fernando, Gaithri. "Assessing Mental Health and Psychosocial Status in Communities Exposed to Traumatic Events: Sri Lanka as Example." *American Journal of Orthopsychiatry* 78.2 (2008): 229–239.

Foucault, Michel. *Madness: The Invention of an Idea*. Trans. Alan Sheridan. New York: Harper, 2011.

———. *History of Madness*. Trans. Jonathan Murphy and Jean Khalfa. London: Routledge, 2009.

———. *Psychiatric Power: Lectures at the Collège de France, 1973–1974*. Ed. Jacques Lagrange. New York: Picador, 2006.

———. *Madness and Civilization: A History of Insanity in the Age of Reason*. Trans. Richard Howard. New York: Vintage, 1988 [1965].

———. *Mental Illness and Psychology*. Trans. Alan Sheridan. Berkeley: University of California Press, 1987 [1962].

Fowler, Katherine, William O'Donohue, and Scott Lilienfeld. "Introduction: Personality Disorders in Perspective." *Personality Disorders: Towards the DSM-V*. Eds.

William O'Donohue, Katherine Fowler, and Scott Lilienfeld. Thousand Oaks, CA: Sage, 2007.

Freund, Peter. "The Expressive Body." *Emotions: A Social Science Reader*. Eds. Monica Greco and Paul Stenner. London: Routledge, 2008.

Frosch, John. "The Psychotic Character: Clinical Psychiatric Considerations." *Essential Papers on Borderline Disorders*. Ed. Michael Stone. New York: New York University Press, 1986 [1964].

Gauchet, Marcel, and Gladys Swain. *Madness and Democracy: The Modern Psychiatric Universe*. Trans. Catherine Porter. Princeton, NJ: Princeton University Press, 1999.

Gauchet, Marcel. "Redefining the Unconscious." *Thesis Eleven* 71 (2002): 4–23.

Gay, Peter. *The Naked Heart. The Bourgeois Experience: Victoria to Freud*. Volume 4. New York: Norton, 1995.

Gerould, Daniel C. "The Americanization of Melodrama." *American Melodrama*. Ed. Daniel C. Gerould. New York: Performing Arts Journal Publications, 1983.

Gledhill, Christine. "Signs of Melodrama." *Stardom: Industry of Desire*. Ed. Christine Gledhill. London: Routledge, 1991.

———. "Introduction." *Home Is Where the Heart Is: Studies in Melodrama and the Woman's Film*. Ed. Christine Gledhill. London: BFI, 1987.

Goldstein, Jan. *Console and Classify: The French Psychiatric Profession in the Nineteenth Century*. Cambridge: Cambridge University Press, 1987.

Gould, Deborah. "On Affect and Protest." *Political Emotions*. Eds. Janet Staiger, Ann Cvetkovich, and Ann Reynolds. New York: Routledge, 2010.

Greco, Monica, and Paul Stenner. "Introduction: Emotion and Social Science." *Emotions: A Social Science Reader*. Eds. Monica Greco and Paul Stenner. London: Routledge, 2008.

Greenberg, Gary. *The Book of Woe: The DSM and the Unmaking of Psychiatry*. New York: Blue Ridge/Penguin, 2013.

———. *Manufacturing Depression: The Secret History of a Modern Disease*. New York: Simon & Schuster, 2010.

Grossberg, Lawrence. "Affect's Future: Rediscovering the Virtual in the Actual." *The Affect Theory Reader*. Eds. Melissa Gregg and Gregory Seigworth. Durham, NC: Duke University Press, 2010.

———. *We Gotta Get Out of This Place: Popular Conservatism and Postmodern Culture*. New York: Routledge, 1992.

Gutman, Huck. "Rousseau's *Confessions*: A Technology of the Self." *Technologies of the Self: A Seminar with Michel Foucault*. Eds. Luther Martin, Huck Gutman, and Patrick Hutton. Amherst: University of Massachusetts Press, 1988.

Gutting Gary. *Michel Foucault's Archaeology of Scientific Reason*. Cambridge: Cambridge University Press, 1989.

Hacking, Ian. *Mad Travelers: Reflections on the Reality of Transient Mental Illnesses*. Charlottesville, VA: University Press of Virginia, 1998.

Hansen, Miriam. "The Mass Production of the Senses: Classical Cinema as Vernacular Modernism." *Reinventing Film Studies*. Eds. Christine Gledhill and Linda Williams. New York: Arnold, 2000.

Hauptman, Ira. "Defending Melodrama." *Melodrama*. Ed. James Redmond. Cambridge: Cambridge University Press, 1992.

Hemmings, Claire. "Affective Solidarity: Feminist Reflexivity and Political Transformation." *Feminist Theory* 13.2 (2012): 147–161.

Herbert, James. "Avoidant Personality Disorder." *Personality Disorders: Towards the DSM-V.* Eds. William O'Donohue, Katherine Fowler, and Scott Lilienfeld. Thousand Oaks, CA: Sage, 2007.

Higgitt, Anna, and Peter Fonagy. "Psychotherapy in Borderline and Narcissistic Personality Disorder." *The British Journal of Psychiatry* 161 (1992): 23–43.

Horwitz, Allan, and Jerome Wakefield. *The Loss of Sadness: How Psychiatry Transformed Normal Sorrow into Depressive Disorder.* Oxford: Oxford University Press, 2007.

Horwitz, Allan. *Creating Mental Illness.* Chicago: The University of Chicago Press, 2002.

Hutton, Patrick. "Foucault, Freud, and the Technologies of the Self." *Technologies of the Self: A Seminar with Michel Foucault.* Eds. Luther Martin, Huck Gutman, and Patrick Hutton. Amherst: University of Massachusetts Press, 1988.

Hyslop, Gabrielle. "Pixérécourt and the French Melodrama Debate: Instructing Boulevard Theatre Audiences." *Melodrama.* Ed. James Redmond. Cambridge: Cambridge University Press, 1992.

Ingram, David. "Foucault and Habermas on the Subject of Reason." *The Cambridge Companion to Foucault.* Ed. Gary Gutting. Cambridge: Cambridge University Press, 1994. 215–261.

James, Louis. "Was Jerrold's Black Ey'd Susan More Popular Than Wordsworth's Lucy?" *Performance and Politics in Popular Drama.* Eds. David Bradby, Louis James, and Bernard Sharratt. Cambridge: Cambridge University Press, 1980.

James, William. "What Is an Emotion?" *Collected Essays and Reviews.* London: Longmans and Green, 1920 [1884].

Kantrowitz, Ricki, and Mary Ballou. "A Feminist Critique of Cognitive-Behavioral Therapy." *Personality and Psychopathology: Feminist Reappraisals.* Eds. Laura Brown and Mary Ballou. New York: Guilford, 1992.

Kaplan, Marcie. "A Woman's View of *DSM-III.*" *American Psychologist* (July 1983): 786–792.

Kasumi, Fujiwara. "The Van Gogh Industry." *Mythologies.* Ed. Tsukasa Kōdera. Amsterdam: John Benjamins, 1993.

Kirk, Stuart, Tomi Gomory, and David Cohen. *Mad Science: Psychiatric Coercion, Diagnosis, and Drugs.* New Brunswick, NJ: Transaction, 2013.

Kleinman, Arthur. "The Art of Medicine: Four Social Theories for Global Health." *The Lancet* 375 (1 May 2010): 1518–1519.

Knight, Robert. "Borderline States." *Essential Papers on Borderline Disorders.* Ed. Michael Stone. New York: New York University Press, 1986 [1953].

Kutchins, Herb, and Stuart Kirk. *Making Us Crazy. DSM: The Psychiatric Bible and the Creation of Mental Disorders.* New York: Free Press, 1997.

Lanzoni, Susan. "Diagnosing Modernity: Mania and Authenticity in the Existential Genre." *Configurations* 12.1 (Winter 2004): 107–131.

Leeman, Fred. "Reflections of Van Gogh in the Work of some Masters of Early Modern Art." *Mythologies.* Ed. Tsukasa Kōdera. Amsterdam: John Benjamins, 1993.

Lenzenweger, Mark, and John Clarkin. "The Personality Disorders: History, Classification, and Research Issues." *Major Theories of Personality Disorder.* Eds. Mark Lenzenweger and John Clarkin. 2nd ed. New York: Guilford, 2005.

Levy, Kenneth, Joseph Reynoso, Rachel Wasserman, and John Clarkin. "Narcissistic Personality Disorder." *Personality Disorders: Towards the DSM-V.* Eds. William O'Donohue, Katherine Fowler, and Scott Lilienfeld. Thousand Oaks, CA: Sage, 2007.

Lewis, Glyn, and Louis Appleby. "Personality Disorder: The Patients Psychiatrists Dislike." *The British Journal of Psychiatry* 153 (1988): 44–49.

Leys, Ruth and Marlene Goldman. "Navigating the Genealogies of Trauma, Guilt, and Affect: An Interview with Ruth Leys." *University of Toronto Quarterly* 79.2 (2010): 656–679.

Leys, Ruth. "The Turn to Affect: A Critique." *Critical Inquiry* 37 (Spring 2011): 434–472.

Livesley, John. "Disorder in the Proposed *DSM-5* Classification of Personality Disorders." *Clinical Psychology and Psychotherapy* 19 (2012): 364–368.

——. "Tradition versus Empiricism in the Current *DSM-5* Proposal for Revising the Classification of Personality Disorders." *Criminal Behavior and Mental Health* 22 (2012): 81–90.

Lucas, Rod. "In and Out of Culture: Ethnographic Means to Interpreting Schizophrenia." *Schizophrenia, Culture, and Subjectivity: The Edge of Experience*. Eds. Janis Hunter Jenkins and Robert John Barrett. Cambridge: Cambridge University Press, 2004.

MacDonald, Michael. *Mystical Bedlam: Madness, Anxiety, and Healing in Seventeenth-Century England*. Cambridge: Cambridge University Press, 1981.

Maddux, James, Jennifer Gosselin, and Barbara Winstead. "Conceptions of Psychopathology: A Social Constructionist Perspective." *Psychopathology: Foundations for a Contemporary Understanding*. Eds. James Maddux and Barbara Winstead. Mahway, NJ: Lawrence Erlbaum, 2005.

Major-Poetzl, Pamela. *Michel Foucault's Archaeology of Western Culture: Toward a New Science of History*. Chapel Hill, NC: The University of North Carolina Press, 1983.

Manning Nick. "Psychiatric Diagnosis under Conditions of Uncertainty: Personality Disorder, Science and Professional Legitimacy." *Rethinking the Sociology of Mental Health*. Ed. Joan Busfield. Oxford: Blackwell, 2001.

Martin, Emily. "Talking Back to Neuro-reductionism." *Cultural Bodies: Ethnography and Theory*. Eds. Helen Thomas and Jamilah Ahmed. Oxford: Blackwell, 2004.

Massumi, Brian. *Parables for the Virtual: Movement, Affect, Sensation*. Durham, NC: Duke University Press, 2002.

Mayer, David. "Learning to See in the Dark." *Nineteenth Century Theatre* 25:2 (Winter 1997): 92–114.

McCallum, David. "Mental Health, Criminality and the Human Sciences." *Foucault, Health and Medicine*. Eds. Alan Petersen and Robin Bunton. London: Routledge, 1997.

McCormick, John. "Joseph Bouchardy: a Melodramatist and His Public." *Performance and Politics in Popular Drama*. Eds. David Bradby, Louis James, and Bernard Sharratt. Cambridge: Cambridge University Press, 1980.

Miller, Peter, and Nikolas Rose. "Introduction." *The Power of Psychiatry*. Eds. Peter Miller and Nikolas Rose. Cambridge: Polity, 1986.

Miller, Peter. "Critiques of Psychiatry and Critical Sociologies of Madness." *The Power of Psychiatry*. Eds. Peter Miller and Nikolas Rose. Cambridge: Polity, 1986.

——. "Psychotherapy of Work and Unemployment." *The Power of Psychiatry*. Eds. Peter Miller and Nikolas Rose. Cambridge: Polity, 1986.

Millon, Theodore, and Seth Grossman. "Millon's Evolutionary Model for Unifying the Study of Normal and Abnormal Personality." *Differentiating Normal and Abnormal Personality*. Ed. Stephen Strack. New York: Springer, 2006.

————. "Sociocultural Factors." *Textbook of Personality Disorders*. Eds. John Oldham, Andrew Skodol, and Donna Bender. Washington, DC: American Psychiatric Publishing, 2005.

Morey, Leslie, Gerianne Alexander, and Christina Boggs. "Gender." *Textbook of Personality Disorders*. Eds. John Oldham, Andrew Skodol, and Donna Bender. Washington, DC: American Psychiatric Publishing, 2005.

Moyn, Samuel. "The Assumption by Man of His Original Fracturing: Marcel Gauchet, Gladys Swain, and the History of the Self." *Modern Intellectual History* 6.2 (2009): 315–341.

Naifeh, Steven, and Gregory White Smith. *Van Gogh: The Life*. New York: Random, 2011.

Nuckolls, Charles. "Toward a Cultural History of the Personality Disorders." *Social Science & Medicine* 35.1 (1992): 37–48.

Oldham, John, and Andrew Skodol. "Charting the Future of Axis II." *Journal of Personality Disorders* 14.1 (2000): 17–29.

Oldham, John, Andrew Skodol, and Donna Bender. "Introduction." *Textbook of Personality Disorders*. Eds. John Oldham, Andrew Skodol, and Donna Bender. Washington, DC: American Psychiatric Publishing, 2005.

Oldham, John. "Personality Disorders: Recent History and Future Directions." *Textbook of Personality Disorders*. Eds. John Oldham, Andrew Skodol, and Donna Bender. Washington, DC: American Psychiatric Publishing, 2005.

Orr, Jackie. "Performing Methods: History, Hysteria, and the New Science of Psychiatry." *Pathology and the Postmodern: Mental Illness as Discourse and Experience*. Ed. Dwight Fee. Thousand Oaks, CA: Sage, 2000.

Palmer, Derrol. "Identifying Delusional Discourse: Issues of Rationality, Reality and Power." *Rethinking the Sociology of Mental Health*. Ed. Joan Busfield. Oxford: Blackwell, 2001.

Papoulias, Constantina, and Felicity Callard. "Biology's Gift: Interrogating the Turn to Affect." *Body & Society* 16.1 (2010): 29–56.

Patrick, Christopher. "Antisocial Personality Disorder and Psychopathy." *Personality Disorders: Towards the DSM-V*. Eds. William O'Donohue, Katherine Fowler, and Scott Lilienfeld. Thousand Oaks, CA: Sage, 2007.

Pilkonis, Paul, Michael Hallquist, Jennifer Morse, and Stephanie Shepp. "Striking the (Im)Proper Balance between Scientific Advances and Clinical Utility: Commentary on the *DSM-5* Proposal for Personality Disorders." *Personality Disorders: Theory, Research, and Treatment* 2.1 (2011): 68–82.

Plagens, Peter. "Tortured Souls." *Newsweek* 12 Oct. 1998: 78–80.

Pollock, Griselda. "History versus Mythology: Reading Van Gogh for Dutchness." *Vincent Everywhere: Van Gogh's (Inter)National Identities*. Eds. Rachel Esner and Margriet Schavemaker. Amsterdam: Amsterdam University Press, 2010.

————. "Crows, Blossoms and Lust for Death: Cinema and the Myth of Van Gogh the Modern Artist." *Mythologies*. Ed. Tsukasa Kōdera. Amsterdam: John Benjamins, 1993.

————. "Artists' Mythologies and Media Genius: Madness and Art History." *Screen* 21.3 (1980): 57–96.

Porter, Jeffrey, and Edwin Risler. "The New Alternative *DSM-5* Model for Personality Disorders: Issues and Controversies." *Research on Social Work Practice* 24.1 (Jan 2014): 50–56.

Porter, Roy. "Introduction." *Rewriting the Self: Histories from the Renaissance to the Present*. Ed. Roy Porter. London: Routledge, 1997.

Postlewait, Thomas. "From Melodrama to Realism: The Suspect History of American Drama." *Melodrama: The Cultural Emergence of a Genre.* Eds. Michael Hays and Anastasia Nikolopoulou. New York: St. Martin's, 1996.

Pribram, E. Deidre. "Melodrama and the Aesthetics of Emotion." *Melodrama Unbound.* Eds. Christine Gledhill and Linda Williams. New York: Columbia University Press, 2016.

———. "Feeling Bad: Emotions and Narrativity in *Breaking Bad.*" *Breaking Bad: Critical Essays on the Contexts, Politics, Style, and Reception of the Television Series.* Ed. David Pierson. Lanham, MD: Lexington, 2014.

———. *Emotions, Genre, Justice in Film and Television: Detecting Feeling.* New York: Routledge, 2013 [2011].

———. "An Individual of Feeling: Emotion, Gender, and Subjectivity in Historical Perspectives on Sensibility." *Sexed Sentiments: Interdisciplinary Perspectives on Gender and Emotion.* Eds. W. Ruberg and K. Steenbergh. Amsterdam: Rodopi, 2010.

Puente, Maria. "Tortured Artist Would Never Have Understood His Appeal." *USA Today* 2–4 Oct. 1998: 1A-2A.

Radden, Jennifer. *Moody Minds Distempered: Essays on Melancholy and Depression.* Oxford: Oxford University Press, 2009.

Richards, Graham. "Emotions into Words – Or Words into Emotions?" *Representing Emotions: New Connections in the Histories of Art, Music, and Medicine.* Eds. Penelope Gouk and Helen Hills. Aldershot: Ashgate, 2005.

Rivera, Margo. "The Chrysalis Program: Feminist Treatment Community for Individuals Diagnosed as Personality Disordered." *Rethinking Mental Health and Disorder.* Eds. Mary Ballou and Laura Brown. New York: Guilford, 2002.

Rose, Nikolas. "Normality and Pathology in a Biomedical Age." *The Sociological Review* 57.2 (2009): 66–83.

———. "Psychology as a Social Science." *Subjectivity* 25.1 (2008): 446–462.

———. "Disorders without Borders? The Expanding Scope of Psychiatric Practice." *Biosocieties* 1.4 (2006): 465–484.

———. "Assembling the Modern Self." *Rewriting the Self: Histories from the Renaissance to the Present.* Ed. Roy Porter. London: Routledge, 1997.

———. "Psychiatry: The Discipline of Mental Health." *The Power of Psychiatry.* Eds. Peter Miller and Nikolas Rose. Cambridge: Polity, 1986.

———. *The Psychological Complex: Psychology, Politics and Society in England, 1869–1939.* London: Routledge & Kegan Paul, 1985.

Rutter, Michael. "Temperament, Personality and Personality Disorder." *The British Journal of Psychiatry* 150 (1987): 443–458.

Saltzman, Cynthia. *Portrait of Dr. Gachet: The Story of a Van Gogh Masterpiece.* New York: Viking, 1998.

Samuel, Douglas, and Thomas Widiger. "Differentiating Normal and Abnormal Personality from the Perspective of the *DSM.*" *Differentiating Normal and Abnormal Personality.* Ed. Stephen Strack. New York: Springer, 2006.

Sass, Henning and Sabine C. Herpetz. "Personality Disorders: Clinical Section." *A History of Clinical Psychiatry: The Origin and History of Psychiatric Disorders.* Eds. German Berrios and Roy Porter. New York: New York University Press, 1995.

Sawicki, Jana. "Foucault, Feminism, and Questions of Identity." *The Cambridge Companion to Foucault.* Ed. Gary Gutting. Cambridge: Cambridge University Press, 1994. 286–313.

Schiermeier, Kris. "A Mutual Love: Van Gogh and Japan." *Vincent Everywhere: Van Gogh's (Inter)National Identities*. Eds. Rachel Esner and Margriet Schavemaker. Amsterdam: Amsterdam University Press, 2010.

Schnog, Nancy. "Changing Emotions: Moods and the Nineteenth-Century American Woman Writer." *Emotions: A Cultural Studies Reader*. Eds. Jennifer Harding and E. Deidre Pribram. London: Routledge, 2009.

Scull, Andrew. *The Insanity of Place/The Place of Insanity: Essays on the History of Psychiatry*. London: Routledge, 2006.

Singer, Ben. *Melodrama and Modernity: Early Sensational Cinema and Its Contexts*. New York: Columbia University Press, 2001.

Skodol, Andrew, and Donna Bender. "Why are Women Diagnosed Borderline More than Men?" *Psychiatric Quarterly* 74.4 (2003): 349–360.

Skodol, Andrew, Donna Bender, Leslie Morey, Lee Anna Clark, John Oldham, Renato Alarcon, Robert Krueger, Roel Verheul, Carl Bell, and Larry Siever. "Personality Disorder Types Proposed for *DSM-5*." *Journal of Personality Disorders* 25.2 (2011): 136–169.

Skodol, Andrew, Donna Bender, Leslie Morey, Renato Alarcon, Larry Siever, Lee Anna Clark, Robert Kreuger, Roel Verheul, Carl Bell, and John Oldham. "Proposed Changes in Personality and Personality Disorder Assessment and Diagnosis for *DSM-5*: Description and Rationale." *Personality Disorders: Theory, Research, and Treatment* 2.1 (2011): 4–22.

Smith, Roger. "Self-Reflection and the Self." *Rewriting the Self: Histories from the Renaissance to the Present*. Ed. Roy Porter. London: Routledge, 1997.

Solomon, Andrew. *The Noonday Demon: An Atlas of Depression*. New York: Scribner, 2001.

Sprock, June, Jeremy Crosby, and Britt Nielsen. "Effects of Sex and Sex Roles on the Perceived Maladaptiveness of *DSM-IV* Personality Disorder Symptoms." *Journal of Personality Disorders* 15.1 (Feb 2001): 41–59.

Stern, Adolph. "Psychoanalytic Investigation of and Therapy in the Border Line Group of Neuroses." *The Psychoanalytical Quarterly* 7 (1938): 467–489.

Strack, Stephen. "Introduction." *Differentiating Normal and Abnormal Personality*. Ed. Stephen Strack. New York: Springer, 2006.

Summerfield, Derek. "How Scientifically Valid Is the Knowledge Base of Global Mental Health?" *British Medical Journal* 336 (3 May 2008): 992–994.

———. "Effects of War: Moral Knowledge, Revenge, Reconciliation, and Medicalised Concepts of 'Recovery.'" *British Medical Journal* 325 (9 Nov 2002): 1105–1107.

———. "The Invention of Post-traumatic Stress Disorder and the Social Usefulness of a Psychiatric Category." *British Medical Journal* 322 (13 Jan. 2001): 95–98.

Susman, Warren. *Culture as History: The Transformation of American Society in the Twentieth Century*. New York: Pantheon, 1984 [1973].

Suyemoto, Karen. "Constructing Identities: A Feminist, Culturally Contextualized Alternative to 'Personality.'" *Rethinking Mental Health and Disorder: Feminist Perspectives*. Eds. Mary Ballou and Laura Brown. New York: Guildford, 2002.

Turner, Jonathan, and Jan Stets. *The Sociology of Emotions*. Cambridge: Cambridge University Press, 2005.

Tyrer, Peter, Patricia Casey, and Brian Ferguson. "Personality Disorder in Perspective." *The British Journal of Psychiatry* 159 (1991): 463–471.

Tyrer, Peter, Patricia Casey, and Joanna Gall. "Relationship between Neurosis and Personality Disorder." *The British Journal of Psychiatry* 142 (1983): 404–408.

Tyer, Peter. "Diagnostic and Statistical Manual of Mental Disorders: A Classification of Personality Disorders that Has Had Its Day." *Clinical Psychology and Psychotherapy* 19 (2012): 372–374. .

———. "What's Wrong with *DSM-III* Personality Disorders?" *Journal of Personality Disorders* 2.4 (1988): 281–291.

Ussher, Jane. "Women's Madness: A Material-Discursive-Intrapsychic Approach." *Pathology and the Postmodern: Mental Illness as Discourse and Experience*. Ed. Dwight Fee. Thousand Oaks, CA: Sage, 2000.

Verheul, Roel. "Personality Disorder Proposal for *DSM-5*: A Heroic and Innovative but Nevertheless Fundamentally Flawed Attempt to Improve *DSM-IV*." *Clinical Psychology and Psychotherapy* 19 (2012): 369–371.

Warner, Richard. "The Diagnosis of Antisocial and Hysterical Personality Disorders: An Example of Sex Bias." *The Journal of Nervous and Mental Disease* 166.12 (1978): 839–845.

Watters, Ethan. *Crazy Like Us: The Globalization of the American Psyche*. New York: Free Press, 2010.

Wedding, Danny, Mary Ann Boyd, and Ryan Niemiec. *Movies and Mental Illness: Using Films to Understand Psychopathology*. Cambridge, MA: Hogrefe and Huber, 2005.

Weymans, Wim. "Revising Foucault's Model of Modernity and Exclusion: Gauchet and Swain on Madness and Democracy." *Thesis Eleven* 98 (2009): 33–51.

White, Paul. "Sympathy under the Knife: Experimentation and Emotion in Late Victorian Medicine." *Medicine, Emotion and Disease, 1700–1950*. Ed. Fay Bound Alberti. Basingstoke: Palgrave Macmillan, 2006.

Widiger, Thomas. "Classification and Diagnosis: Historical Development and Contemporary Issues." *Psychopathology: Foundations for a Contemporary Understanding*. Eds. James Maddux and Barbara Winstead. Mahway, NJ: Lawrence Erlbaum, 2005.

Williams, Carolyn. "'Another Self in the Case:' Gender, Marriage and the Individual in Augustan Literature." *Rewriting the Self: Histories from the Renaissance to the Present*. Ed. Roy Porter. London: Routledge, 1997.

Williams, Linda. "Melodrama Revised." *Refiguring American Film Genres: History and Theory*. Ed. Nick Browne. Berkeley: University of California Press, 1998.

Williams, Lloyd. "Anxiety Disorders." *Psychopathology: Foundations for a Contemporary Understanding*. Eds. James Maddux and Barbara Winstead. Mahway, NJ: Lawrence Erlbaum, 2005.

Williams, Raymond. *Keywords: A Vocabulary of Culture and Society*. Oxford: Oxford University Press, 1983.

———. "Social Environment and Theatrical Environment: The Case of English Naturalism." *English Drama: Forms and Development*. Eds. Marie Axton and Raymond Williams. Cambridge: Cambridge University Press, 1977.

Williams, Simon. "Reason, Emotion and Embodiment: Is 'Mental' Health a Contradiction in Terms?" *Sociology of Heath & Illness* 22.5 (2000): 559–581.

Wilson, Mitchell. "*DSM-III* and the Transformation of American Psychiatry: A History." *The American Journal of Psychiatry* 150.3 (March 1993): 399–410.

World Health Organization. "Fact Sheet: Mental Health." Fact Sheet No 396, October, 2014. www.who.int/topics/mental_health/factsheets/en. Retrieved June 1, 2015.

———. *Mental Health Action Plan, 2013–2020*. Geneva: WHO, 2013.

———. *World Health Report, 2001: Mental Health: New Understanding, New Hope*. Geneva: WHO, 2001.

Young, Allan. *The Harmony of Illusions: Inventing Post-Traumatic Stress Disorder*. Princeton, NJ: Princeton University Press, 1995.

Zemel, Carol. *Van Gogh's Progress: Utopia, Modernity, and Late-Nineteenth-Century Art*. Berkeley: University of California Press, 1997.

———. *The Formation of a Legend: Van Gogh Criticism, 1980–1920*. Ann Arbor, MI: University of Michigan Research Press, 1980.

Zimmerman, Mark, Louis Rothschild, and Iwona Chelminski. "The Prevalence of *DSM-IV* Personality Disorders in Psychiatric Outpatients." *The American Journal of Psychiatry* 162.10 (Oct 2005): 1911–1918.

Index

collective 7; relational nature 144; resisting dichotomization 16, 125
emotional restraint 13, 45–48
emotional subjectivity 49, 53–54
emotional suffering: in the arts 66; pathological *versus* circumstantial forms 146–9
emotion-controlled normal 133
emotionlessness 129, 132–4
emotions: and affective computing 130–2; aligned with cognition 5; associated with artistic genius 14, 65–68, 72–79; basic 9; biographical 139–40; causing insanity 35; in the cinema 83–86; control of within the experimental setting 132–5; core of aesthetic experience 71–72; as culture 8; distinction from affect 5–6; distorting effects on scientific studies 132–3; and experience 9–11, 138–40; forms of 42–43; fulfilling social functions 7–8; incorporating aesthetics 125; increased recognition of 26–27; as inner experience 117–18; internalization in theatre 52–53; and madness 37; malleability of 10; minor 9; not being reduced to mind or body 143–4; as part of psychological sciences 3; personal/ public dichotomy 139; polarities of 40; porous quality among 10; and the psychic subject 17; in psychopathy personality 104; and reason 29, 44; in theatrical melodrama 50; trying to categorize 120–2
Enlightenment 12, 43–44
Ernst, Waltraud 110
Esner, Rachel 84
experience, aesthetics of 138–40
experimental physiology 132–5

femininity: and impact on artistry 67–68; linked to personality disorders 112–17
Ferguson, Brian 101
Flaubert, Gustave 69
fMRI (functional magnetic resonance imaging) 135
form over function in art 69
Foucault, Michel 11–12, 126; Cartesian duality 45; and emotions 38–39; historio-cultural account of mental illness 17–23; on madness 23–28, 65; reason and unreason 28–33

Frances, Allen 102
Freudian period of mental illness 12
Freudian reversal 27
Fry, Roger 77

Gall, Joanna 102
Gauchet, Marcel 3, 11, 12, 17, 27, 29–31, 35, 40
Gay, Peter 49
gender: and artistic genius 67–68; impacting diagnosing personality disorders 112–17
gender dysphoria 115–6
genius: artistic 14, 39, 65–92; changing definition of 66–67; and mental illness 14
Gerould, Daniel C. 51
Gledhill, Christine 48, 71
Global Burden of Disease (GBD) 2
Goldstein, Jan 54
Gosselin, Jennifer 102, 107
great confinement period of madness 23, 29
Greco, Monica 5
Greenberg, Clement 79
Greenberg, Gary 119, 148
Grossberg, Lawrence 5, 85
Grossman, Seth 110
guiltiness of the insane 33–35
Gutman, Huck 43–44
Gutting, Gary 39

Hacking, Ian 148
Hansen, Miriam 14, 83, 84, 85
harmless mentally ill 62–63
Hemmings, Claire 5
high art 72, 85; distinguishing from popular culture 83–84; and dramatic realism 51–52; and lack of emotionality 85–86; and level of emotionality 73–74
high art modernism 14, 72, 77–83
History of Madness (Foucault) 11, 18–19, 23
histronic personality disorders 112–15
homosexuality as a psychosexual disorder 110–11
Horwitz, Allan 26, 58–62, 142, 145, 148
humoral theory 141
Hutton, Patrick 45
hyperfeminization 115
hypermasculine 115